KU-465-184

The Black Museum

THE BLACK MUSEUM

Scotland Yard's Chamber of Crime

JONATHAN GOODMAN &
BILL WADDELL

HARRAP
London

ACKNOWLEDGEMENTS

Many of the illustrations are reproduced by courtesy of the Commissioner of the Metropolitan Police. Valuable assistance has also been given by Dr Roger Berrett of the Metropolitan Police Forensic Science Laboratory, Albert Borowitz, Peter Jackson, S.R. Smith, and Richard Whittington-Egan.

First published in Great Britain 1987
by HARRAP Ltd
19-23 Ludgate Hill London EC4M 7PD

ISBN 0 245-54518-2

Designed by Paul Watkins

Typeset in Linotype Ehrhardt by
Facet Film Composing Ltd,
Leigh-on-Sea, Essex

Printed by R.J. Acford Limited,
Chichester, Sussex

CONTENTS

RELICS OF THE YARD

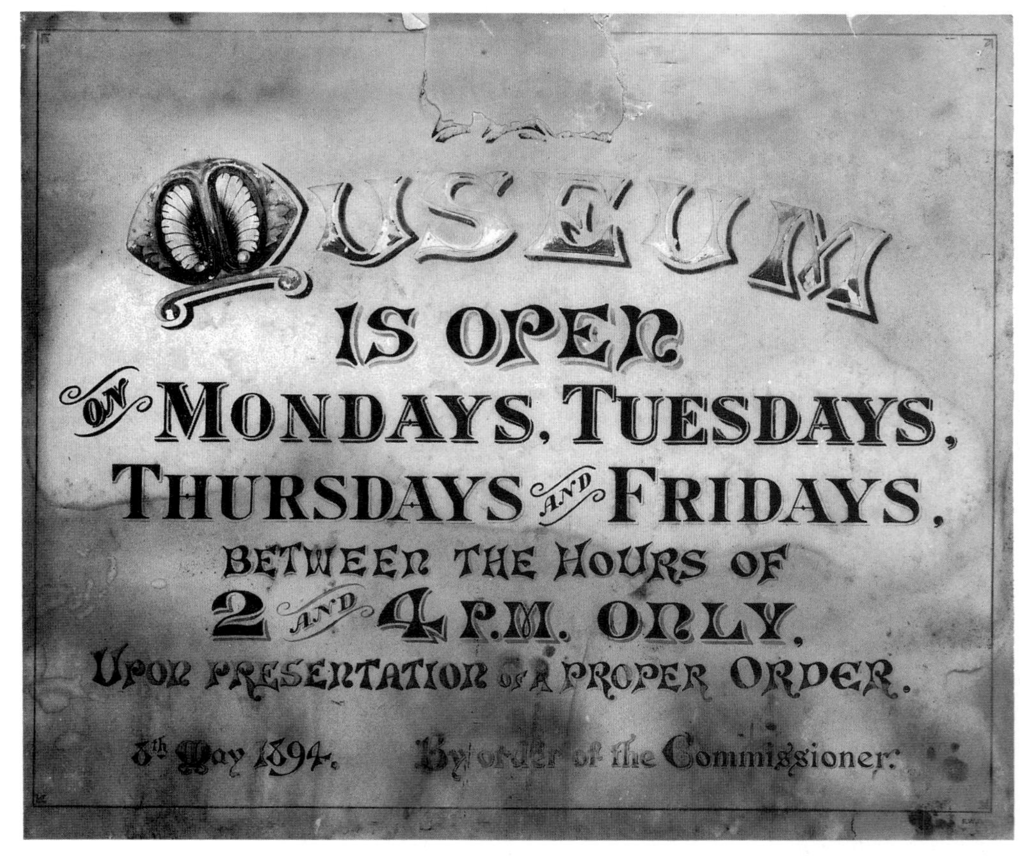

The name Scotland Yard is so synonymous with the Metropolitan Police — with that force itself, with its headquarters, and with members of the force, who are referred to in the press and by the public as 'Scotland Yard officers' — that it is safe to say that few readers of this book will have wondered what on earth Scotland has to do with law-enforcement in London.

One needs to go back a good many years for an explanation — or rather, for explanations. The tracing of them is made complicated by the presence in some histories of London of legends masquerading as facts.

In 1216, just over a year after King John was obliged to set his seal on the Great Charter that was the basis of English political and personal liberty, he died, probably from dysentery, and his elder son became the third of our sovereigns called Henry. As the new king was only nine, the country was run on his behalf by William Marshal, first Earl of Pembroke, with the assistance of, among others, Hubert de Burgh — who by the end of 1219 occupied the post of Judiciar, responsible for law and order. Some time before 1232, when Hubert was sacked, he acquired a plot of land — measuring 14 perches by 6 — between Charing Cross and Westminster. In 1240 he gave it to the recently-formed Dominican Friars; but they, preferring cash to property, sold it to the Archbishop of York, who added it to the grounds of his London residence, York House. (There is some evidence, too slight to be relied upon, that the land had once belonged to Scotsmen. A variation on that evidence suggests that the owners were no ordinary Scotsmen but kings of that country: John Stow, surveyor of London at the end of the sixteenth century, states that 'on the left hand from Charing Cross bee also divers fayre Tenements, lately builded, till ye come to a large plotte of ground enclosed with bricke, and is called Scotland where great buildings hath beene for the receipt of the Kings of Scotland, and other estates of that country'.)

The land seems to have remained the property of the Archbishopric of York till some time before 1413, when a tenancy payment by a non-cleric is recorded. By 1519 the land was Henry VIII's to give away — which he did, to Cardinal Wolsey, his friend at the time. Wolsey built a palace called White Hall upon it — from which he was ousted by Henry in 1529. Apparently the palace remained unoccupied for many years thereafter; certainly it was in a state of decay when Henry's daughter Elizabeth became queen — and by then the grounds were known as Scottelande (perhaps because they had been used for farming by a family called Scott). Near the start of Elizabeth's reign, a canal was built across Scottelande, leading to a dock on the Thames, south-east of Charing Cross. A map published in 1593 shows the canal crossing vacant ground, which is referred to as Scotlande. During the next half-century, parts of Wolsey's palace were renovated, and other parts demolished and some rebuilt — that work being done

(Opposite)
Great Scotland Yard.

in dribs and drabs, one gathers, for in 1660, when Charles II inherited the property, it was described as 'nothing but a heap of houses erected at divers times, and of different models'. Two years later, one of the houses in the heap was occupied by a group of Westminster worthies who had been got together to seek ways of curbing lawlessness in the district. They became known as the Commissioners of Scotland Yard.

A map drawn in 1670 shows two courtyards, both called Scotland Yard, at the northern end of the buildings; the western entrance to them was called Whitehall Place. Twenty-eight years later, Wolsey's palace was almost entirely destroyed by fire. Though the houses round the courtyards remained intact, they fell into disuse till some time before 1729, when, having been refurbished, they were let as residences or offices. One of the new tenants of the houses in the more northerly of the courtyards — by then called Great *Scotland Yard — was Thomas (later Sir Thomas) de Veil, a half-pay captain in the Westminster Militia. As well as running an employment agency for retired or cashiered officers, he was a Magistrate for the Commission of Peace in Westminster — an effective one, himself collecting evidence against, and arresting, quite a number of the persons whom he ordered to be removed from his office in Bow Street to places of confinement.*

In 1812 the Olde Clock House, the most imposing building in Great Scotland Yard, became the Marshalsea Court House, where civil actions within a radius of twelve miles were heard. Writing some twenty years later, Charles Dickens described the Yard as 'a small — a very small-tract of land', adding that its business premises included a tailor's shop, a public house, a bakery specializing in fruit pies, and two eating houses, and that it was made noisy by coal-wagons that trundled through it, using it as a short-cut between Whitehall and the wharfs on the Thames.

In 1829, when the Royal Assent was given to 'An Act for Improving the Police in or near the Metropolis', 4 Whitehall Place was rented at £560 6s.0d. per annum as the headquarters of the 'New Police' (eventually to be nicknamed 'peelers' or 'bobbies' after Sir Robert Peel, the Home Secretary who had introduced the Bill in Parliament). The rear part of the building, overlooking Great Scotland Yard, was converted from servants' quarters into a station house — which, soon after it became operational on 29 September, became known as 'Scotland Yard', thus differentiating it from the main part of the building, 'The Metropolitan Police Office', in which two Commissioners — Charles Rowan, a retired soldier, and Richard Mayne, a lawyer — presided over the seventeen divisions of the force, comprising some two thousand men.

Over the next sixty years, nearly all of the buildings in Great Scotland Yard and Whitehall Place were annexed by the police. They included the Old Clock House, which was taken over in 1850,

PARTICULARS.

LOT ONE.

AN IMPROVED LEASEHOLD RENTAL

OF

£560 6s. PER ANNUM,

Arising out of and amply secured upon

No. 4, Whitehall Place,

A substantial Brick-built House, with Slated Roof, containing—

ON THE UPPER FLOOR, Three Bed Rooms, Sitting Room, Kitchen, Housemaid's Closet and Sink and W.C. From this Floor to the Basement is the Secondary Staircase, principally Stone.

ON THE SECOND FLOOR, Five Rooms used as Accountants' and other Offices, and W.C.

ON THE FIRST FLOOR, which is about 13 ft. high, an Ante Room, good Front Room (formerly the Drawing Room), about 20 ft. by 17 ft. 6 in. with Statuary Marble Mantelpiece, Two Windows to Balcony, and Folding Doors (not used) to the Back Drawing Room with Bow, about 25 ft. by 17 ft. 6 in., and Statuary Marble Mantelpiece, and communicating with another Room at rear. From this to the Ground Floor is the principal Staircase of Stone and well Lighted by Skylight over.

ON THE GROUND FLOOR, which is about 12 ft. high, Stone Paved Entrance and Inner Halls (in the latter is a Glazed Partition forming the Messenger's Office), a Front Room, about 18 ft. by 16 ft. 6 in., with Black Marble Mantelpiece, a Passage Room leading to another large Room with Bow, about 19 ft. by 17 ft. with Black Marble Mantelpiece, communicating with another Room with Grey Marble Mantelpiece and Lavatory. Some of the Doors to the principal Rooms on this Floor are of Mahogany.

IN THE BASEMENT, Kitchen, Scullery, Wine Cellar, Housekeeper's Room, with Sink and Strong Room, Larder, Back Kitchen with Sink (now a Store Room), W.C. and Cupboards in Passage, Paved Front Area with Three Vaults under and Steps to the Street, and small Paved and Covered Area at rear.

At the rear, and also entered from Scotland Yard, are Clerks' and other Offices with Four Offices above.

On every Floor (except the top Floor) there is a communication by means of Double Doors (one of them Iron), with No. 5, Whitehall Place.

These communications the Lessee is under covenant to Brick up if called upon to do so at the end of his Term.

	£	s.	d.
The above Premises are Let on Lease to the Receiver for the Metropolitan Police District for a Term of Twenty-one Years from Michaelmas, 1871; thus there were Ten and a Half Years unexpired at Lady Day, 1882, at the Annual Rent of £625, Lessee paying Land Tax and all other Rates and Taxes (except Landlord's, Property Tax), Insuring from Fire, and keeping the Premises in Repair, and upon the expiration of this Lease an Improved Rent may be expected	625	0	0
They are held direct from the Crown, and are or were lately, together with the adjoining House, No. 3, Whitehall Place, held under one Lease for a Term of Ninety-nine Years from 5th April, 1813, at one entire Rent, This Lease has been or will be surrendered previous to the completion of the Sale, and separate Leases of the Two Houses granted for the same Term under the same Covenants, so far as the same are applicable, and at a Ground Rent for this Lot One of £64 14s. a year	64	14	0
Improved Annual Rental	£560	6	0

following the closure of the Marshalsea Court House: the lease was granted on condition that the clock was maintained so that it almost invariably worked and showed exactly the right time, only being allowed to stop because maintenance made the hiatus imperative. In the 1870s a reporter noted that 'Scotland Yard is not like any of the Continental handsome, well-built, commodious bureaux de police, *but is a curious medley of stables, outhouses, temporary offices, sheds, and private houses, each more inconvenient than the other, and all connected together by a labyrinthine web of passages as tortuous and intricate as the secret and burrowing nature of its occupants can suggest'.*

During the first forty years of more organized policing, all property belonging to convicted felons went to the Crown; but under a provision of an Act passed in 1869, whatever was found on the felons, apart from articles that were stolen or of an unlawful nature, had to be retained till their sentences were completed, when they could apply for re-possession. That entailed the setting-up of a Central Prisoners' Property Store at 1 Great Scotland Yard, which was already a repository for unclaimed stolen property.

Since no official arrangements were made for the disposal of tools of the criminal trades, the attic was turned into a lumber-room of 'weapons, forged notes and bills, false sovereigns, beards, wigs, moustachios, rope-ladders, skeleton keys, empty cashboxes, knives, razors, hatchets — most of the three latter more or less blood-stained'.

In 1874, as the outcome of hard work by an Inspector Neame, the officer in charge of the stores — and, one suspects, harder work by one of his assistants, Police Constable George Randall — a 'crime museum', the first in the world, was opened on the top floor of 1 Great Scotland Yard; its exhibits, selected from the conglomeration of stuff in the attic, were intended to give policemen and magistrates some idea of the ingenuity of 'break-in artists'. During the following decade the scope of the exhibits was widened to include implements of other types of crime and souvenirs of celebrated cases.

On 8 April 1877 a 'special reporter' for *The Observer* coined the term Black Museum. It seems likely that the reporter's holier-than-the-police tone stemmed from umbrage at Inspector Neame's refusal to treat him as a visitor special enough to qualify for admission to the museum, thereby forcing him to base an article entitled 'THE BLACK MUSEUM' on what he saw in other rooms and on what he gathered from their attendants:

Among the premises of the police is a tall, dull, gloomy house in the very corner of the yard as you enter from Whitehall-place. Everything looks dirty and forlorn about this building, which has the natural sombreness of its exterior heightened by iron bars to the windows, and by all the dingy blinds being drawn down as if some one lay dead there. There is no one dead there, however, though it contains innumerable relics and mementoes of those who are civilly dead to the eyes of the law, of those who have suffered the last penalty of the law, and of those whose lives have been murderously wrested from them while their murderers remain still undiscovered. . . . One might as well try in the space of an article to give a description of the contents of the British Museum as of this black one. The rooms are just like the storerooms of a large pawnbroker's, and just as there, every conceivable thing that can fetch money has been pledged, so here every conceivable thing that is worth money has been stolen. . . . We were quite prepared to see a very heterogeneous collection in the first room, but the wonderful variety of its contents we must own surprised us. For instance, in one corner are three large sacks of cochineal, a smaller sack of opium, and one large case of jalap, in all worth between £700 and £800, the proceeds of a robbery, of course,

The Black Museum in 1883.

yet here they have stayed for thirteen years unclaimed. Opposite these is a large tin bath, which we must own is puzzling. Its size precludes the possibility of its having been stolen from a shop unobserved, and if stolen from a house why was not something of more value and more portable taken? Portmanteaus, travelling bags, and railway rugs are, of course, here to any extent, as might be expected, so also are paper bundles of gold and silver chains of all sorts of lengths, patterns, and values. These will ultimately go into the bullion department, but the Black Museum has not yet been completely arranged. . . . Provisions, such as hams, tongues, cheeses, &c., are never kept, nor are such things as easily decay detained long. A few days ago a bundle of raw unclaimed silk was sold for £150. Still, in such rooms there are an immense mass of things that should never be kept there at all, for they answer no good purpose, and merely cumber the space. Among these are tiers of bundles of prisoners' clothing, which, in spite of every effort in the way of cleanliness and disinfectants, give the rooms a close, ill-smelling atmosphere. . . .

It is, however, in the top front room — like all the others, with its blinds drawn close — that the real and repulsive horrors of this *Black Museum* are garnered. Here is almost every kind of firearm, and every kind of cutting or thrusting weapon, with which murder can be committed or attempted, and every single one of which has been used for a criminal purpose. What with blood-stained clothes, razors, penknives, hatchets, choppers, daggers, sword-canes, hammers, pikes, spades and pick-axes, the very room, which is close and stuffy, seems to smell of blood, and leave a horrid flavour in the mouth. Here, as elsewhere, there are very many things which should be destroyed unless the authorities mean to open it at a small fee as the most unrivalled chamber of horrors in Europe, in which case Bloomsbury-square would be too small to accommodate the morbid lovers of the horrible who would be pretty sure to flock to it. . . .

Long before 1886, it was obvious that the Metropolitan Police needed larger headquarters. In the middle of that year the decision was taken to build a bespoke 'centre of police' in some other part of London. The site eventually chosen was on the recently-constructed Thames Embankment. The 70,000 square feet of land had been intended for a National Opera House; the scheme had fallen through because of lack of funds, and the area was derelict. The Receiver, the financial administrator for the police, raised £200,000 by loan for the acquisition of the land and the erection of New Scotland Yard (that name chosen by the new Commissioner, James Monro); a further £97,755 had to be borrowed before the building, designed by Norman Shaw, RA, and made from granite quarried by convicts at Dartmoor, was ready for use in 1890. (Two years before, when the site was being cleared, parts of a woman's body were found hidden among the debris. An investigation failed to reveal the identity of either the woman or her dissector, and so New Scotland Yard came into being upon the scene of an unsolved mystery.

"*Behind each exhibit is the personal story of triumph or despair; of hope or desperation – inextricably linking the victim, culprit and investigator. I look to the Black Museum as a focal point of the hard-won reputation of our Force in the arena of crime investigations, providing the lasting record that fading memories cannot.*"

Sir David McNee QPM
12 October 1981

INSIDE THE BLACK MUSEUM

The Black Museum consists of two principal rooms (one square, one L-shaped) in which its exhibits are displayed on shelves or tables and in show-cases. There are over five hundred items in the Museum, only a small proportion of which can be displayed at any one time.

There are no windows in the Museum and the rooms are kept at a constant temperature of 62 degrees to maintain the humidity levels required for the preservation of the artefacts.

For display purposes, the exhibits are arranged under such headings as Abortion, Bank Robberies, Drugs, Embassy Siege, Espionage, Famous Murders, Forgeries and Counterfeits, The Great Train Robbery, Murder of Police Officers, Notorious Poisoners, Sieges, Hostages and Hi-jacking, Terrorism, Vice, etc.

The captions in this insert are based on explanatory notes supplied by Bill Waddell.

The Museum contains pathological exhibits relating to various murders, such as the arms above. On the right is the bath in which the mass-murderer Dennis Nilsen disposed of some of his victims. His cooker is also on display at the Museum.

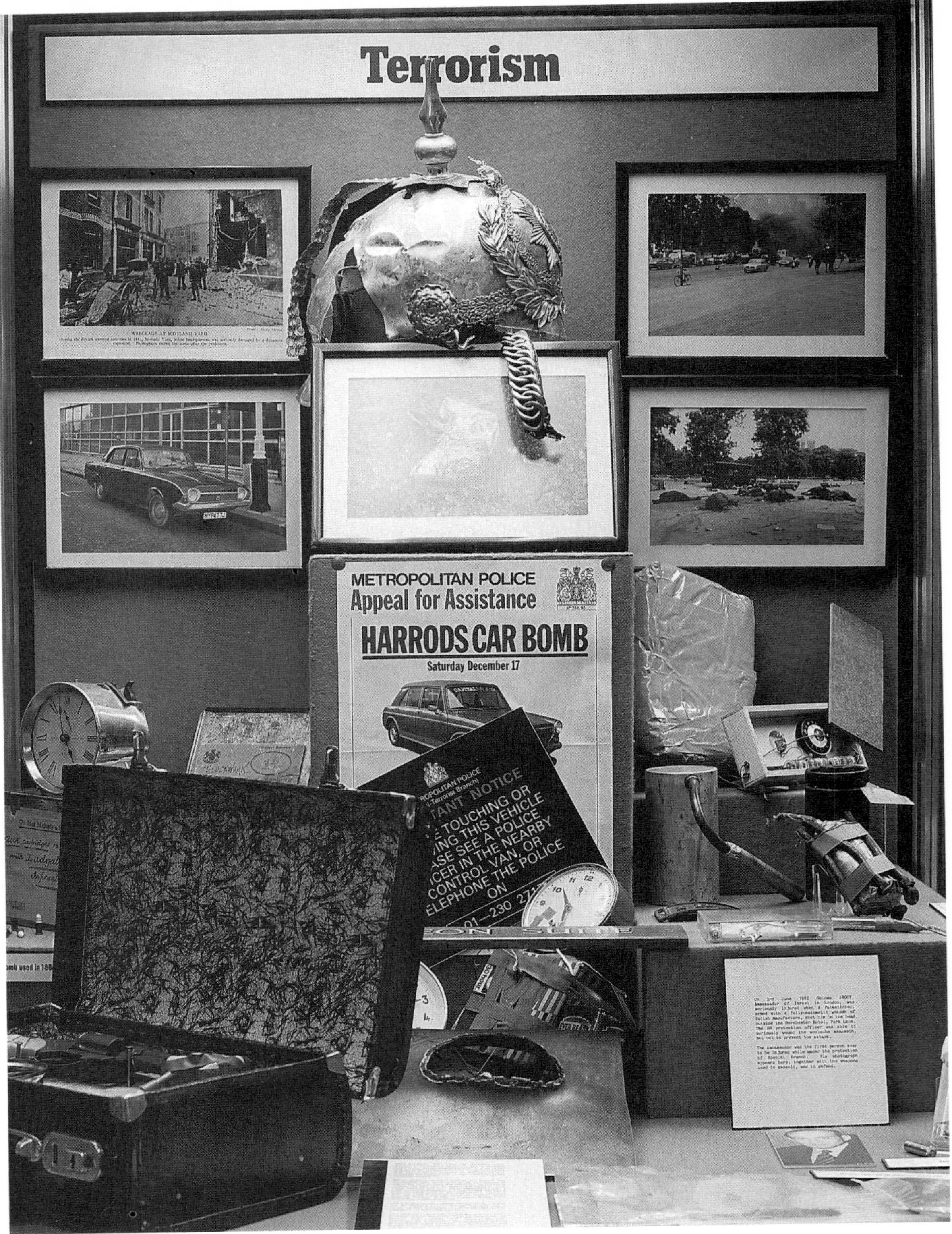
Terrorism
METROPOLITAN POLICE
Appeal for Assistance
HARRODS CAR BOMB
Saturday December 17

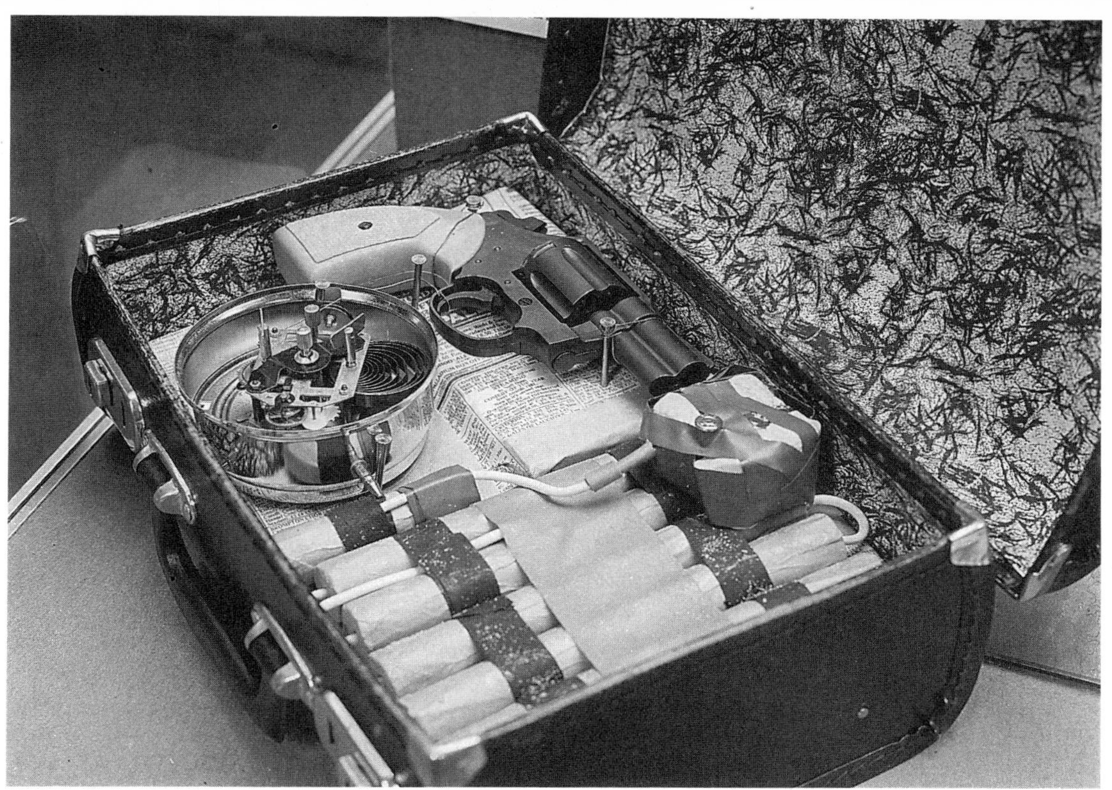

A close-up of the show-case relating to terrorist attacks in London. The items include a bomb that was sent to the Prime Minister's residence at No 10 Downing Street and another that killed bomb-disposal expert Kenneth Howarth at a Wimpy Bar in Oxford Street in 1981. The damaged helmet is from the Provisional IRA bomb attack on the Household Cavalry in Hyde Park in 1982. In this attack and another on the band of the Green Jackets in Regent's Park eleven people were killed. In December 1983 a car bomb outside Harrods store in Knightsbridge killed six people and wounded ninety-seven others. A poster relating to this crime is also included in this display.

Part of the Forgeries and Counterfeits display which includes, among other items, forged warrant cards, fake gold rings and diamonds, and a set of Belgian francs in which the counterfeiter made the elementary mistake of spelling 'franc' with a 'k'. The postal order on the left was altered from 3/6d to 8/6d (the forger was caught when he tried to cash it at a post office).

Opposite: Passage-way leading past a section on Vice and Gaming towards the show-case on Espionage.

Overleaf: In 1980 the Iranian Embassy in London was seized by six Arab Iranians demanding autonomy for Khuzestan/Arabistan. The operation was planned by Iraqis as part of the war against Iran. The SAS stormed the Embassy and five terrorists were killed and one taken prisoner. Two hostages were murdered by their captors.

As well as the Murder of Policemen show-case photographed on page 21, there is a separate display cabinet at the Museum relating to the murder of P.C. Blakelock in 1985.

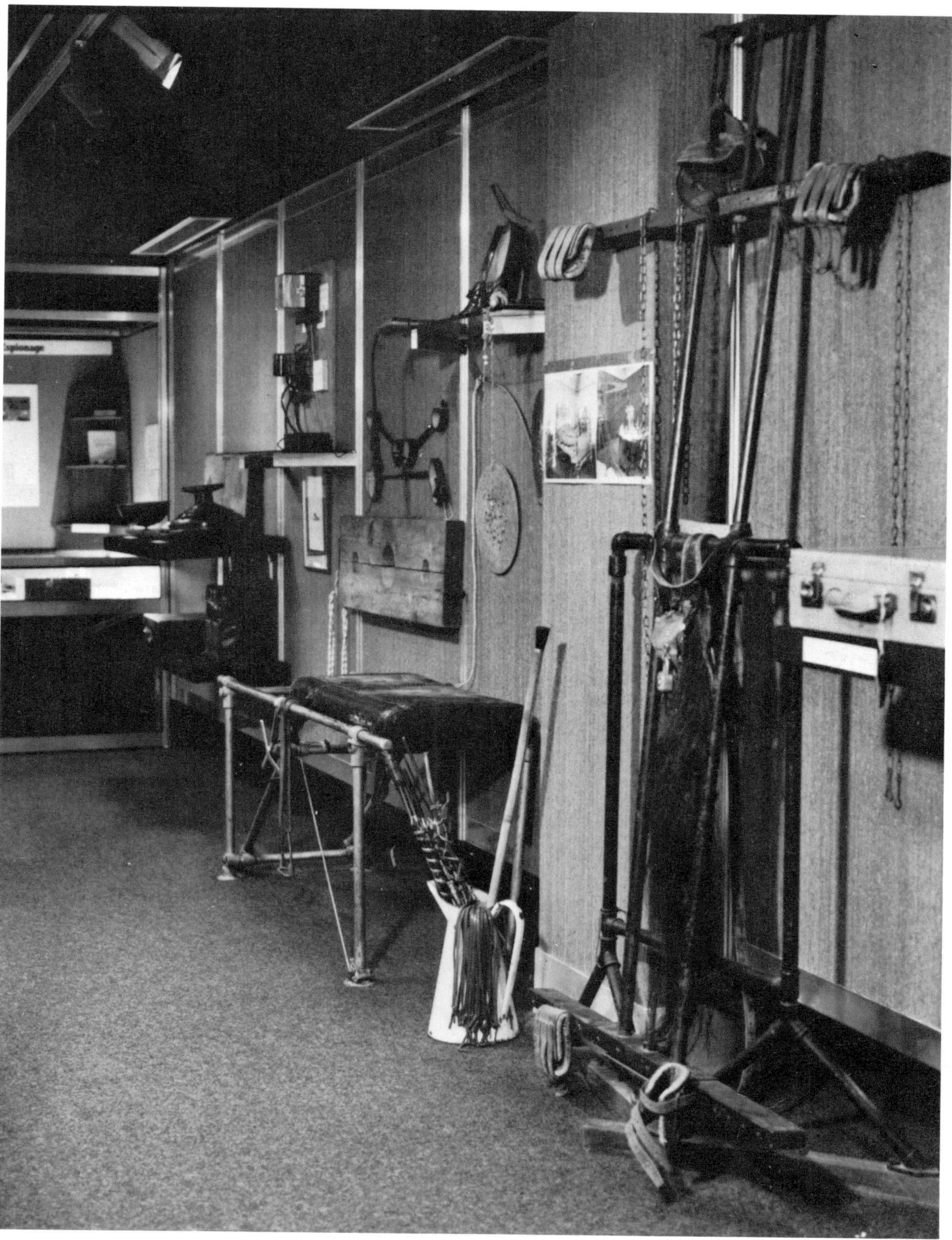

K
469
Embassy Siege

Murder of Police Officers
Metropolitan Police Officers killed by criminal act since 1900
Murder of PC Gutteridge by Browne and Kennedy 1927
METROPOLITAN POLICE
£1,000 REWARD
MURDER
THE MAN WHO SOLD DEATH

A random selection of some of the items in the Black Museum not covered elsewhere in this book.

Above right: A pair of binoculars sent to a young girl in the 1940s with the instructions to look through them and pull the string. Fortunately they were intercepted before they could be used for their horrific purpose.

Below right: A suitcase fitted with a hypodermic needle. It was intended for use in killing witnesses in the trial against the Kray brothers (East End gangsters). The idea was to inject cyanide into victims at bus stops and on Underground stations. Fortunately the suitcase was never used.

Opposite above: John Robinson concealed Minnie Alice Bonati's body in this trunk in the 'Rochester Row' murder of 1927.

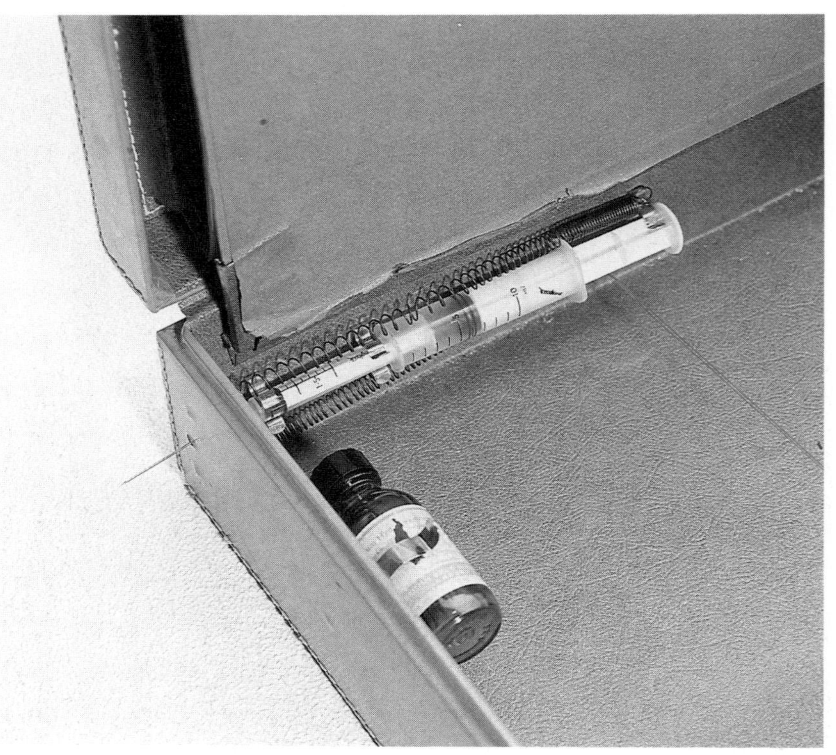

Below left: The minute pellet (1.53 mm in diameter) which was fired through the tip of an 'umbrella' into the thigh of Bulgarian defector Georgi Markov as he waited at a bus stop on Waterloo Bridge in 1978. The pellet is shown mounted on a scanning electron microscope. The exhibit is resting on a photographic enlargement of the pellet (somewhat distorted as the actual pellet is completely round). The photograph shows the holes through which the poison – ricin – reached the bloodstream. Ricin is derived from the castor oil bean and is a particularly toxic agent, a minute quantity of which can cause death. The crime was thought to be committed by the Bulgarian Secret Service.

Overleaf: The Great Train Robbery took place in August 1963 when the Glasgow to London mail-train was robbed by fifteen men. During the attack, in which over two million pounds-worth of used notes were seized, the driver received injuries which contributed to his death a few years later.

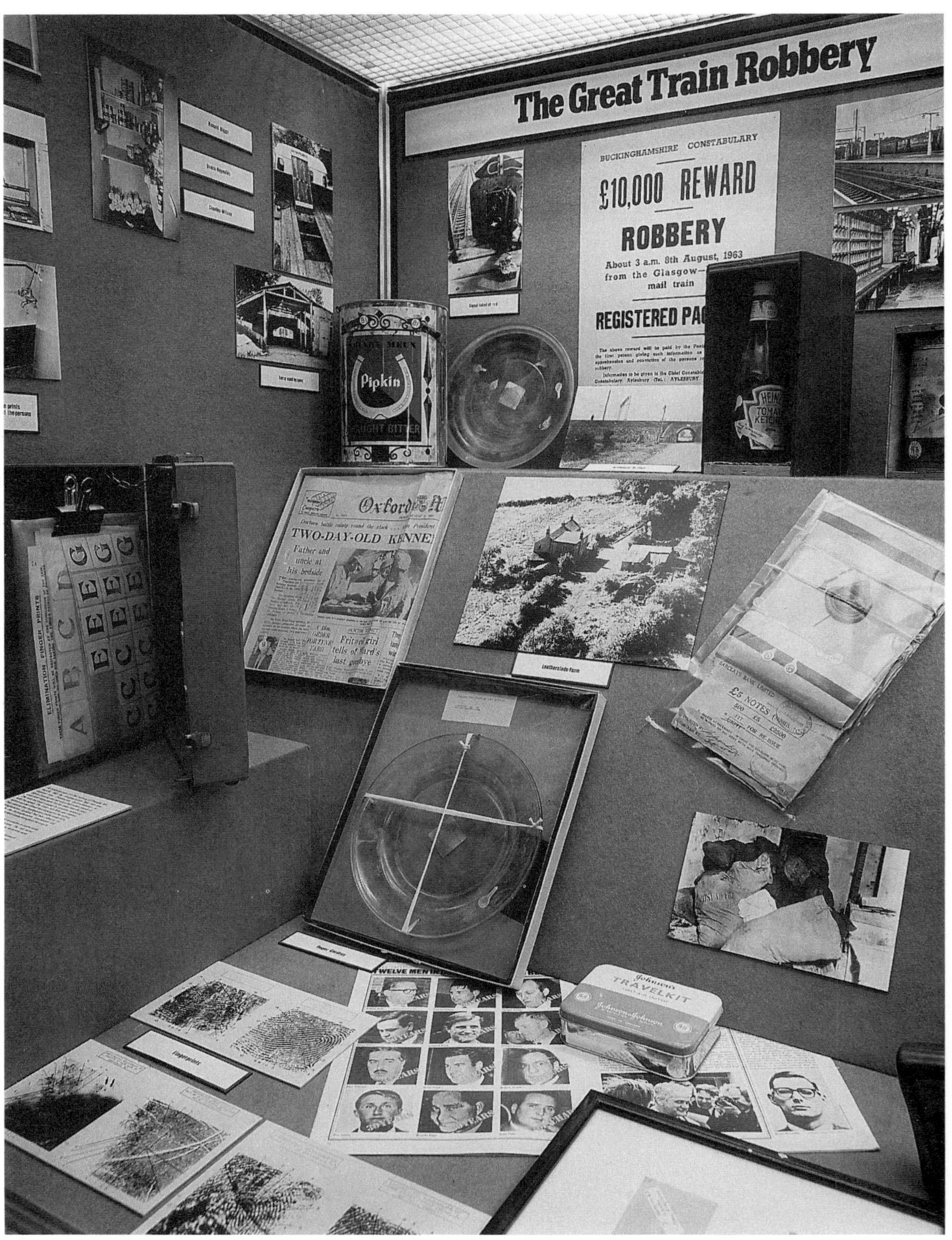
The Great Train Robbery
BUCKINGHAMSHIRE CONSTABULARY
£10,000 REWARD
ROBBERY
About 3 a.m. 8th August, 1963
from the Glasgow—
mail train
REGISTERED PAC
Pipkin
DRAUGHT BITTER
HEINZ
TOMATO KETCHUP
Oxford
TWO-DAY-OLD KENNE
Father and uncle at his bedside
Fritwell girl tells of lord's last goodbye
Leatherslade Farm
ELIMINATION FINGER PRINTS
£5 NOTES
TRAVELKIT
Johnson & Johnson
TWELVE MEN
Fingerprints

A set of rooms in the basement was provided for the Black Museum — or, as it was supposed to be called, the Police Museum. Though there was no curator as such, Police Constable Randall was responsible for keeping the place tidy, adding to the exhibits, and vetting applications for visits and arranging dates for them; sergeants from the Criminal Record Office took turns as tour-conductors.

After Randall's retirement in 1900, comparatively few exhibits were added; none at all during the First World War, when the museum was closed. But in 1921 a 'Police Museum Committee' was formed, and a sergeant in the CRO was assigned, part-time, to do the day-to-day work. The museum was redesigned in 1936 — only to be closed during the Second World War. In 1951 exhibits considered to be of interest only to policemen were transferred to the Detective Training Museum at the Hendon Police College, leaving space for the display of a larger number of relics of particular cases. During the next few years the museum started to become less particular to the Metropolitan Police, by the bringing in of some exhibits that were unmetropolitan, and some that recalled events prior to the formation of the police. In 1955 a full-time curator was appointed; he and several of his successors had no previous association with the police, but by the start of the 1960s it was usual for the post to be occupied by a retired detective.

Though two extensions were added to New Scotland Yard, by the mid-1960s larger and more modern premises were needed. And so in 1967 the Metropolitan Police moved from the fine building to a rented tower-block of nineteen storeys jutting above St James's Underground Station, in Victoria. All that distinguishes it from the surrounding concrete slabs is a revolving metal sign, on each of the three faces of which are the words 'NEW SCOTLAND YARD'. The sign stands in the forecourt — or perhaps one should say aft-court, considering that everyone who works in the new New Scotland Yard refers to the front hall as the back hall — a convention that goes back to the early days of the force, when most officers entered or left by the rear door of 4 Whitehall Place in Great Scotland Yard.

The Black Museum is on the first floor. Redesigned in 1981, part of the area is meant to capture the 'feel' of the earlier museums, and the rest is (or was, in 1981) ultra-modern.

Over the years many famous people have signed the visitors' books. Several members of the British royal family have been shown around, the Prince of Wales (later King Edward VII) being the first, and Princess Diana of Wales the most recent.

Sept. 18.	Edward Smith	Athenaeum Club.
27	W. S. Gilbert.	London - Savoy Theatre
	Arthur Sullivan	London.

"	[illegible]	[illegible]
"	Harry Houdini	New York
	[illegible]	[illegible]

	[illegible]	[illegible]
"	Jerome K Jerome	[illegible]
"	A. Conan Doyle.	So. Norwood.
"	E. W. Hornung.	Abingdon Mansions, W.

Among other eye-catching signatures are those of Gilbert and Sullivan, Laurel and Hardy, and the escapologist Harry Houdini (who must have been particularly interested in the collection of manacles, some guaranteed to be 'escape-proof'). In excessive contravention of the rule that 'non-legal' persons may not enter the museum unless they are vouched for, and are in the company of persons qualified for admission, in 1893 the entire Australian cricket team was squeezed in. On 10 December of the previous year, three members of a cricket team made up of contributors to the *Idler* magazine were brought to the museum by a magistrate-friend of one of them: Jerome K. Jerome, the *Idler*'s editor, who, three years before had achieved wider fame as the author of *Three Men in a Boat*; E.W. Hornung, who six years later published the first of his tales about the amateur cricketer and cracksman Raffles; and Hornung's prospective brother-in-law, Arthur Conan Doyle, who five years before had published the first of his tales about Sherlock Holmes. (At the end of 'The Adventure of the Empty House', which appeared in *The Strand Magazine* in October 1903, Watson comments that Holmes has hit upon the truth regarding the criminal's motive, and Holmes replies: 'It will be verified or disproved at the trial. Meanwhile, come what may, — — will trouble us no more. The famous air-gun of Von Herder will embellish the Scotland Yard Museum, and once again Mr Sherlock Holmes is free to devote his life to examining those interesting little problems which the complex life of London so plentifully presents.')

Some visitors, upon entering the museum, experience an uneasy feeling that they are under surveillance. The feeling is probably attributable to a side-of-the-eye glimpsing of a row of heads on a tall shelf. The heads, which are made of plaster, are the death-masks of murderers, most of whom were executed outside Newgate Gaol in the first half of the nineteenth century, when there was widespread acceptance of the 'science' of phrenology, the study of bumps on real or facsimile heads as a guide to people's excess or shortage of various mental faculties. The death-masks that have been in the museum longest were acquired by Howard Vincent, the Director of the Criminal Investigation Division between 1879 and 1884, who, influenced by Cesare Lombroso's theory that, cranially speaking, there were definite 'criminal types', showed the masks to trainee-detectives, telling them to be suspicious of any men bearing a resemblance to them. Vincent may have acquired his batch of masks from the Chief Warder at Newgate — from whose office most of the others were salvaged for the museum just before the prison was pulled down in 1902.

The masks, thirty-seven of them, are doubly representative — of the crime of murder and of the capital punishment of murderers. Since those are the subjects in which visitors express the greatest interest, we will devote most of this book to some of the Black Museum's exhibits relating to the first, and will begin with a section that outlines significant events in the history — ended not all that long ago — of the second.

A SELECT CALENDAR OF CAPITAL PUNISHMENT

There is no knowing how long established in Britain capital punishment was by the fifth century BC. Quagmires then being a feature of many tribal lands, they were put to the dual purpose of stifling those condemned and interring their remains. Other means and methods must have also been used, if only in parched places, but none has been trustworthily inferred by archaeologists. Hanging was favoured in Anglo-Saxon times, but beheading, casting from cliffs, burning, stoning, and drowning were not uncommon. If, as most authorities have it, capital punishment fell into disuse immediately following the Norman Conquest, it was reintroduced during the reign of Henry I (1100–35). According to John Laurence, a historian of capital punishment (*see Bibliography*):

(Opposite)
The 'New Drop' at Newgate.

In 1350 the statute Pro Clero read . . .'all manner of clerks, as well secular as religious, which shall be from henceforth convicted before the secular justices aforesaid for any treasons or felonies touching other persons than the King himself or his royal majesty, shall from henceforth freely have and enjoy the privilege of Holy Church, and shall be, without any impeachment or delay, delivered to the ordinaries demanding them'.

In practice this came to mean immunity for all who could read. Anyone could claim benefit of clergy and was examined as to his scholarship. This examination consisted in the reading of a passage, usually from the 51st Psalm, which was appropriately called 'the neck verse'. . . . The Church naturally did not extend its protection to heretics, who were burnt alive. Heresy had a very wide meaning. In 1222 a deacon was burned at Oxford for embracing Judaism in order to marry a Jewess, and many who lived with Jewesses were sentenced to death for having committed an unnatural office. . . .

Clerics came to include all who were tonsured or had their hair cut in clerical fashion. The privilege of clergy was only allowed in case of a first conviction after 1487, and to prevent a second claim it was the practice to brand murderers with the letter M upon the brawn of the left thumb, and other felons with the 'Tyburn T'. Ben Jonson was, in 1598, so marked for manslaughter.

By the late fifteenth century there were eight categories of capital crime: treason, petty treason (the killing of a husband by his wife), murder, larceny, robbery, burglary, rape, and arson.

The country-wide annual average number of executions during the reign of Henry VIII was about 2000, and it was slightly fewer for the forty-five years till 1603, when that Henry's daughter Elizabeth was on the throne. (For some forty years from near the end of Elizabeth's reign, a man called Derrick seems to have been the busiest of the hangmen. As early as 1608, not only was his name associated with his trade, but that trade was associated with his name — by Thomas

Dekker, at any rate, whose best-selling *Belman of London: Bringing to Light the Most Notorious Villanies that are now practiced in the Kingdoms* has an article entitled 'Prigging [thieving] Law' that contains these lines: 'For he [the prigger] rides his circuit with the devil, and Derrick must be his host, and Tiburne, the land at which he will light . . . at the gallows, where I leave them, as to the haven at which they must cast anchor, if Derrick's cables do but hold.' Derrick's first assignment had been forced upon him: while employed domestically by the Earl of Essex, he was sentenced to death but then pardoned on condition that he hanged a job-lot of twenty-three other delinquents, and he carried out that task with a type of crane that, from his subsequent remunerated use of it on countless similar occasions, came to be known as a derrick.) Though the first year of the reign of Henry VIII's son, the juvenile Edward VI, was marked by a tender Act — deleting boiling to death from the selection of methods — the volume of executions appears to have reached a peak, albeit comparatively slight, while he was the ostensible king. In those years, 1547–53, the annual average at Tyburn alone was 560.

For over two hundred years from 1571, the Tyburn Tree stood at the foot of the Edgware Road, about where Marble Arch is now. Fast-growing, the 'tree' was, in its heyday, a triangular contraption of three tall posts that were joined at the top by beams, each capable of suspending eight persons lately left dangling by the whipping away of the deliverers' carts; and so the whole thing could accommodate twenty-four. The procession of the condemned along the three-mile westerly route from Newgate Prison was as much a part of 'Tyburn Fair' as the culminating reason for it: a good time was had by all those who, lining the narrow streets or sitting in bought comfort at windows or in the stands called Mother Proctor's Pews, got a view of the cartloads of offenders, each with a rope ready round his neck, a wreath in his hands, and, if he could afford one, a coffin by his side. From some time before 1678 until 1686, many of those who made the one-way journey to Tyburn were received there by Richard Jacquet, whose nickname of Jack Ketch was eventually applied to all executioners. Towards the end of 1783, the authorities, pandering to the wish of an increased number of genteel residents of the West End, did away with the processional preamble to metropolitan hangings, simply by felling the Tyburn Tree in favour of a scaffold, less crowdable but sophisticated by a 'drop floor', next to Newgate — a handiness that displeased not only those whose sport was spoiled but also those of their superiors who approved of the 'moral lesson' of capital punishment. This 'lesson' was outlined by Samuel Johnson, who started off by exclaiming against the extreme reduction in travelling time from condemned cells to gallows as an instance of change for change's sake:

The age is running mad after innovation: all the business of the world is to be done in a new way: Tyburn itself is not safe from the fury of innovation! . . . No, Sir, it is not an improvement: they object that the old method drew together a number of spectators. Sir, executions are intended *to draw spectators. If they do not draw spectators, they don't answer their purpose. The old method was most satisfactory to all parties: the public was gratified by a procession: the criminal was supported by it. Why is all this to be swept away?*

In keeping with a growing regard for property, the number of capital offences grew to 222 by 1810; these included stealing a pocket handkerchief, cutting down someone else's tree (the 'Black Act', 1723), robbing a rabbit warren, shoplifting goods worth more than five shillings, counterfeiting stamps used for the sale of perfumes and hair-powders; and anyone who personated a Greenwich pensioner ran the risk of dying for doing so. But the law was more severe in theory than in practice: from about the middle of the eighteenth century, there were only 24 offences for which death was actually suffered.

Between 1811 and 1832, hangings in England averaged 80 a year, of which 70 were for murder. During those years the number of persons who received the punishment — usually as the alternative to execution — of transportation for life rose steadily from 29 to 547.

1818. Hanging was abolished as a punishment for shoplifting.

James Foxton, or Foxen, who took up hanging during this year, and earned his living from it for more than a decade, seems to have been more perfectionist than his predecessors. In August 1828, shortly after he announced his intention to retire at the end of the year, he was given the plum job of dispatching William Corder, the murderer of Maria Marten in the Red Barn at Polstead, a Suffolk village not far from the market-town whose name of Bury was apt to the event of Corder's execution. Perhaps partly because Foxton was over-keen to make his ending of Corder the crowning glory of his own career, the salient moment of the ceremony came several moments too soon. According to the contemporary J. Curtis (*see Bibliography*):

The apparatus for the execution was exceedingly simple, and much smaller than the ponderous machine used at Newgate. Instead of being straight, the cross-beam is a kind of slender curve, holes perforated in it for the insertion of the rope. . . .

After the executioner had fixed the rope to the beam, and was busy in tying what he called the 'mysterious knot', it was suggested to him that he had left too much of what is technically called 'the fall', in consequence of which he reluctantly took part of it up, and it was quite evident that *Mister Ketch* did not relish this interference with his public functions.

Everything being completely adjusted, the executioner descended from the scaffold, and just before the reverend chaplain had commenced his last prayer, he severed, with a knife, the rope which supported the platform, and Corder was cut off from the land of the living. Immediately he was suspended, *Ketch* grasped the culprit round the waist, in order to finish his earthly sufferings, which were at an end in a very few minutes. In his last agonies the prisoner raised his hands several times; but the muscles soon relaxed, and they sank as low as the bandage round his arms would permit.

Later in the day, during a visit to the Shire Hall for the purpose of claiming Corder's trousers (just one of his perks), Foxton tried to make the best of what the multitude had considered a bad job by suggesting that the slight signs of his handiwork in the region of Corder's throat proved that he had 'done the job in a masterly manner'. Actually, though, he was upset; and that feeling stayed with him, being made worse by his overhearing and reading of general criticisms of him that sprang solely from the particular error at Bury. As soon as he was about to retire and had no need to mind his p's and q's, he sought to pass the buck for Corder's Amen-less descent and pre-mortem suspension, ascribing the prematurity of the fall to official interference in his 'mysteries', and the unsudden dying to official insistence upon a shortened drop: 'I never like to be meddled with, because I always study the subjects which come under my hands, and according as they are tall or short, heavy or light, I accommodate them with the fall. No man in England has had so much experience as me, or knows how to do his duty better.'

One of the few first-hand accounts of how it felt to be inefficiently hanged was passed on to a reporter by an Irish youth who, having been found guilty of sheep-stealing, was supposed to have been executed at Omagh in 1825:

After the body had dangled at the end of the rope for the prescribed time, it was cut down and handed over to the convict's relatives.

As it happened, however, the youth recovered, and, beyond a slight distortion of the neck, was none the worse for his experience, as far as his physical condition was concerned. He said that though he felt the jerk of the rope when the ladder was turned, he did not become unconscious. He seemed to have the power of seeing all round, above and below him. Then everything turned a bright red colour, and a sort of half sleepy sensation crept through his frame, till he became insensible.

That account partially tallies with that of an actor who was accidentally hanged during a stage performance in the 1890s:

Under proper conditions, Mr H— was hauled up over the branch of an imitation tree by means of a cord fastened to his belt, but one night the attachment to the cord slipped, and the noose tightened round the neck of the son of Thespis. Fortunately, a 'super' standing in the wings noticed that Mr H— was almost blue in the face, and rescued him. Describing his experience, Mr H— said that he felt a burning sensation in the head for a second or two, then everything seemed to become a brilliant red, changing suddenly to a bright green. In his ears he could hear the sound of rushing waters, and the lights of the vast auditorium were blotted out. Of actual pain, he felt very little, save for the fact that his head seemed to feel too small. Then he lost consciousness.

1818. The influential caricaturist George Cruikshank subsequently recalled:

I was returning home between 8 and 9 a.m. down Ludgate Hill, and saw several human beings hanging opposite Newgate, and to my horror two of them were women. On enquiring, I was informed that it was for passing forged one-pound notes! It had a great effect on me, and I determined, if possible, to put a stop to this shocking destruction of life for merely obtaining a few shillings by fraud. I felt sure that in many cases the rascals who had forged the notes induced these poor, ignorant women to go into the gin shops and get 'something to drink', and then *pass* the notes and hand them the change.

Cruikshank at once sketched a 'Bank Note — not to be imitated' which, when published by his friend William Hone, caused such a stir that the Bank of England stopped issuing one-pound notes. But still, in 1820 the sentence of death was carried out on 46 persons found guilty of having forged bank-notes — some of which turned out to be good. Not until 1836 did the offences of coining and forgery become non-capital.

1822. By an Act proposed by Sir Robert Peel, the Home Secretary, no more 'Tyburn Tickets' were issued, and those in existence became invalid. Since 1699 anyone bringing to justice a person guilty of burglary, housebreaking, horse-stealing, or stealing goods to the value of five shillings or more from shops, warehouses or coach-houses (all offences that were still or had only recently ceased to be capital), was entitled to such a 'ticket' — a certificate exempting him from compulsory service as an officer of the parish in which the crime was committed. There is no doubt that to some of the people who dreaded being conscripted to the ranks of, for instance, petty constables, rate collectors, or overseers of the poor, the promise of a 'Tyburn Ticket' acted as an irresistible temptation to give perjured evidence. In 1816 about 500 of the transferable 'tickets' were in force in London — many having been handed down in families from generation to generation, but many more having been purchased (for between £12 and £40 — far below the going rate in Manchester, where 'tickets' were auctioned for as much as £300).

1827–30. In these three years, from the May of the first to the May of the last, of 451 persons sentenced to death, only 51 were executed.

1829–74. William Calcraft was helped to become an executioner by events that seemed to show that it was his destiny. Born near Chelmsford, Essex, about 1800, the first of his parents' dozen children, he migrated to London while still a boy, and there followed various occupations, shoemaking among them. At the age of twenty-five or so he married a

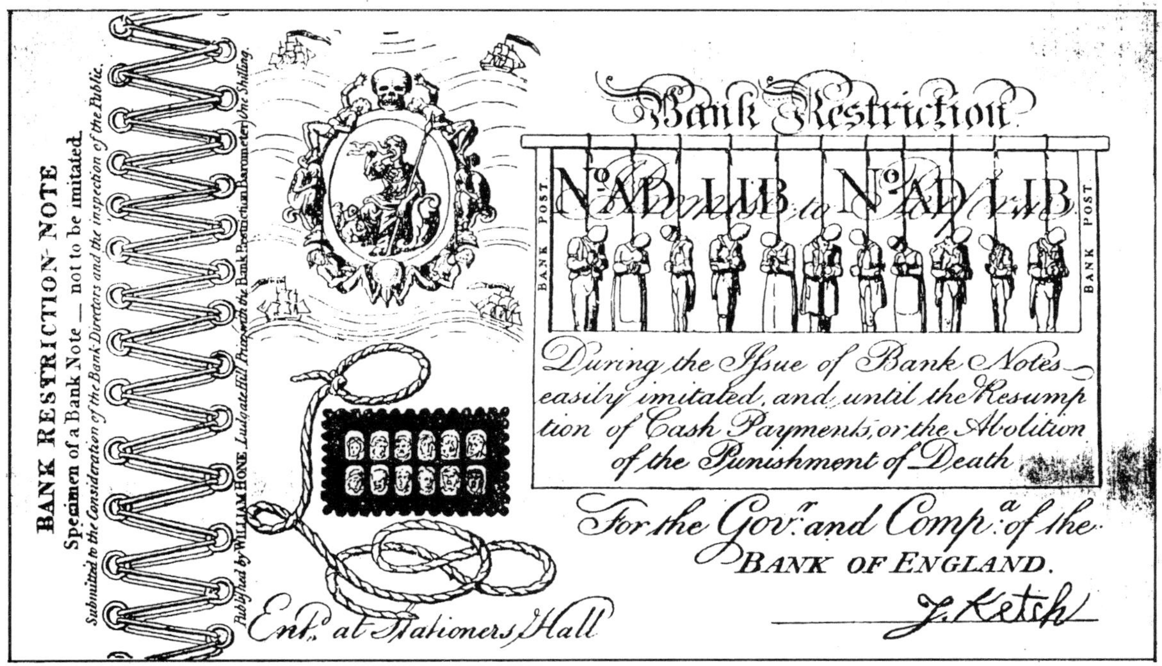

Cruikshank's version (see top of facing page).

woman who, so she said, was twenty-nine. By 8 December 1828, he was an itinerant vendor of pies. On the morning of that day (a Monday), he was peddling near Newgate, where a great crowd was gathered for the hanging of Joseph Hunton, a Quaker convicted of forgery. The hangman was James Foxton. Three weeks from his retirement, he had been called in at short notice as stand-in for the regular man at Newgate, Tom Cheshire — who, never mind polite reports that he was 'temporarily incapacitated through illness', was in a state described in less polite ones as 'bordering on delirium tremens'. According to a journalist who, writing soon after Calcraft's death, claimed to have spent much time with him, he was often in reminiscent mood:

During the time that the execution of Hunton was in progress, Calcraft had remained silent, and had temporarily suspended the sale of his pies, but immediately the struggles of the man had ceased he again commenced to sell his edibles. A man was busily engaged in close proximity to the scaffold in selling beer from a huge can to those of the crowd whose thirst required and whose pockets permitted a draught of the liquid. As Calcraft worked his way past the gallows, he saw the executioner, James Foxton, come from beneath them, apparently weak and faint, and heard him call to the beer-man, who, however, failed to hear him; whereupon Calcraft stepped up to him and offered to procure a draught of ale or porter for him, an offer which the hangman gratefully accepted. A conversation followed between the pair, in which Calcraft, in order to emphasize his assertion regarding the hard times he had experienced, expressed his willingness to take to the hangman's 'line of business', whereupon the latter informed him that he intended to 'turn it up shortly', and promised to say a word for Calcraft if ever an opportunity occurred.

Calcraft thought little more of Foxton's promise, but some time after the meeting above referred to he received a request by special messenger, to attend at Newgate on the following morning. He duly presented himself at the appointed time — ten o'clock — and was shown into the presence of the Governor of Newgate (Mr Wontner), one of the under-sheriffs, and several aldermen. He was informed that his name had been mentioned to them by Foxton, and was asked if he thought he could flog two or three boys. Calcraft replied that he was willing to try, and was eventually told to present himself at Newgate the following morning. At that time he was told by one of the prison warders that he would have to flog four boys, and after a few instructions in the flogging yard he inflicted the necessary chastisement on the youths, and did it so effectually and satisfactorily that he was engaged by the authorities for the same purpose on all future occasions, at a fixed salary of ten shillings per week.

Foxton had hardly become accustomed to retirement when, on 14 February, St Valentine's Day, he dropped dead. Till then the Court of Aldermen of the City seem to have felt that they could muddle along with Tom Cheshire, using Foxton as a free-lance whenever Cheshire was too hung-over to do any hangings; but in the absence of a London-residing reserve, the Aldermen felt obliged to sack Cheshire (though kindly allowing him, on those odd occasions when a fit of soberness coincided with an execution morning, to stand in the scaffold's background, hard-pressed on both sides by burly officials as a precaution against his falling in sleep; he died the following year, drunk at his passing). The hundreds of applicants for the consequent vacancy were whittled to a short-list of two — Calcraft and a man whose name (which was Smith) was all that was publicly divulged of him. At the end of an extraordinary but brief meeting of the Court of Aldermen, Calcraft, recipient of Foxton's reference, was picked unanimously. Supposing that the following description of the swearing-in ceremony is about right (there was, and for centuries had been, a ceremony of some sort — in Calcraft's case, occupying the small hours of Sunday, 5 April 1829), then Calcraft was probably the last recruit to be put through it:

Assembled with great pomp were the Recorder of London and his secretary, the Clerk of Arraigns, the Lord Mayor and his chief clerk, the Sheriffs and the City Marshal, the Governors of Newgate and

Horsemonger Lane Gaols, and one of the Crown Judges, together with the Town Crier, officers of the peace, javelin men, and other officers. They met in secret conclave, the Crown Judge being seated at a bench, elevated somewhat and covered with black cloth, and wearing dark caps trimmed with scarlet, and underneath on a large scroll were the words: 'Whoso sheddeth man's blood by man also shall his blood be shed.' All the other officials were dressed in their full civic costumes, scarlet robes, wigs, and gowns, some holding their wands, others their batons of authority, and various insignia of office. The Recorder announced that the court for choosing and swearing in of an executioner of felons and traitors was now sitting, according to the laws of the ancient realm, etc., after which the crier cried out, 'God save the King!' and the whole assembly responded, 'Amen!' A bell now began to toll the funeral knell, and in a few moments the Judge asked for the name of the selected candidate to fill the solemn office of Executioner, and the Sheriff replied:

'The man we have chosen to be his most gracious Majesty the King's Executioner, my Lord, is William Calcraft.'

'Bring in a well-sharpened axe,' responded the Sheriff; whereupon the Keeper of the Axe brought in a very wide-bladed axe, sharpened to a very keen edge, and placed it on the Judge's table. This was the axe that had been used for beheading traitors. Then the Sheriff said:

'Bring in the usual leg-irons, handcuffs, and other fetters,' and in obedience to the command the Keeper of the Irons brought in the leg-irons, handcuffs, and other manacles, and laid them on the table, the bell during this time continuing to toll.

'Now,' said the Sheriff, 'bring in the halter and a pair of white caps and the beheading knife, well sharpened.' These were then laid on the table by the Keeper of the Halter, Straps, and Knife.

'Bring in the candidate now,' said the Sheriff, and the doorkeeper threw open the door and called William Calcraft. In a few moments Calcraft walked in. He was a somewhat short, thick-set man, about 5ft 6in. in height and weighing about 11½ stone. He was slightly pock-marked, had a somewhat large mouth, thick lips, and coarse, short, black curly hair, and was clean-shaven. He was ordered to kneel and take the oath of secrecy in his office, and this having been done, the Sheriff said:

'Let him now be sworn, and take in the most solemn manner the solemn oath of his most gracious Majesty the King's Executioner.' Calcraft, still kneeling, then took the oath, the prescribed form being that the candidate laid his left hand on the axe and his right hand on the Bible, and then, in the most solemn manner, repeated the following oath after the Clerk of Arraigns:

'I do hereby most solemnly swear to hang or behead, or otherwise destroy, all felons and enemies of our lord the King and of his subjects, duly sentenced according to law, and that I will do the like unto father, mother, sister, or brother, and all other kindred whatsoever, without favour or hindrance, irrespective of sex or age. So help me God!'

John Holloway.

During this time the Judge held over his head the great sword of justice. The knife, the axe, the halter, and the manacles were then given into his hands. He was then commanded to rise. A thick black veil was thrown over his head, so as to conceal his features, and he was then led out of the court amidst the groans of the assemblage, the tolling of the bell, and the withering words of the Judge: 'Get thee hence, wretch!'

The City paid Calcraft a retainer — at first of a guinea a week, but eventually, by two rises of a florin each, of twenty-five shillings — and he received a guinea per execution and five shillings per flogging. Perhaps because he felt that the fee for flogging was generous, and feared transmitting that feeling to his paymasters (who might then reduce the fee), he never complained that by comparison — in terms both of his rehearsal time and of the public's interest in his performance — the executional piecework rate was low. Or perhaps — and this seems more likely — he recognized that the fact that he was employed by the City was of far greater importance than any arithmetic in regard to the City's total annual emoluments to him. Even if the position had been honorary, it would have been worth having for all the non-City jobs, nice little earners, that stemmed from it: for instance, the post, virtually complementary to that at Newgate, of executioner at the Surrey County Gaol in Horsemonger Lane (annual retainer of five pounds; a guinea per hanging); and, since all English and Welsh counties, excepting Yorkshire, were within the province of the City executioner, plenty of out-of-town assignments (for which the call-out fee ranged from £8 to £12, expenses extra; as discount was offered on hangings over and above one, so long as all were in a single-morning, same-scaffold batch, the treasurers of local authorities in which one person was awaiting execution and another, not yet tried, was odds-on to be condemned, had to weigh the gain from a discount against the costs incurred in keeping the first prisoner alive till the second could die with him). And public executions provided fringe-profits to the executioners — chiefly from the sale, often to specializing dealers, of souvenirs (items, patently personal, from an executed person's pockets or purse, suddenly secondhand articles of clothing, and, most profitable of the perks, snippings of hemp: *see page 117n*), but also from a service to sufferers from cysts, as exemplified in a report of the hanging of John Holloway, the first Brighton 'trunk murderer' — of his wife, a midget called Celia — at Lewes, Sussex, on 16 December 1831:

A great number of persons had assembled, and as the doomed man appeared on the scaffold he was received with loud yells and groans. A man who throughout his lifetime had been afflicted with a very unsightly wen on his neck had persuaded Calcraft to permit him to come upon the scaffold for the purpose of endeavouring to cure the wen by rubbing or stroking it with the hand of the hanged man. As soon as Calcraft saw that life was extinct, he unfastened the culprit's hands and unpinioned his arms, and, taking hold of one of the dead man's hands, commenced stroking the other man's neck with it. The people began to hiss and yell, thinking that Calcraft and the 'patient' were having a lark, and the sheriffs mounted the scaffold and demanded an explanation of the performance. Calcraft and the man replied that they were adopting the charm which was said, in some books written in the Middle Ages, to be the best and only cure for a wen. The sheriffs at once ordered Calcraft to desist from his operation, as it was his duty, they said, to kill and not to cure.

John Holloway was but one of a host of celebrated murderers who, by making their final appearance with and owing to Calcraft, made him as celebrated as all of them put together. Reference is made to three of them, and to Calcraft's engineering of their downfall, elsewhere in this book: John Tawell (*page 99*), the Mannings (*page 137n*), and Franz Müller (*page 130*). Among the others were *François Courvoisier* — Swiss born, in common with Marie Manning — who was hanged at Newgate on 6 July 1840 for having terminated his employment as valet to Lord William Russell by near enough decapitating that member of the distinguished Bedford family; *James Blomfield Rush*, the auctioneer who was hanged at Norwich — close to the scene of his crimes, the shooting to death of a

Frederick Manning *Solicitors* *Marie Manning*

CLARK'S EDITION.

A FULL REPORT

OF THE

TRIAL OF JAMES BLOMFIELD RUSH

FOR THE

MURDER OF MR. JERMY AND HIS SON,

OF

STANFIELD HALL, IN THE COUNTY OF NORFOLK;

COMMENCING ON WEDNESDAY, MARCH 28, AND CONCLUDED APRIL 4, 1849, AT NORWICH ASSIZES.

PORTRAIT OF RUSH, SKETCHED IN THE COURT.

[TWENTY-SECOND EDITION.]

LONDON:

PRINTED AND PUBLISHED BY W. M. CLARK, 17, WARWIC

PRICE SIXPENCE.

(Far right)
The death-mask of Greenacre.

creditor and his son — on 21 April 1849 (having the night before enjoyed the dinner he had requested, of 'roast pig and plenty of plum sauce'; pernickety to very nearly the end, which he may have delayed by telling Calcraft to take his time, he insisted upon the noose being fitted 'a little higher'); *James Greenacre*, the wheeler-dealer in real estate who was hanged on 2 May 1837 for the murder, probably with a rolling-pin, of Hannah Brown, a washerwoman whose pregnancy by him had threatened his desire to prolong co-habitation, eventually in America, with a young woman named Sarah Gale. (Amid the exorbitant audience at Newgate, pie-pedlars, successors to Calcraft in that regard, caused their cold wares to sell like hot cakes by calling them 'Greenacres' — an early use of the marketing tactic of selling a brand-name rather than a product. The success of the tactic on that occasion must have been due to the number of frustrated cannibals present, their appetites whetted for the 'Greenacres' by the delicacy-by-association fact that after Greenacre had killed Hannah Brown he had cut her into portions — admittedly more than pie-sized — and distributed them round the town. To the present day, when stevedores in the few remaining London docks let fall a case of soft fruits — with the result that the case splits open and the fruits roll, the unblemished of them to be pounced upon and pocketed — the object of the accident is referred to as 'a Greenacre'.)

As time passed, and especially after executing was made an indoor occupation, Calcraft, ever more evidently prosperous, encountered fewer and fewer rebuffs on account of the source of his prosperity. The only apparently clear indication that he tried, using artificial means, to seclude his official duties from his social and domestic life is a report that he purchased his black suits — always black — two at a time: the minute he arrived at the place of work (latterly in his career, in obedience to a new rule, always on the eve of an execution), he changed from one suit to its duplicate, and as soon as he had performed his function and got the prison governor's signature on his work-sheet, he again changed suits. One wonders whether Calcraft, a frugal man, actually kept each suit particular of usage; if he did, then the executional suit was still perfectly good when its contemporary was becoming threadbare. Perhaps he occasionally bought just one suit, replicating how its predecessor had looked in its prime, and how that predecessor's better-preserved half still did; or perhaps he bought his suits not two at a time but in threes; or perhaps the two-at-a-time tale was, like a good many more concerning Calcraft, made out of whole cloth.

Calcraft's first interview with the executioner.

During his period in office (which, with the possible exception of the aforementioned Derrick's, was the longest ever), journalists assigned to write 'Calcraft the Man' articles experienced great difficulty, always overcome, in making him seem as out of the ordinary as their editors insisted that he had to be. He exhibited devotion to his wife and children — two sons and a daughter; he was a churchgoer, an animal-lover, a supporter of charities (none in aid of causes at all considerate of the criminal classes). In 1855, or thereabouts, he bought a nice house in Poole Street, Shoreditch, a mile or so north of Newgate, and soon made the garden prettier than those of his neighbours — to whom he endeared himself, if in no other way than by explaining how they might rid themselves of the snails in their gardens. These had originally been in his garden, but since he had not liked the idea of exterminating any of God's smaller creatures, he had forced them into exodus. Proof positive that he was a pillar of society, he was admitted without opposition from existing members to membership of a gentlemen's club in the West End. That place was the setting of one of the few verified anecdotes concerning his extra-professional life: upon entering the club one day, intending to take a nap, he was accosted by a loquacious provincial member, who cried out, bursting with laughter as he did so, 'Whenever I come to London, the hangman is always the first person I see!' — to which Calcraft replied, with no pretence of merriment, 'You may be sure that he will also be the last.'

On the rare occasions when Calcraft allowed himself to be drawn into talking shop, he took care to stress that, so far as he was concerned, hanging was 'just a job', peculiar only in the sense of being exclusive, and no more unpleasant than lots of others he could mention. There is no doubt that he meant what he said. If he had discerned any 'mysteries' in his occupation he might have contributed something towards the science of it; as it was, when he retired on 25 May 1874 — directly after hanging, in Newgate, a young man named John Godwin who had done away with his wife — the only tricks of the trade that he had added to those he had picked up some forty-five years before from James Foxton were to do with after-the-fall emergencies arising from inadequate consideration of factors relating to stature, age, and sex that affected how far a person had to drop so that the noose neither slowly strangled nor decapitated.

Calcraft — who enjoyed five years of retirement, pensioned at twenty-five shillings a week — deserved the gratitude of his successors, and of everyone who approved of capital punishment, for having gained such an extent of respectability that some of it had overlapped on to the way he had earned his living. It would be going too far, much too far, to say that he had given the office of public executioner a touch of class, but he had certainly — though only by his conduct away from the gallows — made that office seem less disestimable.

Meanwhile, both the ostensible scope of capital punishment and the degree of audience participation in it had been reduced, as indicated by some of the first of the following entries:

1832–7. Capital punishment was abolished for a large number of crimes, including returning from transportation, attempted

Daniel M'Naghten.

murder, horse-stealing, cattle-stealing, sheep-stealing (whence came the Somerset proverb that one might as well be hanged for a sheep as a lamb), rick-burning, burglary, and stealing letters from the Post Office; consequently, the number of persons sentenced to death dropped from 438 in 1837 to 56 in 1839. Acts were passed which respectively provided for the bodies of all executed criminals to be buried within the prison precincts and discontinued the practice of dissecting executed murderers before exposing their bodies to public view.

1840. For the first time, a resolution was put before Parliament (by William Ewart, the son of a Liverpool businessman who was William Ewart Gladstone's godfather) that capital punishment should be abolished entirely. The debate was side-tracked towards the question of whether or not the sight of someone being hanged encouraged lawfulness — it did *not*, according to Ewart, who described public executions as 'Saturnalias of the Gallows' and cited a poll conducted by a Bristol parson, whose main finding was that of 168 convicts interviewed just prior to their execution, all but four had first-hand knowledge of what was in store for them. The saying that good causes attract bad advocates seems to have been exemplified by a supporter of Ewart, Sir Stephen Lushington — a founder of the Society for the Diffusion of Useful Knowledge — who asserted, (in defiance of logic and arithmetic) that if a hundred hangings per annum brutalized the public mind, 'six would do so in a twenty-four greater degree'. The motion for total abolition was defeated, but far less comprehensively than had been prophesied by pundits of Parliament, the vote being 161–90.

1841–60. Hanging for rape was abolished (in 1841), and there was extensive repeal of other statutes carrying the death penalty.

1843. Daniel M'Naghten, a thirty-year-old woodworker who had migrated from Glasgow to London, shot and killed Edward Drummond, the private secretary of the prime minister Sir Robert Peel, in mistake for that politician, and was acquitted on the ground of insanity — a verdict that provoked such a furore that it became the subject of debate in the House of Lords, in consequence of which the Lords asked the judges five abstract questions about insanity.

From 1671 till 1812 the Law had relied upon a 'test' that Sir Matthew Hale had devised, not quite on the spur of the moment, to decide whether or not a person was afflicted by 'melancholy distemper'; but in the latter year the prime minister, Spencer Perceval, less fortunate with mistaken

The assassination of Mr Perceval.

identity than was Peel, was shot dead in the lobby of the House of Commons. Before sentence of death was carried out on the guilty party (a previously inoffensive eccentric named John Bellingham), Lord Chief Justice Mansfield expressed the following dictum, thereby establishing the first departure from Hale's criteria: 'The single question is whether, when he [Bellingham] committed the offence, he possessed a sufficient degree of understanding to distinguish good from evil, right from wrong, and whether murder was a crime not only against the law of God, but against the law of his country.'

The 'M'Naghten answers' given by the judges in 1843, their spokesman Lord Chief Justice Tindal, straightway became the 'M'Naghten *rules*' — the essence of which has ever since been explained by judges to juries trying cases where the defence of insanity has been entered in something like the following terms:

> It must be clearly proved that, at the time of the committing of the act, the party accused was labouring under such a defect of reason, from disease of the mind, as not to know the nature and quality of the act he was doing, or, if he did know it, that he did not know he was doing what was wrong.

1861. The number of capital offences was reduced to four (murder, treason, piracy with violence, and arson within the Sovereign's vessels, arsenals and dockyards) by a Criminal Law Consolidation Act.

1866. The Report of a Royal Commission on Capital Punishment, under the chairmanship of the Duke of Richmond, recommended the passing of an Act to end public executions.

On 22 May the last *entirely* public execution in Scotland took place against the south wall of Perth Prison, on a scaffold borrowed from Aberdeen. The condemned man was Joseph Bell, who twelve days before had been found guilty of the murder of Alexander M'Ewan, a baker's vanman who had been shot to death — 'his head veritably riddled with pellets' — in furtherance of the theft of his takings and pocket-money (amounting to £5 10s.0d.) near Vicars Bridge, Blairingone. Bell, who protested his innocence till the end, had been a potter by day, a poacher by night, and in time spared from those occupations, an unrewarded poet. When condemned, he turned to poetry full-time, filling blank spaces in books of an uplifting nature brought to him by a clergyman of Perth. On the title page of a book he bequeathed to his parents, he wrote:

> Dear Father and Mother, it is the 12th of May,
> I wrote these lines for you today;
> Sad news they will have to tell,
> About our parting, Joseph Bell.
>
> In remembrance of me pray keep this book,
> With earnest eyes do on it look,
> For this day we must take farewell.
> Your loving son, Joseph Bell.

And he inscribed a book earmarked for an uncle:

> I cannot help speaking without amaze;
> See how the Court did on the jury gaze
> When the verdict of guilty did sound its knell
> Upon your nephew, Joseph Bell.

It was estimated that about 2000 people surrounded the barricades when Calcraft, on one of his comparatively infrequent excursions across the border, drew the bolt on the borrowed scaffold.

1868. On 11 May, the Capital Punishment Within Prisons Bill, embodying the recommendation of the Royal Commission, received its third reading in the House of Lords and was sent to the Queen for her assent. Next day, up in Scotland, Robert Smith, who was nineteen, was hanged outside Dumfries Prison for the sexually-motivated murder of a little girl named Scott near the village of Cummertrees. Half-bowing to the wish of the Provost of Dumfries that the hanging should be the first done privately, the governor of the prison arranged for the barricades to be erected more for the purpose of restricting the spectators' view of what they had come to see (many having trudged long distances to do so) than to make breathing-space for those directly involved in the event. Rather a shame, that, for the hanging was more suspenseful than most: a *Scots Black Kalendar* (*see Bibliography, under Tod, T.M.*) records that 'the execution, which was the last public one in Scotland, was, however, not carried through with dispatch, as the rope had to be taken off and readjusted before the bolt was drawn. (Askern, of York, officiated.)'

On 26 May, three days before the Capital Punishment Within Prisons Bill received the Royal Assent, a 27-year-old Irish stevedore named Michael Barrett, convicted of having played a leading part in a Fenian bomb outrage on 13 December 1867 that had killed a dozen people (and injured 120 more) at the Clerkenwell House of Detention, was hanged outside nearby Newgate by Calcraft, performing publicly for the last time. Barrett should have become the last person to be hanged publicly in the British Isles earlier than he did. His execution had been postponed for a few days, giving time for an extra-judicial inquiry regarding his contention — from the moment he was arrested and charged in Glasgow, and throughout his trial — that he was nowhere near Clerkenwell around the time of the explosion; the morning after he was eventually hanged, *The Times* suggested that, far from being upset at his treatment, he should have been grateful to British justice for having given him what amounted to two trials — 'It is rare in the history of our criminal jurisprudence that Government allows a sort of special commission to inquire into the validity of a jury's verdict and the judge's approval.' (Nearly forty years passed before, in 1907, a Court of Criminal Appeal was established.) If some people had had their way in 1917, Barrett's place in the history of capital punishment would have been undermined by Sir Roger Casement, condemned to death for treachery on behalf of aims similar to those of Barrett and his fellow-Fenians: it was seriously suggested that as the Act of 1867 referred only to the hanging of murderers, Casement should be executed in some large public place — Hyde Park, perhaps. No one influential took any notice, and Casement was hanged in the privacy of Pentonville Prison. (In 1965 remains said to be his were dug from the Pentonville graveyard and shipped to Eire, a token of the British Government's desire for Anglo-Irish detente.)

THE ILLUSTRATED

POLICE NEWS.

LAW COURTS AND WEEKLY RECORD.

No. 223. | Registered for [illegible] Abroad. | LONDON, SATURDAY, MAY 30, 1868. | Office—[illegible], Strand, London. | PRICE ONE PENNY.

THE EXECUTION OF BARRETT.

FATAL STRUGGLE WITH AN EXCISEMAN

MURDER & ATTEMPTED SUICIDE AT SALFORD

On Thursday, 13 August 1868, the first private execution in Great Britain was carried out in Maidstone Prison, Kent — of Thomas Wells, aged eighteen, the murderer of Edward Adolphus Walshe, the station-master at Dover, in the same county. Next morning *The Times* reported that 'at the moment of the drop there were very few, if any, strangers in the vicinity of the prison, and the town of Maidstone presented quite its usual appearance, presenting a marked extraordinary contrast to that which it exhibited on the occasion of a public execution'; but the *Morning Star*, after breathing a sigh of relief that 'the citizens [have been] freed from the odious accompaniment of an execution', rambled towards a conclusion about a 'spectacle' that wasn't: 'No, the English people cannot long tolerate the spectacle of criminals put to death in a private pit.' Presumably there was strict obedience to ancillary provisions of the causative Act, most of which were meant to allay concern that capital punishment might turn into a hole-and-corner pursuit, not only deficient in moral lessons but seeming (among those who needed such lessons) to be something that was done secretly because it was something to be ashamed of doing. The sheriff, the gaoler, the chaplain, and the prison surgeon had to be present; local Justices of the Peace could attend if they wished, but it was left to the sheriff or visiting justices of the prison to decide whether or not to admit relatives of the prisoner or anyone else. (Passes were almost invariably given to journalists — some of whom, fiction-writers in their spare time too, contributed much to a mythology of private executing that would have grown substantial even if they had been uncreative. Abolitionists who before the Act had prophesied that some papers would vie with some others for 'exclusives' on the private hangings of celebrated criminals were only too happy to be able to lament when it happened. 'The cheap newspapers carry the account of the final scene of disgrace and pain far and wide,' wrote one of the reformers, 'and it is eagerly read by all who are eagerly attracted by baneful excitement.' Twenty years elapsed before the Home Office ordered that the Press were to be excluded, at the same time reminding sheriffs that, as signatories to the Official Secrets Act, they were not allowed to give information about executions to outsiders.) Directly after a hanging, the surgeon had to ensure that its practical purpose had been fulfilled, and once he had signed a declaration that he had done so, the sheriff, gaoler, and chaplain had to sign a declaration to the effect that he was satisfied (the form of words of both documents appears on pages 56–7); no more than hours after a hanging, a coroner's inquest had to be held on the body, which then had to be buried within the precincts of the particular prison.

WILLIAM MARWOOD,
FROM THE WAX MODEL
IN MADAME TUSSAUD'S.

1874–83. Calcraft was succeeded as the Newgate executioner by William Marwood, who, whenever he was required, commuted from the small town of Horncastle, in Lincolnshire, where he had been born in 1820 and where he continued to trade as a cobbler in a one-storey shop near the parish church. He appears to have been chosen, firstly, because he had some experience, having done a few hangings in the Midlands in the absence of the regular local man, and secondly, because he impressed the recruiters by his keen yet unmorbid interest in the executionary task. This had led him to work out a 'long-drop' method — guaranteed, so he said, to break a person's neck by the sudden jerk on the rope. (The recruiters might have queried the guarantee if they had known that, a few years before, Marwood had offered to explain to the Chancellor of the Exchequer a scheme that he guaranteed would wipe out the National Debt.)

Marwood took pride in being a Public Executioner (he insisted upon that title, and showed signs of crossness when anyone spoke or wrote of him as 'a hangman of England'): 'I am doing God's work,' he explained, 'according to the Divine command and the law of the British Crown. I do it simply as a matter of duty and as a Christian. I sleep as soundly as a child and am never disturbed by phantoms. Where there is guilt there is bad sleeping, but I am conscious that I live a blameless life. When I get out of bed on the morning of an execution — not that I do it every day of my life — I kneel down quietly and ask God's blessing on the work I have to do, and His mercy for the poor prisoner. Detesting idleness, I pass my vacant time in business. It would have been better for those I execute if they had preferred industry to idleness.' He had *Public Executioner* business-cards printed; he replaced the tatty sign above his cobbling establishment with a splendid one on which the words 'MARWOOD, Crown Office' were scripted in gilt; leaving little room for the last that he no longer stuck to, he turned part of the shop into a museum of his other occupation, and, when guiding visitors around it, let them touch, but not fondle, a rope that he had used to dispatch nine uncelebrated 'subjects', whose names he reeled off as if he were reciting a variation on 'Uncle Tom Cobbley and All' — and gaze at, but not touch, the prize exhibit, which was the rope he had used on four occasions made special by the celebrity of those condemned. The four, in the order of their going, were

Charles Peace, whose long criminal career (most industriously as a burglar, using home-made gadgets, some of his own invention) was brought to an end in October 1878, when he was arrested, only after a fierce struggle, in the garden of a house in Blackheath, South-East London, where his illicit presence had been observed. Following his conviction in Sheffield for the murder in that city of the husband of a woman with whom he had become infatuated, Peace confessed to the earlier murder, in a suburb of Manchester, of Police Constable Nicholas Cock: luckily for a young Irishman, William Habron, who, at a trial watched by Peace from the public gallery, had been found guilty of the shooting of the policeman, the sentence of death passed upon him had been commuted to life imprisonment. Peace's brief encounter with Marwood in Armley Prison, Leeds (in the county of Yorkshire, which was no longer independent of the Newgate hangman), was the second time they had met: some years before, they had shared a compartment in a train running from Nottingham to London, where Marwood was due to perform an execution, and Marwood, not knowing Peace's identity, had chattered the journey away with gallows tales — most enjoyably for Peace, who at journey's end had said jokingly, 'If you ever have to do the job for me, be sure you grease the rope well, to let me slip through.' Shortly before their second meeting, Peace — troubled by laryngitis that may have been psychosomatic — remarked to one of the death-watch warders, 'I wonder if Marwood can cure this cough of mine.' When Marwood appeared, Peace begged him to 'do his work quickly', and was told: 'You shall not suffer pain from my hand.' 'God bless you!' Peace exclaimed, and added, for the benefit of everyone present, but without making his wish theirs: 'I hope to meet you all in Heaven.'

Charles Peace (inset) and his home-made 'concertina' ladder.

According to a published description of what followed, Peace's talkativeness, as customary as Marwood's to the bitter end, delayed that end: 'He allowed himself to be pinioned with no show of fear, and walked to the scaffold with a steady step. After he had taken his place on the trap-door and his feet had been strapped together, Marwood prepared to adjust the white cap, when Peace cried out, "Stop a minute!" For several minutes then he made a farewell speech to the newspaper reporters and others present. Marwood then drew the white cap over his head.' Though the rest was silence (for if, as was certainly so on some other occasions, Marwood's 'long drop' did not have the instant effect that he insisted it invariably had, any protests from Peace were muffled by the hood of white jute), his many fans among those who had never suffered from his crimes were touched to learn, soon after his fall ('Bold Charlie's final leap' was the description of it by one of his literary romancers, subtly alluding to his agility, as monkey-like as his features), that he had composed his own valediction: 'In memory of Charles Peace who was executed in Armley Prison Tuesday February 25th 1879. Aged 47. For that I don but never intended.'

Kate Webster, the Irish cook-general at a house near Richmond Hill, Surrey, who on a Sunday evening in March 1879 probably used a cleaver to kill her admittedly cantankerous mistress, whose corpse she unhurriedly chopped into scraps which (having for some reason boiled most of them) she distributed, à la Greenacre, in places away from the scene of the crime, meanwhile negotiating for the sale of her victim's effects — and, it seems likely, residue: she offered two large pots of dripping, source unstated, to a fellow-frequenter of the local public house. As she had left Richmond by the time the police sought to question her, they circulated a notice stating that she was 'Wanted for stealing plate, &c., and supposed murder of her mistress', and describing her as 'aged about 32, 5ft. 5 or 6 inches high; complexion sallow; slightly freckled, teeth rather good and prominent. Usually dressed in dark dress, jacket rather long, and trimmed with dark fur around pockets; light brown satin bonnet.' She was traced to her native-town of Killane, County Wexford, and escorted to London, where, at the Old Bailey, she was tried, found guilty, and sentenced to death. Almost till her end, she insisted that she was innocent of the murder; after failing in an endeavour to put the blame on one person, she tried, with no more success, to put the blame on

Kate Webster.

another. In the words of the Irish writer Elliot O'Donnell (*see Bibliography*),

Wandsworth prison, the place where she was confined, had originally been erected simply as a house of correction, therefore no provision was made in it for prisoners capitally condemned. It was not, in fact, until after the Prison Act became law and Horsemonger Lane Jail was closed that convicts undergoing the death sentence were admitted. Hence Kate Webster, instead of being confined in a 'condemned cell', was put in one that was larger and more comfortable, and near to the prison infirmary. In order that two female attendants should be with her day and night, it was necessary to engage 'reliefs' . . . and Captain Colville [the governor] requested the Rev. Father M'Enery, the Roman Catholic chaplain of the prison, to try and find some kindly, sympathetic woman, of the same religious persuasion as Kate herself, to do duty as one of them. Consequently a Sister of Compassion from the convent at Hammersmith participated in this work of supervision. . . .

The execution was fixed for Tuesday, 29 July 1879, at nine o'clock in the morning; and on the evening prior to it, realizing at last that there was no possible chance of evading the scaffold, she made a full confession of her guilt. . . . She went to bed at the usual time, namely, ten o'clock, and apparently slept tolerably well, rising about five. . . .

The place of execution was on the south side of the entrance to the jail, in a court-yard. The bell commenced to toll at a quarter to nine o'clock, and the prisoner, who appeared at last resigned to her fate, came forth, leaning on the arm of her confessor, Father M'Enery. They had to descend a flight of stairs to reach the place of execution, where Marwood commenced the process of pinioning the prisoner, and placing her under the drop. The priest read the Roman Catholic service, and when, at the words, 'Jesus, Good Shepherd, come', the prisoner responded in a loud voice, 'Lord, have mercy upon me,' the bolt was immediately drawn. Later the black flag was hoisted on the prison, and the notices were posted in conformity with the Act, the first being —

'Her Majesty's prison, Wandsworth. Declaration of Sheriff and others — Whereas at a session of the Central Criminal Court, holden on Monday, the 30th day of June, 1879, Katherine Webster was convicted of the wilful murder of Julia Martha Thomas, and it was ordered and adjudged that the said Katherine Webster should be hanged by the neck until she was dead, now we, the undersigned, do hereby declare that judgment of death has been this day executed on the said Katherine Webster in our presence. Dated this 29th day of July, 1879.

CHARLES J. ABBOT, Under-Sheriff.
H.G. COLVILLE, Governor.
M. M'ENERY, Chaplain.'

The other was —

> 'Her Majesty's prison, Wandsworth. I, the undersigned, a surgeon of Her Majesty's prison, Wandsworth, in and for the county of Surrey, do hereby certify that I have this day examined the body of Katherine Webster, on whom judgment of death was this day executed in the said jail, and on that examination I found that the said Katherine Webster was dead. Dated this 29th day of July, 1879.
>
> HUGH B. WYNTER, MD, Surgeon.'

Percy Lefroy Mapleton (*as portrayed in the* Daily Telegraph).

Percy Lefroy Mapleton, the penny-a-line freelance journalist who committed the second British 'railway murder' — of Isaac Gold, a semi-retired merchant and dealer in coins, who on 27 June 1881 was found dead, with a bullet-wound in his neck and knife-wounds in his body, near the entrance to the Balcombe Tunnel of the London, Brighton & South Coast Railway. A watch and chain and other valuables had been taken from him. There was clear evidence that Mr Gold had entered a first-class compartment of a Brighton-bound train at London Bridge Station; that he had been murdered while the train was passing through Merstham Tunnel, just north of the Balcombe one; and that the 22-year-old Mapleton was the culprit (among the many indications of his guilt, perhaps the most telling were those noticed by the ticket-collector at the station on the outskirts of Brighton at which he alighted from the train: for one thing, his suit was saturated with blood, and for another, his gait was made peculiar by a watch-chain hanging from his left boot). Soon arrested, Mapleton then escaped — by the simple stratagem of entering his lodgings in Croydon by the front door, where his escort waited, and going out at the back. A drawing of him was published in the *Daily Telegraph* (the first time, it seems, that a portrait of a person wanted for murder appeared in a newspaper), and, being seen by his new landlady, led to his re-arrest. He was found guilty when tried at Maidstone Assizes, and sent to the prison at Lewes, not far from Brighton, for execution. An unlikely story has it that Marwood was concerned that Mapleton's chin was so negligible that the noose might ride up, perhaps gagging him to death. One reporter of the execution commented, 'Death is proverbially swift, [and] in the guise of Marwood it moved with appalling celerity', and others said that the celerity was made especially appalling by the fact that Mapleton had fainted while being pinioned, and was still unconscious when he dropped. 'All my eye!' Marwood exclaimed at those reports. 'Mapleton meant mischief, and if I hadn't had him

THE ILLUSTRATED
POLICE NEWS
LAW COURTS AND WEEKLY RECORD
No. 951.
SATURDAY, MAY 6, 1882.
Price One Penny.
EXECUTION OF DR LAMSON
THE LAST MEAL
LAST VISIT TO LAMSON
MORNING OF THE EXECUTION
THE PINIONING
PROCESSION TO THE SCAFFOLD
SCENE ON THE SCAFFOLD
THE BLACK FLAG AT WANDSWORTH GAOL

by the heel, he might have given me a lively dance all round the yard.'

George Lamson.

George Lamson, the drug-addicted general practitioner who in December 1881, having squandered the money he had married for, thought to recapitalize his wife by murdering her teen-aged, legacy-expectant brother (a cripple living in a private school at Wimbledon), using a slice of Madeira cake filled with a vegetable poison, aconitine, for that purpose. If the thirty-year-old Lamson had not embroidered on the lethal-cake idea, so much so as to produce an ornate murder-plan that was clearly recognizable as such, he would probably have profited from his crime; as it was, and despite the ingenious advocacy of his counsel Montagu Williams (who a few months before had defended Mapleton), the jury at his trial at the Old Bailey needed less than half an hour to reach a verdict that Mr Justice Hawkins, 'the Hanging Judge', was pleased to tag with the sentence of death: more than usually pleased, perhaps, for he was among those who suspected that the murder of a brother-in-law that Lamson was tried for was not the first that he had committed. On 29 April 1882, the day after the sentence was carried out, the *Daily Telegraph* reported:

At Wandsworth it seems they have a curious custom. In other gaols it is the method to pinion the prisoner inside his cell, a mode both convenient and commendable. But, for reasons best known to themselves, the officials of this prison prefer to have the operation performed in the open air. Thus it happened that Lamson, who had donned the suit of black which he wore at his trial, was allowed to walk freely from his cell between two warders, at about five minutes to nine, in the direction of the scaffold. . . . Marwood, who just then was waiting within the inner gates, with his straps thrown over his arm, hesitated until the cortege should come near him. As it happened, Lamson had not seen him, and apparently had not expected him, when the leading warders came up to the place where the executioner was. Then there was a sudden pause, for Marwood, with uplifted hand, had called out, 'Halt!' and the procession had stopped. That word 'halt' told its tale upon the prisoner. Realizing to the full his position for the first time, to all seeming, Lamson now staggered, and almost fell against one of the warders, who supported him. His tremor was, indeed, terribly apparent, and it was a great question for a moment whether he would not fall. But the executioner at this instant came to his aid, and with the help of the warders kept him in an upright position. Not removing the collar which Lamson had put on, and only turning in the points which might presently stand in the way of the rope, Marwood began to pinion him. 'I hope you will not hurt me,' the convict murmured, half in fear and half by way, possibly, of remonstrance. 'I'll do my best not to hurt you; I'll be as gentle as I can,' responded Marwood, and the work went on. Marwood's plan here was apparent. Lamson was a more powerfully built man than he appeared, weighing upwards of 11 stone 12lbs., and the executioner, evidently fearing that his strength would operate somewhat against a sharp and quick fall, fastened back his shoulders in a manner which precluded all possibility of the culprit resisting the action of the drop. For this reason, then, Lamson was fastened by the strap somewhat more tightly than Percy Lefroy Mapleton, whose slimness of figure and comparatively light weight of ten stone furnished no necessity for any such precautions.

When the convict was pinioned the procession moved on, the clergyman the meanwhile reading the service of the Church appointed for the burial of the dead, the doomed man responding almost inaudibly to the words. It was with great difficulty now that he could walk at all; indeed, it is certain that had he not been supported by the two warders who stood on either side of him, he would have fallen to the earth. Suddenly he came in sight of the gallows — a black structure, about 30 yards distant. The grave, newly dug, was close at hand. The new and terrible spectacle here acted once more with painful effect upon the condemned man, for again he almost halted and fell. But the warders, never leaving hold of him, moved on, while Marwood came behind. At last the gallows was reached, and here the clergyman bade farewell to the prisoner, while Marwood began his preparations with the rope and the beam overhead. With a view to meet any accretion of fear which might now befall the culprit, a wise precaution had been made. The drop was so arranged as to part in the middle, after the fashion of two folding doors; but, lest the doomed man might not be able to stand upon the scaffold without assistance, two planks of deal had been placed over the drop, one on either side of the rope, so that up to the latest moment the two warders supporting the convict might stand securely and hold him up, without danger to themselves or inconvenience to the machinery of the gallows. In this way Lamson was now kept erect while Marwood fastened his legs and put the cap over his eyes. He must have fallen had the arrangement been otherwise, for his effort to appear composed had by this time failed. Indeed, from what now occurred it is evident that the convict yet hoped for a few moments more of life, for, as Marwood proceeded to pull the cap down over his face, he pitifully begged that one more prayer might be recited by the chaplain. Willing as the executioner possibly might have been to listen to this request, he had, of course, no power to alter the progress of the service, and was obliged to disregard this last demand of the dying man. Signalling to the warders to withdraw their arms, he drew the lever, which released the bolt under the drop, and so launched the prisoner into eternity. . . .

It may have been a coincidence that 'gallows humour' was all the rage while Marwood was in office. This sort of thing, which appeared in a Yorkshire comic magazine entitled *Toby*: 'PUBLIC EXECUTIONER (reading his noosepaper): "What! Another reprieve! They won't let me earn an honest living!" ' Sometimes wittingly, sometimes not, Marwood contributed to the fund of tales: for instance, during a business visit to Kirkdale prison, Liverpool, he complained of the rickety ascent to the scaffold, 'One of these days, a chap will be killed coming up these stairs if he doesn't mind out.' Everyone knew that he was the answer to the conundrum, 'If Pa hanged Ma, who would hang Pa?'

He received much mail — not all of it from admirers and autograph-hunters. There were threatening letters; perhaps something like as many as he reckoned, saying that he 'cared nowt about them'. The letter of that sort which received most publicity arrived in mid-May, 1882, a fortnight after the murder in Dublin's Phoenix Park of Lord Frederick Cavendish, the newly-arrived Chief Secretary for Ireland, and Thomas Burke, the Permanent Under-Secretary, by members of a secret society called The Invincibles:

> Dublin
>
> MARWOOD,
>
> It was decided last night at a meeting of the Secret Association here to forward this communication to you to the effect that no doubt you are longing intensely for the job to murder us here by your rope for the wilful murder of Burke and Cavendish. Well, don't be in a hurry, for although we are all in Dublin we are not caught yet and not likely for this paltry [reward of] £10,000. Should we be arrested and convicted, on the peril of your life you must not set foot on the soil of this city or any part of this country of Ireland. If you do you will never get out of it alive. You very narrowly escaped from Armagh the last time you were here, but you will not escape the next time you come over here. Even if you have an escort we shall manage the whole lot of you about right. We shall have revenge somehow, you may depend upon it, and this I tell you once and for all; so now beware. We know you. There can be no mistake in the carrying out of this resolution, so now you are cautioned. Your movements will be telegraphed here from the time you leave Horncastle until you get here, if you get so far under a false name and false business. We want no hangman in this country to carry out English law. Enough. Beware!
>
> From Jack of —, the murderers of Burke and Cavendish

When reporters asked Marwood if he was apprehensive about 'traversing the length and breadth of Great Britain with his little black bag without any protection whatever', he downed the gin that one of the reporters had bought him and told another to refill his glass before replying, in the exclamation-marked way that seems to have been characteristic of him: 'No! No! No! D'you think I'm afraid? Not a bit of it! I've been too many years at my trade to have any funk now! I'm too old a hand at the job!'

Marwood died, in harness, on 2 September 1883. According to an obituary 'by one who knew him',

> Never within the memory of the oldest inhabitant of Horncastle had so much excitement been occasioned as by the illness and death of William Marwood. During the few days immediately prior to his decease, inquiries were made from various parts of the kingdom, and even many telegrams were sent to the Press Association. When his death occurred, the news was transmitted by wire to all parts of the country.
>
> It appears that he had recently been visiting Lincoln, and had been enjoying himself too freely with friends; when he arrived home the day before he was taken ill, he had evidently been drinking. The coroner thought it advisable to hold an inquest, for all kinds of wild rumours had been circulating, many affirming that he had been poisoned by the Irish Invincibles in revenge for his execution of Fenians at Manchester. This was disproved beyond all doubt, for Dr Hadden, who had been attending him, and who assisted at the post-mortem made by the medical gentleman appointed by the coroner, stated that death was due to a complication of diseases, and that inflammation of the lungs, aggravated by jaundice, was the real cause.
>
> He had amassed a fair amount of money, having cottage property at Horncastle and in the neighbourhood. He died at the age of sixty-four, and he undoubtedly would have lived much longer had it not been for his intemperate habits.

1883–4. A week after Marwood's death, the following notice appeared in the national press:

> In consequence of the numerous applications which have been received at the Home Office for an appointment to the place of public executioner, we are requested to state it is neither the right nor the duty of the Secretary of State to make any such appointments. There is no such office as that of public executioner appointed by the Government. The person charged with the execution of capital sentences is the Sheriff. It is the right and the duty of the Sheriff to employ and to pay a fitting person to carry out the sentence of the law.

Among the wrongly addressed applications were these:

The Illustrated POLICE NEWS

LAW COURTS AND WEEKLY RECORD

No. 953. SATURDAY, MAY 20, 1882. Price One Penny.

UNITED IN GRIEF.

THE LATE LORD F. CAVENDISH M.P.

THE LATE MR T. H. BURKE.

MURDER OF LORD F. CAVENDISH AND MR BURKE

RESIDENCE OF THE LATE LORD F. CAVENDISH—DUBLIN

Mr T. H. Burkes' Residence Phoenix Pk

REMOVING BODY OF LORD F. CAVENDISH

Mr FOLEY INFORMS HIM OF WHAT HE HAD SEEN

Scene of the Murders.

ARRESTED ON SUSPICION

POLICE ON GUARD WHERE THE VICTIMS FELL.

I, H— R—, of Trindley Colliery, County of Durham, 6 feet 1 inch in my stocking feet, 14 stone weight, 35 years of age, would like the office of public executioner, in place of the late Marwood, deceased. I would hang either brothers or sisters, or anyone else related to me, without fear or favour.

(Signed) H— R—
(his mark)

Dere Sir,
I am waiting outside with a coil of rope, and should be glad to give you a personal proof of my method.

Sir,
. . . I have some knowledge of Anatomy, am an exceedingly strong man, and can command sang-froid under any circumstances. I have witnessed Executions among all nations; consequently, there is no fear of my getting sick at the right moment.

Sir, . . . I beg to state that by trade I am a Barber, and that my age is 34, and also that helth and nerve is good. In my Line of Business as a Barber I have had some years of Great Experience in the Formation of the necks and windpipes of all kinds of people, and, therefore, I think that the Situation, if dear Sir, it will be your Pleasure to appoint Me, would be the means of my Fulfilling it to your full satisfaction. I can Refer you for my testimonials to several Manchester Gentlemen of High honer and Long Standing.

Deer Sur,
I am ankshus to be yure publick exechoner, and i hereby apply for the job. i am thurty yeres old, and am willing to hang one or two men for nothink, so as you will see how I handle the job. i am strong, brave, and fear no man, and i will hang anybody you like to show how i can do it. i inclose photo.

Sir,
. . . I have at various times made some very successful experiments in the art of hanging (by means of life-size figures) with the view to making myself thoroughly proficient in the despatch of criminals, and I have no hesitation in saying that I believe my system would be the most expeditious, never failing, and most humane that has ever been adopted or that could possibly be used, as it has been my greatest study. My system of hanging is not a lingering death by strangulation, but instantaneous and painless, rendered so by a small appliance of my own for the instant severing of the spinal cord. I may say that I adopt a variety of drops, varying from 7ft. $10\frac{1}{2}$ins. to 16ft. $11\frac{3}{32}$ins. I shall be glad to conduct a series of experiments under your personal inspection on the first batch of criminals for execution, that you may see for yourself the superiority of my system over that of all others.

All of those letters, and the hundred or so others that also shouldn't have been sent to the Home Office, were forwarded to the Guildhall, there to be added to the pile of a thousand or so correctly-addressed ones. The Sheriffs of London and Middlesex invited some thirty of the applicants to attend interviews, separately but all on the same morning, at the Old Bailey. Of those, seventeen turned up, making one of the strangest gatherings that the Old Bailey — a place often frequented by strange gatherings — had ever housed. Within two hours the seventeen hopefuls had been interviewed, three of them twice — which indicates that the least appealing of them shambled into the Sheriffs' presence and were instantly ordered out of it. The short-listed three were James Berry, of Bradford, Yorkshire (who, straightway after his second interview, wrote home, saying that he had 'virtually' been offered the job and had 'agreed upon the price'); Jeremy Taylor, of Lincoln, a builder who claimed to have been 'very intimate with the late Mr Marwood'; and Bartholomew Binns, a coal-miner near his native-town of Gateshead. The Sheriffs chose Binns — and soon wished they hadn't. Having bungled three of the first four jobs he was given, he turned up for the fifth too drunk to be allowed near the scaffold, and was fired. It was subsequently reported that 'Binns, piqued at his dismissal, obtained a wax figure and a small gibbet, and appeared at fairs, etc., etc., exhibiting in a booth the manner in which he had carried out the executions during his short tenure of office. The police soon put a stop to his disgraceful exhibitions, and Mr Binns dropped out of the public sight.'

Bartholomew Binns.

1884–92. James Berry, so recently rejected, was instated. Calcraft had in his youth made shoes; Marwood throughout his life had mended them; and the footwear association was continued by Berry, who, having spent most of his twenties as a constable in the Bradford and West Riding police force, had become a seller of shoes in someone else's shop — a job that he did not give up till he felt secure as an executioner. Berry was less poorly educated than his predecessors: his handwriting was copperplate, he read unstumblingly (demonstrating that ability while conducting Methodist services as a lay-preacher), and, as the following extract from his memoirs shows, he was quite — only quite — good at sums:

> I was slightly acquainted with Mr Marwood before his death, and I had gained some particulars of his method from conversation with him; so that when I undertook my first execution [on 31 March 1884], at Edinburgh, I naturally worked upon his lines. This first

commission was to execute Robert Vickers and William Innes, two miners, who were condemned to death for the murder of two gamekeepers. The respective weights were 10 stone 4 lb and 9 stone 6 lb., and I gave them drops of 8ft 6in. and 10ft. respectively. In both cases death was instantaneous, and the prison surgeon gave me a testimonial to the effect that the execution was satisfactory in every respect.

Upon this experience I based a table of weights and drops. Taking a man of 14 stone as basis, and giving him a drop of 8ft., which is what is thought necessary, I calculated that every half-stone lighter weight would require a two inches longer drop, and the full table as I entered it in my books at the time, stood as follows:

14 stone	... ...	8ft.	0in.
13½	... ...	8	2
13	... ...	8	4
12½	... ...	8	6
12	... ...	8	8
11½	... ...	8	10
11	... ...	9	0
10½	... ...	9	2
10	... ...	9	4
9½	... ...	9	6
9	... ...	9	8
8½	... ...	9	10
8	... ...	10	0

This table I calculated for persons of what I might call 'average' build, but it could not by any means be rigidly adhered to with safety.

That last comment of Berry's was an understatement. By the start of 1886 his percentage of 'mishaps' — though slightly lower than Marwood's, and nowhere near Binns's 75% — was considered by the Home Secretary to be high enough to warrant the appointment of a Departmental Committee, under the chairmanship of Lord Aberdare, its brief 'to inquire into the existing practice as to carrying out of sentences of death, and the causes which in several recent cases have led either to failure or to unseemly occurrences; and to consider and report what arrangements may be adopted (without altering the existing law) to ensure that all executions may be carried out in a becoming manner without risk of failure or miscarriage in any respect'. The Committee recommended, *inter alia*, that all scaffolds should be much alike and that the ropes should be of standard thickness and length, and proposed a 'scale of drops' that differed in some respects from the one worked out by Berry.

QUOTE

No. ....

Bradford, ... *189*

YORKS.

Sir,

I beg leave to state in reply to your letter of the .... *that I am prepared to undertake the execution you name of* ....

at .... *on the* ....

I also beg leave to state that my terms are as follows: £10 for the execution, £5 if the condemned is reprieved, together with all travelling expenses.

Awaiting your reply,

I am, Sir,

Your obedient Servant,

James Berry.

The High Sheriff,

for the County of ....

James Berry.

None of Berry's 'subjects' was as famous beforehand as was one of them, John Lee, afterwards — his fame being chiefly due to the fact that he was able to savour it. Lee, having been found guilty of the stabbing to death of Emma Keyse, the 68-year-old spinster for whom he had worked domestically in the suburb of Torquay called Babbacombe, was scheduled to die in Exeter Prison at eight o'clock on the morning of Monday, 23 February 1885. But, depending upon which way one looks at it — from Lee's point of view or from Berry's — things went miraculously right or embarrassingly wrong. Berry gave his version of the non-event in a replying letter, dated 4 March, to the Under-sheriff of Devon (who seems to have confused him, perhaps by allotting thirty days to February, into writing *inst*, then *ult*, rather than *ult* twice):

Executioner's Office,
1 Bilton Place, City Road,
Bradford, Yorks.

Re JOHN LEE

Sir,

In accordance with the request contained in your letter of the 30th inst., I beg to say that on the morning of Friday, the 20th ult., I travelled from Bradford to Bristol, and on the morning of Saturday, the 21st, from Bristol to Exeter, arriving at Exeter at 11.50 a.m., when I walked direct to the County Gaol, signed my name in your Gaol Register Book at 12 o'clock exactly. I was shown to the Governor's office, and arranged with him that I would go and dine and return to the Gaol at 2.0 p.m. I accordingly left the Gaol, partook of dinner, and returned at 1.50 p.m., when I was shown to the bedroom allotted to me which was an officer's room in the new Hospital Ward. Shortly afterwards I made an inspection of the place of Execution. The execution was to take place in a Coach-house in which the Prison Van was usually kept. . . . Two Trap-doors were placed in the floor of the Coach-house, which is flagged with stone, and these doors cover a pit about 2 yards by 1½ yards across, and about 11 feet deep. On inspecting these doors I found they were only about an inch thick, but to have been constructed properly should have been three or four inches thick. The ironwork of the doors was of a frail kind, and much too weak for the purpose. There was a lever to these doors, and it was placed near the top of them. I pulled the lever and the doors dropped, the catches acting all right. I had the doors raised, and tried the lever a second time, when the catch again acted all right. The Governor was watching me through the window of his office and saw me try the doors. After the examination I went to him, explained how I found the doors, and suggested to him that for future executions new trap-doors should be made about three times as thick as those then fixed. I also suggested that a spring should be fixed in the Wall to hold the doors back when they fell, so that no rebounding occurred, and that the ironwork of the doors should be stronger. The Governor said he would see to these matters in future. I retired to bed about 9.45 that night. . . .

On the Monday morning I arose at 6.30, and was conducted from the Bedroom by a Warder, at 7.30, to the place of execution. Everything appeared to be as I had left it on the Saturday afternoon. I fixed the rope in my ordinary manner, and placed everything in readiness. I did not try the Trap-doors as they appeared to be just as I had left them. It had rained heavily during the nights of Saturday and Sunday. About four minutes to eight o'clock I was conducted by the Governor to the condemned Cell and introduced to John Lee. I proceeded at once to pinion him, which was done in the usual manner, and then gave a signal to the Governor that I was ready. The procession was formed, headed by the Governor, the Chief Warder, and the Chaplain followed by Lee. I walked behind Lee and 6 or 8 warders came after me. On reaching the place of execution I found you were there with the Prison Surgeon. Lee was at once placed upon the trap-doors. I pinioned his legs, pulled down the white cap, adjusted the Rope, stepped on one side, and drew the lever — but the trap-door did not fall. I had previously stood upon the doors and thought they would fall quite easily. I unloosed the strap from his legs, took the rope from his neck, removed the White Cap, and took Lee away into an adjoining room until I made an examination of the doors. I worked the lever after Lee had been taken off, drew it, and the doors fell easily. With the assistance of the warders the doors were pulled up, and the lever drawn a second time, when the doors again fell easily. Lee was then brought from the adjoining room, placed in position, the cap and rope adjusted, but when I again pulled the lever it did not act, and in trying to force it the lever was slightly strained. Lee was then taken off a second time and conducted to the adjoining room.

It was suggested to me that the woodwork fitted too tightly in the centre of the doors, and one of the warders fetched an axe and another a plane. I again tried the lever but it did not act. A piece of wood was then sawn off one of the doors close to where the iron catches were, and by the aid of an iron crowbar the catches were knocked off, and the doors fell down. You then gave orders that the execution should not be proceeded with until you had communicated with the Home Secretary, and Lee was taken back to the Condemned Cell. I am of opinion that the ironwork catches of the trap-doors were not strong enough for the purpose, that the woodwork of the doors should have been about three or four times as heavy, and with ironwork to correspond, so that when a man of Lee's weight was placed

Cover of paperback.

PRICE SIXPENCE
THE MAN THEY COULD NOT HANG
THE LIFE STORY OF JOHN LEE
PUBLISHED AT 17 AND 18, HENRIETTA STREET, LONDON, W.C.

upon the doors the iron catches would not have become locked, as I feel sure they did on this occasion, but would respond readily. So far as I am concerned, everything was performed in a careful manner, and had the iron and woodwork been sufficiently strong, the execution would have been satisfactorily accomplished.

I am, Sir,
Your obedient Servant,
JAMES BERRY

Henry M. James, Esq.,
Under-Sheriff of Devon,
The Close, Exeter.

As likely an explanation for the failure of the apparatus appears in a book entitled *In the Light of the Law* (London, 1931), the author of which, Ernest Bowen-Rowlands, quotes a letter from a 'well-known person' who claimed to have heard from someone that

an old lag in the gaol confessed to him (I think when dying) that he was responsible for the failure of the drop to work in the execution of the Babbacombe murderer. It appears that in those days it was the practice to have the scaffold erected by some joiner or carpenter from among the prisoners. The man inserted a wedge which prevented the drop from working and when called in as an expert he removed the wedge and demonstrated the smooth working of the drop, only to re-insert it before Lee was again placed on the trap. This happened three times [*only twice, according to Berry*] and finally Lee was returned to his cell with doubtless a very stiff neck.

The Home Secretary, deciding that it would be unfair on Lee to put him through further attempts to hang him, granted him a reprieve. In his case, 'imprisonment for life' amounted to twenty-three years. Following his release in December 1907, he did quite well from 'The Man They Could Not Hang' stories in newspapers, the longest of which was turned into a paperback.

Berry was only forty when he resigned in March 1892. He stated that his decision was solely 'on account of Dr Barr interfering with my responsible duty at Kirkdale Gaol, Liverpool, on my last execution there' (of a man named John Conway, who had been almost decapitated). As that unfortunate incident had occurred nearly seven months before, either Berry was in the throes of a delayed psychological reaction or he used the incident as an excuse for resigning. The latter possibility is strengthened by two facts: shortly after becoming an ex-executioner, he became the first such man to publish a book of memoirs (*see Bibliography*); and shortly after the book appeared, he embarked upon a long lecture-tour, for which he was very well paid. Though there was nothing in his book that suggested that he disapproved of capital punishment, his lecture was a mixture of the 'Exciting Episodes' promised on the billboards, and passages of abolitionist propaganda. It is noted in the introduction to a facsimile edition of the book, published in 1972, that 'when the lecture engagements petered out, he turned his hand to various jobs; as well as being an innkeeper, he was at another time a cloth salesman at north-country markets, at another a bacon salesman on commission. The last years of his life were devoted to evangelistic and temperance work, and he died at his home in Bradford in October 1913.'

1892–1901. Berry's successor was James Billington, a barber of Farnworth, Lancashire, who needed no induction training, for he had acted as an executional locum in the neighbouring — some might say rival — county of Yorkshire for eight years. Marwood's celerity had been termed appalling; Billington's was record-breaking. Whereas the previous best time for pinioning was a minute and a half, Billington, using a double-buckled strap of his own devising, rarely needed more than thirty seconds — and, so it was said, he was so prompt in pulling the lever that hardly any of those thereby caused to fall had been in a position to hear the second syllable of the chaplain's 'A-men' at the end of the burial prayer.

Billington's alacrity was chiefly responsible for Dr Thomas Neill Cream's inclusion among those persons unofficially accused of the 'Jack the Ripper' murders in Whitechapel in 1888. Cream, an habitual poisoner of women of the unfortunate class, was led to the Newgate gallows on 15 November 1892. At the last minute he called out what sounded like, 'I am Jack –': no more than that because Billington had started him on his descent. Billington afterwards said: 'If I had only known he was going to speak, I should have waited for the end of the sentence' — and, showing that his reliance upon facts was as slight as that of present-day 'Ripperologists', added: 'I am certain that Neill Cream and Jack the Ripper were the same man.' It doesn't seem to have occurred to anyone that if Cream had not been stopped in mid-stream, his remark might have turned out to be the partly surprised, partly pleased 'I am ejaculating' — ejaculation being the final involuntary act of a number of condemned men. That phenomenon is discussed in a letter written by Dr James Devon on notepaper of the Scottish Arts Club, 24 Rutland Square, Edinburgh, on 29 January 1931, to Harry Hodge, the founder and first general editor of the *Notable Trials* series:

(Below) *Dr Cream.*

Cream's potion case.

. . . I'll try to tackle the question you pose: 'Is it true that a man gets an erection at the moment of being hanged . . . ?'

The answer is NO — but, stated absolutely and without reason, I dare say you will consider it rather insufficient. Take the question in parts, then.

First let it be understood that I have only been present at four hangings. It was my duty to attend them as Medical Officer of Duke Street prison [Glasgow], and they took place between 1895 and 1913, when I became Commissioner. The persons were one Scotsman, two Irish, and one African Negro. In the four cases, death was instantaneous, from fracture-dislocation of the spine. There was no congestion present *post-mortem*, save that due to the action of the rope on the tissues after death, for in these cases the body hung for an hour before being taken down. In all the other cases during my period of office, I was informed that death had occurred as suddenly and that there was no priapism [persistent erection of the penis]. This is what one would expect. There is no time for erection to take place. That process takes a comparatively appreciable period. The Corpora Cavernosa are filled with blood which the sphincters prevent from returning. That does not take long for its occurrence, but death is quicker.

On the other hand, death by hanging *is* sometimes preceded by erection; and sometimes by emission. There is ample testimony to the fact. Hanging produces a general congestive state. It may also induce irritation in that part of the spinal cord, or in the cerebellum, to which the induction of erection is ascribed; and as death does not take place for minutes — occasionally for a good many minutes — there is ample time for erection and emission, or for continued erection, to take place. But I am too old a hand to pin any more absolute trust to theories of causation than to the evidence of the senses as recorded by observers. I have heard tales honestly told that ran against all theories and expectations. I have seen things I could not believe, and my eyes were not playing tricks on my mind.

There is a story (I thought it was in the Cent Nouvelles Nouvelles, but cannot find it there; it is an old story and well told) of a man who was hanged and, being cut down, was removed to the house of a charitable old maid. She laid him out on the bed and undressed him. He had died with lance erect. Follows a description of what she did — and she did so well that she brought the apparently dead to life, in the manner that Restif de la Breton and his companions revived the girls who were apparently drowned. Now I would not advance a Merry Tale as evidence of a fact, but even a Merry Tale has to be founded in part on an accepted belief. It can only outrage all probability when it is obviously intended to be a burlesque. It is as worthy of consideration as much that is accepted as scientific testimony (*teste* Bernard Spilsbury) and will sometimes come out better from the ordeal of examination. Old Dunlop, the Glasgow surgeon, who died at the beginning of this century, was a teacher of mine in the early '90s, and had then been medico-legal examiner for

Dr Pritchard.

the Crown for a long time. I succeeded to one of the posts on his death and had been working on cases side by side with him before that. He told me that in his earlier days he had seen erection in the case of the hanged, and I remember him, in discussing it, saying, 'Eh, man, ye should have seen Pritchard's.' [Dr Edward William] Pritchard was hanged on 28 July 1865 [for the murder by poisoning of his wife and mother-in-law; he was the last person to be executed publicly in Glasgow]. In those days the 'short drop' was used and death was due to strangulation. The method of death was entirely different from that which takes place nowadays by the use of the 'long drop'. In the former case there may be erection. In the latter case there is probably not time for it to take place, apart from any other consideration.

It was Billington who put an end to, and to the squabbles between, Henry Fowler and Albert Milsom, both of whom had amassed long criminal records before the night of 14 February 1896, when in the furtherance of a burglary in Muswell Hill, North London, one or other of them battered to death an old man named Henry Smith. A toy lantern left by the body proved to belong to Milsom; several weeks later, he and Fowler were arrested at Bath. Each sought to foist the blame for the murder upon the other, Milsom being the more eager in that regard. In the dock at the Old Bailey, Fowler tried to strangle Milsom, and would have succeeded but for the intervention of warders. Fearing a further bust-up on the scaffold, the authorities at Newgate arranged a triple execution for the morning of 9 June: a neutral murderer, William John Seaman, was put between the former partners — causing him to remark, 'This is the first time I've ever been a bloody peacemaker.' As Billington moved, cap in hand, towards Fowler, the latter shouted out, 'Is Milsom there?' — and, having been assured that he was, said, 'Very well, you can go on.'

Billington's conscientiousness may have been the death of him. On 3 December 1901, while in Manchester (there to execute a fellow-Farnworthian, Patrick M'Kenna, for uxoricide), he developed a nasty cold; as soon as he got home, he took to his bed, but the cold became pneumonia. He was less concerned that he was ill than that the illness might prevent him from travelling to Newcastle, where he was booked to hang two members of a Miller family, both called John, for the murder of John Ferguson, a travelling showman. Their execution was scheduled for 8 December. On the morning of the 7th, according to a subsequent report,

Mr Billington crawled out of bed and commenced to dress, declaring that he had never broken his compact with the Government, and

The ropes that hanged (left to right) *Fowler, Seaman and Milsom.*

would not begin then. He only managed to put on his trousers before he fell, semi-conscious, on the floor. He was replaced in his bed. Several executions were pending, which his sons carried out for him, making flying visits back from the gaols to the sick-room. The best possible attendance was procured for Mr Billington, but a few days sufficed to see the end, and he passed away at the age of 54. At his funeral many influential people were present, and messages of sympathy were sent to his family from all over the Kingdom.

1902 et seq. The fact that James Billington's sons filled in for him during his terminal illness, and that their doing so caused no raised eyebrows at the Home Office or among either prison officials or reporters of the hangings, is indicative of a post-Marwood smudging of the roles of Public Executioner and Assistant Public Executioner (the latter position only recently made an official, paid one). The smudging continued till shortly before the Second World War, and so it is not possible to be exact in regard to the career-span of all of the hangmen who became household names during those forty years.

James Billington was succeeded as a Public Executioner by his elder son, William, who during his first few years in office was usually assisted by his brother John. On 7 May 1902, at Newgate, the brothers put an end to George Woolfe, who, having made Charlotte Cheeseman pregnant, had chosen to murder rather than marry her. (A week or two before her death, she had sent Woolfe a rhymed plea: 'My pen is blunt, my ink is pale,/My love for you will never fail,/Apples is ripe, pears is better,/George, dear, will you answer this letter?') Woolfe was the last person hanged at Newgate before the prison was demolished so as to make space for the present Old Bailey; the scaffold, capable of accommodating three, was removed to Pentonville, where it was re-inaugurated, the brothers officiating, on 30 September 1902, its load on that occasion being one James MacDonald, who had stabbed a man to death near Spitalfields Market, in the East End of London. The brothers' partnership was most publicized in the clement months of the following year: in April they travelled to Wandsworth Prison to hang Severin Klosowski, also known as George Chapman, a Polish-born publican who, though charged with and found guilty of the murder by poisoning of only one of his barmaids, had certainly disposed of others by the same means (and who was, and is, suspected by some of having committed the 'Jack the Ripper' murders); in July the brothers paid one of their rare visits to the prison at Chelmsford, Essex, there to execute Samuel Dougal, the 'Moat-Farm Murderer' — of Miss Camille Holland, the owner of the farm, whose body, with a bullet-wound through the skull, had been discovered, in a ditch leading from the moat, nearly four years after her disappearance. F. Tennyson Jesse, the editor of the Dougal volume in the *Notable British Trials* (*see Bibliography*), notes that

> it was a fine, sunny morning as Dougal, bare-headed and bare-throated, took his last brief walk in the open air. . . . The executioner, Billington, had his hand upon the lever when the

UP IN THE PUBLIC GALLERY
MRS MARSH MOTHER OF THE DECEASED
WOOLF LEWISOHN WHO KNEW THE ACCUSED
MR MARSH FATHER OF DECEASED
THE FIRST MRS CHAPMAN (LUCY BALDERSKY) NOW ALIVE
DET. INSP GODLEY WHO ARRESTED PRISONER
G. CHAPMAN. (THE ACCUSED)
MAR. 1903
SOUTHWARK POISON MURDER CASE.
MRS RAUCH
SISTER OF THE FI
MRS CHAPM
WHO IS STILL ALI
S. BADESKY

(Opposite)
A paste-up of drawings made at George Chapman's trial by William Harrison.

(Above)
Miss Camille Holland.

(Above, right)
The Moat Farm.

(Left)
Samuel Dougal.

(Right)
Dougal's gravestone – taken from the precincts of Chelmsford Prison.

(Above, right)
George Joseph Smith.

(Above)
Smith's three bath-victims, in the reverse order of their going:
(top)
Margaret Lofty,
(centre)
Alice Burnham,
(foot)
Bessie Mundy.

chaplain bent forward towards Dougal, who could not see him, for already the white cap had been drawn over his face. Twice the chaplain asked Dougal: 'Are you guilty or not guilty?' while Billington's hand stayed upon the lever. Dougal half-turned his head in the direction of the chaplain's voice and said 'Guilty!' at the moment that the lever was pulled. This action of the chaplain's was severely criticised both in the Press and in Parliament. . . . It is a nice theological point how far a minister of God is justified in agitating a man during his last moments on earth for the sake of his soul, but it must be admitted that, in spite of the indignation of the public, such persistence is logical enough in view of a chaplain's beliefs.

Dougal was buried, according to custom, in the precincts of the prison. The body of his victim lies in Saffron Walden cemetery; above it is a cross of white marble ornamented with a carved bas-relief taken from an early and very characteristic painting by Miss Holland herself; it represents a very feminine-looking angel gathering the figure of a young girl to her bosom; the inscription on the cross runs as follows: 'In sympathetic memory of Camille Cecile Holland, of Maida Vale, London, who died at Clavering under distressing circumstances on the 19th May, 1899, aged 56 years. *Nunc demum requiescat in pace.*' Miss Holland herself would surely have approved of the delicacy, if not of the grammar, of that well-chosen phrase — 'under distressing circumstances'.

When John Billington gave up hanging so as to devote himself to the family barbering business, William was often assisted by John Ellis — who, quite by chance, also was a barber. His shop (originally his father's) was in Rochdale, Lancashire, where he had been born in 1874. Following William Billington's retirement in 1907, Ellis became an executioner in his own right; in the years till 1923, when he too retired, he hanged many famous criminals — among them Dr Crippen (*see page 140*), Sir Roger Casement (*mentioned on page 49*), and, on Friday the 13th of August 1915, George Joseph Smith, the dealer in secondhand goods who had engaged in the sideline of bigamously marrying spinsters as shelved as Camille Holland had been, persuading them to make him their sole beneficiary, and then drowning them (leaving the last 'bride in the bath' soaking while he crept downstairs and played *Nearer, My God to Thee* on the harmonium in the parlour).

Ellis was one of two hangmen who learnt the ropes from William Billington. The other's family-name, which was Pierrepoint, would become almost synonymous with the job. Prior to his appointment, Henry Pierrepoint had followed various trades in towns on both sides of the Pennines; he believed that the knowledge of anatomy that he had picked up as a butcher came in handy to him as a hangman. Partly owing to ill-health and partly because he could not accept a newspaper's offer for his 'life story' until he did so, he retired in 1916 — by which time he had executed, or assisted at the execution of, ninety-nine murderers. At his suggestion, his younger brother Thomas took up hanging, while continuing to manage the carrier's business that he, Henry, had set up in the town of Clayton, near Bradford. Thomas Pierrepoint's term in office was a long one, lasting some thirty years. In 1931 another member of the Pierrepoint family, Henry's 27-year-old son Albert, was accredited by the Home Office as an executioner. Though he assisted his Uncle Tom less often than was reckoned by reporters, the number of their joint ventures was probably sufficient to justify reference to them as the 'Pierrepoint firm'. When Thomas retired in 1945, Albert succeeded to the unofficial title of Number-One Hangman; his other trade at that time was grocery, but in the following year he took over a public house at Hollinwood, between Manchester and Oldham, the curious name of which, 'Help the Poor Struggler', was amended by regular customers to 'Help the Poor Strangler'. He subsequently wrote that 'the move was entirely successful. I proved it to myself when I found that I could take a three o'clock 'plane from Dublin after conducting an execution there [Eire having no home-grown hangmen] and be opening my bar without comment at half-past five.'

1908. The death penalty was abolished for persons below the age of sixteen.

1922. Under the Infanticide Act, women who killed their newborn children could not be executed for doing so.

At 9 a.m. on 9 January 1923, Frederick Bywaters, aged twenty, was hanged by Thomas Pierrepoint in Pentonville Prison, and his 28-year-old mistress, Edith Thompson, was hanged by John Ellis in Holloway Prison. Both had been found guilty of the murder of Mrs Thompson's husband Percy, who had certainly been stabbed to death by Bywaters; the jury must have devoted most of their two hours of discussion to the question of whether Mrs Thompson's love-letters to Bywaters (one telling him: 'yes darlint be jealous, so much so that you will do something desperate') had incited him to commit the act. The morning after the concurrent executions, it was reported that whereas 'Bywaters was calm to the end, partaking of a little breakfast and smoking a final cigarette before walking firmly from his cell', 'Mrs Thompson, after a night of semi-consciousness, with a doctor in constant attendance, was dazed, requiring assistance to walk to the scaffold'. Before very long, more imaginative reports, gratefully accepted by abolitionists, helped towards the creation of a legend that Edith Thompson was quite unconscious when Ellis hanged her. That legend, tacked on to the widely held and strongly based belief that she had been tried as much for adultery as for murder, caused her to become a sort of patron-saint of the abolitionist cause. (Ellis's resignation in March 1923, which may have been prompted by the offer of a lucrative contract to star in a mock-execution show at holiday resorts along the south coast, was taken by abolitionists to mean that he was 'afflicted by remorse' in regard to Edith Thompson; and so was his attempt, seventeen months later, to commit suicide by shooting himself in the neck [before discharging him from what was then the *crime* of attempted suicide, the presiding magistrate commented, 'If your aim had

(Opposite, top)
Henry Pierrepoint.

(Opposite, centre)
Thomas and Albert Pierrepoint.

(Right)
Scene: the garden of the Thompsons' house in Ilford, Essex. Left to right, Frederick Bywaters, Percy Thompson, his wife Edith.

been as true as the drops you gave, it would have been a bad job for you.']; and so was his actual suicide, late in 1931, which he accomplished by slitting his throat with a razor that he had often used unblemishingly in his barber-shop.)

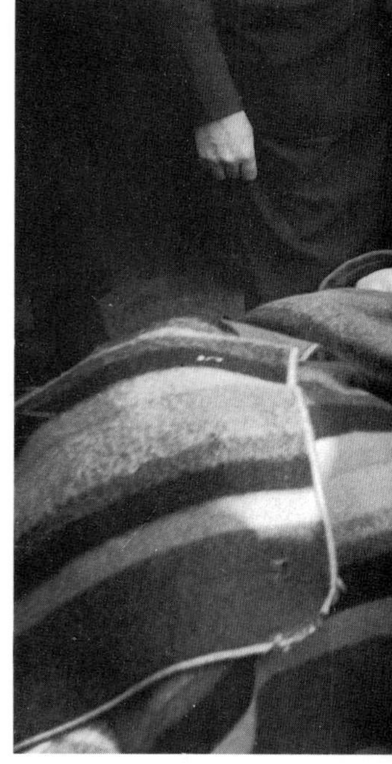

Christopher Craig, en route to the committal proceedings and (below) *his revolver.*

(Below right) *Derek Bentley, trying to hide his face after being charged with murder.*

1925. E. Roy Calvert, a young Quaker, brought together representatives of religious and reform societies, who agreed to help in forming a National Council for the Abolition of the Death Penalty. Calvert accepted the post of full-time secretary (but only after he had the promise of an annual subsidy of £250 from the well-known Quaker family, the chocolate-making Cadburys), and ran the organization, virtually single-handed, during the twenty-three years of its existence. Working from a tiny office in Victoria Street, close to the Houses of Parliament, he gathered statistics on capital punishment from all over the world and made press-releases and *Notes for Speakers* from those which accorded with his belief that it was not a deterrent to murder; he wrote pamphlets for publication by the Council and books for publication under the commercial imprint of Victor Gollancz, a member of the Council; he wrote letters to editors and to politicians, signing some of them himself but more often getting prestigious members to append their signatures; he arranged for members to stand by prison gates when execution notices were posted, and for the resulting tableaux to be photographed by the press. Considering Calvert's success in gaining publicity for the Council and for its cause, it seems surprising that membership of the Council never rose above 1,200.

1928. The most successful piece of abolitionist propaganda, Charles Duff's 'satirical essay', *A Handbook on Hanging*, was published in London. Between 1934 and 1961 there were seven revised editions, each from a different London publisher. A German edition, *Henkerfibel*, the translation supervised by Berthold Brecht, appeared in 1931, and had the honour of being burned by the Nazis two years later.

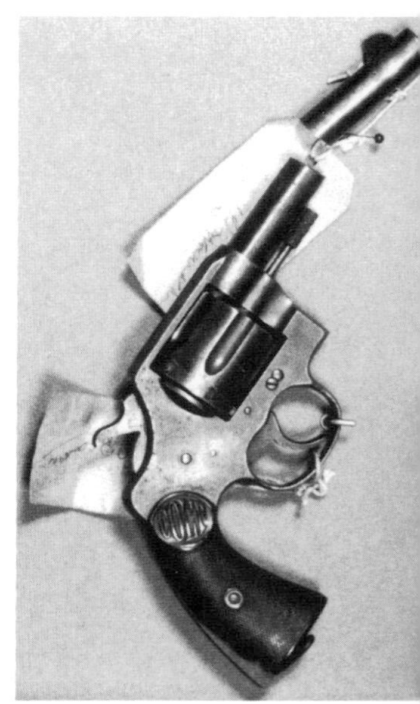

1929. A Select Committee on Capital Punishment recommended that the death penalty should be 'suspended experimentally' for five years. The recommendation was not acted upon; but there is no doubt that it impressed many abolitionist writers and speakers (politicians among them), who saw that they were far more likely to achieve their objective in stages than at a stroke — also, that the publicizing of their support for a trial no-hanging period would sway the minds of some of the many 'don't-knows' about once-and-for-all abolition (politicians among *them*).

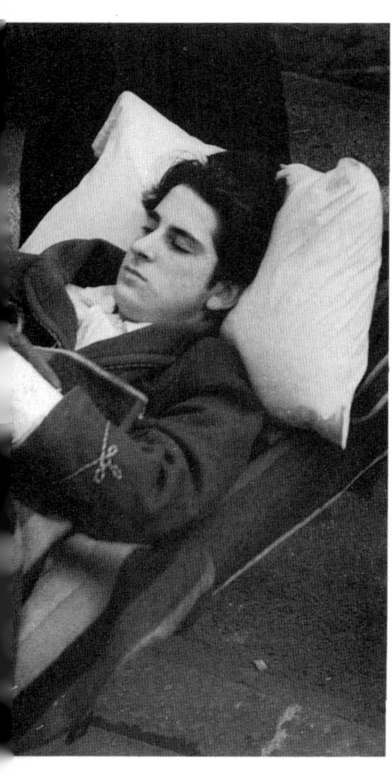

1931. The Sentence of Death (Expectant Mothers) Act gave pregnant women immunity from hanging.

1933. By the Children and Young Persons Act, sentence of death could not be passed on a person found guilty of a capital crime who was under eighteen when the crime was committed; the Court had to sentence the accused to detention during His Majesty's Pleasure.

Some twenty years later, the Act created an anomaly that gave a great boost to the anti-hanging campaign. The anomaly arose from the case of Craig and Bentley, which has been outlined as follows:

> On the night of 2 November 1952, the police were called to investigate a break-in at a confectionery warehouse in Croydon, Surrey. During a fracas on the roof of the building, one of the intruders, nineteen-year-old Derek Bentley, was taken into custody. But the other intruder, sixteen-year-old Christopher Craig (whose older brother had three days before been sentenced to twelve years' imprisonment for armed robbery), produced a revolver and held the police at bay. Bentley shouted, 'Let them have it, Chris' (an ambiguous remark; but, according to police testimony, Bentley certainly did not mean that Craig should hand over the gun). Craig fired at Detective Constable Frederick Fairfax, who was holding Bentley, and wounded him in the shoulder. He then shot Police Constable Sidney Miles between the eyes. Later, after firearms had been brought for the police, Craig jumped from the roof. Before losing consciousness, he said, 'I hope I've killed the fucking lot.'
>
> At the trial at the Old Bailey before the Lord Chief Justice, Lord Goddard, both Craig and Bentley were found guilty of the murder of PC Miles. Bentley was executed at Wandsworth Prison on 28 January 1953. Craig, because of his age, was sentenced to be detained. He was released in 1968.

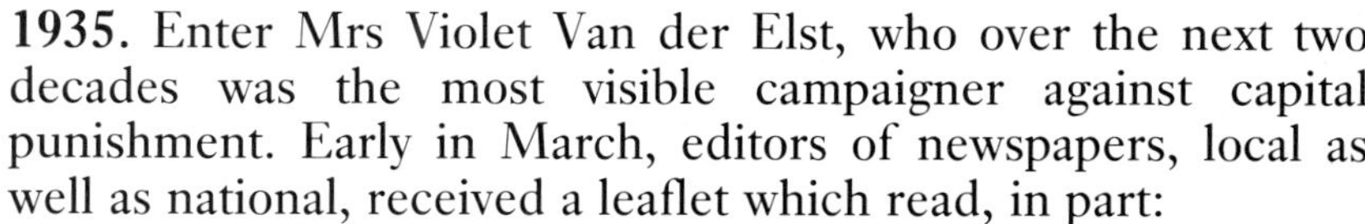

1935. Enter Mrs Violet Van der Elst, who over the next two decades was the most visible campaigner against capital punishment. Early in March, editors of newspapers, local as well as national, received a leaflet which read, in part:

> Mrs Van der Elst, the well-known manufacturing chemist, proprietor of the Shavez-Zeekol Company Ltd and other large distributing organisations, has decided to devote a great deal of time to organise a Campaign for the Abolition of Capital Punishment in this country. . . .
>
> One cannot cure the cause of a murder by hanging a murderer, one can only prevent murder by making the punishment sufficiently deterring to prevent others from committing similar crimes.

Mrs Van der Elst complaining at being moved on.

Mrs Van der Elst is organising a demonstration to take place at 9 o'clock on 13 March, Wednesday morning, on the occasion of the execution of the murderer, George Harvey. . . .

Mrs Van der Elst, at her own expense, is organising Petitions for the Reprieve of condemned men on every occasion that a murderer is sentenced to death.

From the Press Office of the

VIOLET VAN DER ELST CAMPAIGN
FOR THE ABOLITION OF CAPITAL PUNISHMENT
4 Palace Gate, W8

'George Harvey' was the assumed name of Charles Lake, who had been found guilty of having killed a bookmaker following an argument over money. Mrs Van der Elst's biographer, Charles Neilson Gattey (*see Bibliography*), notes that at 8.30, half an hour before Lake's execution,

she went to Pentonville, with her supporters, in cars which drove slowly round the prison in procession. In the first, a big white Rolls, sat Mrs Van der Elst with a woman companion. The others were occupied by men. As the cars moved at a walking pace along the kerb in front of the prison, a film was taken privately for her. A brass band had been engaged to play the 'Dead March' and hymns. Mrs Van der Elst had stated that a symphony of her own composition might also be included. But the musicians departed after being told by the police that on Home Office instructions they were banning the playing of music within earshot of the prison.

For an hour before the execution sixty sandwichmen paraded up and down the road carrying placards bearing the words 'Stop Capital Punishment' and 'Mercy is Not Weakness'. On one of these was a drawing of a gallows, with the figure of a woman standing below the noose. Then they marched to Hyde Park, followed by police cars.

At subsequent executions, Mrs Van der Elst's razzle-dazzle activities on the ground were overflown by her aeroplanes, all trailing STOP THE DEATH PENALTY streamers. In no time at all, the publicity given to her outside-prison appearances, and to her almost invariable consequential appearances in magistrates' courts to answer charges brought by traffic policemen, made her a celebrity. People with nothing better to do with their time turned up at prisons on execution mornings, simply to see — and, if they were lucky enough, to be photographed with — 'the incredible Mrs Van der Elst'. Contrary to the statement by one of her early helpers, Clement Attlee, MP, that 'she had strong claims to be regarded as the woman who did more than anyone else to secure the abolition of capital punishment in Britain', she probably did more harm than good: many respectable people who would have liked to assist the abolitionist cause were put off from doing so for fear of being compared to 'VD Elsie'.

1948. In April, Sydney Silverman, the Labour MP for Nelson and Colne, obtained Commons approval for a clause in a Criminal Justice Bill, suspending capital punishment for an experimental period of five years; but the decision was reversed by the Lords, who also rejected an attempt by the Labour Government to bring in compromise legislation that defined categories of murder.

1949/1953. On 2 December 1949, acting on information contained in a series of contradictory statements made by Timothy John Evans, an illiterate van-driver, the police searched 10 Rillington Place (later renamed Ruston Place), in the West London district of Notting Hill Gate, and found the bodies of Evans's wife Beryl and their year-old daughter Geraldine; both had been strangled, the woman with a rope or twisted nylon stocking, the baby with a necktie. Indicted for the murder of the baby, Evans was found guilty, and was executed by Albert Pierrepoint on 9 March 1950. One of the leading prosecution witnesses at the trial was John Reginald Halliday Christie, an ex-War Reserve policeman, who was the tenant of the ground-floor flat at 10 Rillington Place. Three years later, the remains of six more women were found in the house and garden. One of them was Christie's wife Ethel, and it was for her murder that he was tried and found guilty. Not only did Christie admit responsibility for the deaths of the other five women, all of whom had been prostitutes, but he gave detailed evidence purporting to show that he had murdered Beryl Evans; he denied, however, that he had killed the baby. John Scott Henderson, QC, was appointed by the Home Secretary to inquire into the evidence and report whether, in his opinion, there had been a miscarriage of justice in the Evans case. After hearing in private the evidence of twenty-three persons, one of whom was Christie (who was hanged by Albert Pierrepoint a few days later, on 15 July 1953), Scott Henderson stated, among other findings, that there was no doubt that Evans was responsible for the deaths of his wife and baby. But few people were satisfied, either with the way in which the inquiry had been conducted or with the findings, and abolitionist sloganeers were quick to link the name of Timothy Evans with that of Derek Bentley. (In 1965, mainly due to the efforts of a group led by the writer and broadcaster Ludovic Kennedy [*see Bibliography*] and including Evans's mother, Mr Justice Brabin was appointed to hold a public inquiry. His report [*HMSO, Cmd. 3101*],

published in October 1966, concluded with findings that, rather than resolving the issue, added a permutation to the possibilities: 'I have come to the conclusion that it is more probable than not that Evans killed Beryl Evans. I have come to the conclusion that it is more probable than not that Evans did not kill Geraldine.')

John Christie.

(Opposite)
The back of 10 Rillington Place.

1949–55. In May 1949, Chuter Ede, the Home Secretary of the Labour Government, set up a Royal Commission on Capital Punishment, under the chairmanship of a retired civil servant, Sir Ernest Gowers, its terms of reference being

> to consider and report whether liability under the criminal law in Great Britain to suffer capital punishment for murder should be limited or modified, and if so, to what extent and by what means, for how long and under what conditions persons who would otherwise have been liable to suffer capital punishment should be detained, and what changes in the existing law and the prison system would be required; and to inquire into and take account of the position in those countries whose experience and practice may throw light on these questions.

The Commission's Report (HMSO, Cmd. 8932), published in September 1953, contained a mass of proposals, the main one being that juries should be empowered 'to decide in each case whether punishment by imprisonment for life could properly be substituted for the death penalty':

> a workable procedure could be devised . . . it is the only practicable way of enabling the courts, instead of the Executive, to take account of extenuating circumstances so as to correct the rigidity which is the outstanding defect of the existing law. . . . We recognise that the disadvantages of a system of 'jury discretion' may be thought to outweigh its merits. If this view were to prevail, the conclusion would seem to be inescapable that in this country a stage has been reached where little more can be done effectively to limit the liability to suffer the death penalty, and that the issue is now whether capital punishment should be retained or abolished.

The Report was not debated by the Commons until 10 February 1955. On a free vote, the House agreed to a motion by the Conservative Home Secretary, Major Gwilym Lloyd-George, that the recommendations should only 'be taken note of'. An amendment to the effect that the death penalty should be suspended, proposed by Sydney Silverman, was defeated — also on a free vote — by 245–214. During the debate the former Home Secretary, Chuter Ede, said that he had erred in signing

le match de la vie

ELLE A PLAIDÉ COUPABLE PAR AMOUR

Ruth Ellis, 28 ans, ancien mannequin, était l'hôtesse d'un club de Kensington. Elle est mère de deux enfants. C'est par jalousie qu'elle abattit le coureur automobiliste David Blakely. Elle avait d'abord refusé de signer son recours en grâce.

78

Six balles tirées " avec l'intention de donner la mort " l'ont conduite dans la cellule des condamnées à la peine capitale. Mais toute l'Angleterre s'est émue devant l'inflexibilité de sa justice qui n'admet pas l'excuse de la passion.

RUTH ELLIS CAS DE CONSCIENCE DE L'ANGLETERRE

Quand l'huissier à chaîne d'argent déposa sur son bureau le dossier vert de l'« affaire Ruth Ellis », l'imperturbable major Gwilym Lloyd George, fils du célèbre homme politique, ne put maîtriser un tressaillement de son visage. Comme pour chasser des pensées inopportunes, il passa la main sur son front, puis demanda à n'être dérangé sous aucun prétexte.

En fait, l'histoire était banale, mais le destin l'avait transformée en une véritable bombe. Pour la première fois depuis des siècles une brèche s'ouvrait dans l'inexpugnable citadelle de la justice anglaise. Cette bombe, il appartenait au major, Home secretary de Sa Majesté, d'y mettre ou non le feu. S'il recommandait à la Reine de rejeter le recours en grâce formulé par Ruth Ellis, vingt-huit ans, condamnée pour un meurtre passionnel à être pendue, la vieille machine judiciaire britannique continuerait à fonctionner sur le rythme de la tradition. Si, au contraire, il proposait sa grâce, le premier pas, le plus dur, serait fait dans la voie de réformes qui bouleverseraient le système actuel. En ne pendant pas Ruth Ellis, l'Angleterre désavouerait sa législation et prendrait officieusement en considération le drame passionnel.

(Suite page 80.)

IL LUI PRÉFÉRAIT LES COURSES

David Blakely, 25 ans, fils de famille, n'avait qu'une passion, les courses. Il avait construit lui-même sa voiture Emperor (à g.). C'est le dimanche de Pâques qu'il a été tué. Il avait l'intention de participer aux 24 Heures du Mans.

ENQUÊTE JACQUES LE BAILLY

79

The start of a feature in Paris Match, *23 July 1955.*

(Right) *The scene of the murder of David Blakely.*

the 'death papers' of Timothy Evans, adding that he hoped 'that no future Home Secretary, while in office or after he has left office, will ever have to feel that, although he did his best, he sent a man to the gallows who was not "guilty as charged" '.

1955. The hanging of Mrs Ruth Ellis, which took place in Holloway Prison on 13 July, was partly responsible for the fact that she was the last woman to be hanged in Great Britain.

Ruth Ellis was twenty-eight. Her rackety life as a 'good-time girl' was starting to take its toll on her face and figure. She had two children — the elder, a son, the product of a flirtation with a French-Canadian serviceman in 1944; the younger, a daughter, born during her brief marriage to an alcoholic dentist, from whom she was divorced in February 1955. Just over a year before the divorce was made absolute, she became the mistress of David Blakely, a flashily handsome racing-car driver, younger than herself, whom she had met in a drinking-club near Harrod's that she was then managing on behalf of a pimp named Morris Conley, who had employed her in other capacities. During Blakely's absences — either because he was competing in car-races or because of temporary estrangement — she slept with other men, including Desmond Cussen, a company director who, after being introduced to her by his friend Blakely, became infatuated with her. Within weeks of the beginning of her on-off affair with Blakely, he made her pregnant; she procured an abortion. Towards the end of 1954 she again became pregnant — by Blakely, she said. On 28 March 1955 she suffered a miscarriage — brought on, she said, by Blakely's punching her in the stomach during a quarrel.

The revolver used by Ruth Ellis.

Blakely broke his promise to spend Easter with her. Late in the evening of Good Friday, 8 April, suspecting that Blakely was staying with a married couple named Findlater — friends of his but enemies of hers — she got Desmond Cussen to drive her to Tanza Road, Hampstead, which was where the Findlaters had a flat. Her suspicion was confirmed by the sight of Blakely's van parked outside the house. She created a disturbance, chiefly by trying to break the windows of the van. A policeman called to the scene advised her to leave, and, assuming that the advice would be followed, himself left; by the time a second policeman arrived, summoned by Mr Findlater's telephoned complaint of further disturbance, she was being driven away by Cussen. Next day, she made several telephone calls to the Findlaters' flat; one or other of the Findlaters took the calls and, recognizing her voice, hung up. In the afternoon of Easter Sunday, Blakely drove the attractive young nanny of the Findlaters' child to Victoria Station, where she was to catch a train home; he was away for two hours. In the evening he, the Findlaters, and a mutual friend, Clive Gunnell, listened to records and drank beer. At about nine, he and Gunnell drove the short distance to the Magdala public house to fetch more beer. They had a drink in the saloon bar and left at 9.20, carrying, between them, three quart bottles. A bank clerk and his wife, Donald and Gladys Yule, were walking down Parliament Hill towards the Magdala.

Blakely saw Ruth Ellis standing nearby. He ignored her. A second later, she took a revolver from her handbag and fired a shot. As Blakely ran for cover, she fired again. He collapsed, face-down, near his van. Standing over him, she continued to pull the trigger — even after the revolver was empty. One of the last shots ricocheted off the pavement and hit Gladys Yule in the hand.

An off-duty constable came out of the Magdala and approached Ruth Ellis. She told him to telephone the police. 'I *am* the police,' he said as he grabbed the gun from her. Blakely was taken to hospital, where he was found to be dead, and the off-duty constable escorted Ruth Ellis to Hampstead Police Station. An hour and a half later, she was interviewed by CID officers. In answer to questions about the revolver, she claimed that it had been given to her three years before by a man whose name she could not recall: 'It was security for money, but I accepted it as a curiosity.' Asked why she had put the gun in her handbag before travelling to Hampstead, she said: 'I intended to find David and shoot him.'

Next day, Easter Monday, she received an unexpected visit from a solicitor, a total stranger to her — not a member of the reputable firm, Victor Mishcon & Co, that had acted for her in regard to her divorce. The solicitor's stated concern that she should receive whatever legal assistance she wanted was slight compared with the main reason for his visit, which was to get her to sign a contract giving exclusive rights in her story to a newspaper group. He achieved that objective by telling her that she — or, in the event of her death, her son — would receive a substantial cash-payment. In fact, the contract provided only that the newspaper group would cover the costs of her defence. The solicitor's trickery, for which he was well rewarded, resulted in the paradox that three esteemed barristers (one of whom, was on the newspaper group's payroll as a reader for libel) were briefed for the defence of a woman who, far from wanting anyone to defend her, was determined to be hanged. The day after Ruth Ellis signed the contract, she ended a letter to David Blakely's mother: 'I shall die loving your son. And you should feel content that his death has been repaid. Goodbye.'

The trial, at the Old Bailey, began on 20 June and ended well before lunchtime on the 21st. The judge, Mr Justice Havers, refused to allow Ruth Ellis's leading counsel, Melford Stevenson, QC, to put to the jury the defence of 'provocation by jealousy' — in effect, *crime passionel*. Before the trial Ruth Ellis had written to a friend, 'All I want is that the jury should hear my full story' — which was just about the last thing her defenders wanted. During her examination-in-chief, Melford Stevenson was often shocked by her casual answers to questions that she considered irrelevant — most noticeably when, asked about her *movements* in the early evening of Easter Sunday, she said, 'I was very upset, and I had a peculiar idea I wanted to kill him [Blakely].' Unable to believe his ears, Melford Stevenson asked, 'You had *what*?' — and, before he could recover his senses enough to retract that question, was told: 'I had an idea I wanted to kill him.' The leading prosecutor, Christmas Humphreys, asked her only one question in cross-examination: 'Mrs Ellis, when you fired that revolver at close range into the body of David Blakely, what did you intend to do?' 'It is obvious,' she replied, 'that when I shot him I intended to kill him.' 'Thank you,' said Mr Humphreys, and sat down. In view of the judge's ruling against the defence of provocation by jealousy, Melford Stevenson felt that it would be improper for him to make a closing speech; Christmas Humphreys also waived his right to do so. In his summing-up, Mr Justice Havers told the jury: 'It is not open to you to bring in a verdict of manslaughter on the grounds of provocation. . . . If you are satisfied that the accused deliberately fired those shots at Blakely, and as a result he died, it is not open to you to find a verdict of Not Guilty.' And so the jury returned the verdict of Guilty. They made no recommendation for mercy.

On the following day, Ruth Ellis's solicitor announced that she would not appeal.

A petition was drawn up and copies of it distributed to abolitionist signature-collectors. Many people wrote to the Home Secretary, Major Gwilym Lloyd-George, urging him to grant a reprieve: a few of them put forward reasons that were particular to Ruth Ellis (for instance, that her recent miscarriage may have affected her mind), and one, an acquaintance of Ruth Ellis's who had visited her in prison, stated that she had said in confidence that she had acquired the revolver from a named male friend on the day of the murder, and that he had driven her to Hampstead in the evening. (Although, years later, extra-judicial inquiries revealed the strong probability that the man *was* an accessory before the fact of the murder, a police investigation conducted at the time failed to find evidence against him: a minute was added to the Ellis file at the Home Office, noting that 'even if [the] theory about the gun is true, it is not directly relevant to the question of premeditation. It does not affect the fact that Mrs Ellis went to Hampstead armed with a gun which she then used against Blakely.') Meanwhile, the London *Evening Standard* published a letter from the American author, Raymond Chandler:

> As a part-time resident and full-time friend and admirer of England, I have always, until now, respected its legal system — as has most of the world. But there is at times a vein of savagery that repels me.
>
> I have been tormented for a week at the idea that a highly civilised people should put a rope around the neck of Ruth Ellis and drop her through a trap and break her neck. I could understand perhaps the hanging of a woman for bestial crime like a multiple poisoning, an axe murder (à la Lizzie Borden) or a baby-farm operator killing her charges, but this was a crime of passion under considerable provocation. No other country in the world would hang this woman.
>
> In France she would get off with a light sentence or none. In America it would be first or second degree manslaughter and she would be out of prison in anywhere from three and a half to seven years.
>
> This thing haunts and, so far as I may say it, disgusts me as something obscene. I am not referring to the trial, of course, but to the medieval savagery of the law.
>
> RAYMOND CHANDLER
> Eaton Square, Westminster

That letter was the first of many regarding the case — about half disagreeing with Chandler — that appeared in the *Standard*. If Major Lloyd-George was particularly impressed by one of the letters, it was Mrs Gladys Yule's:

> Don't let us turn Ruth Ellis into a national heroine. I stood petrified and watched her kill David Blakely in cold blood. . . . These hysterical people, getting up petitions for a reprieve, and those rushing to sign them. Do they realise Ruth Ellis shot Blakely to the danger of the public? She might easily have killed me, an innocent passer-by. As it is, I have a partly crippled right hand for life. . . . Crime passionel indeed! What if other countries would let her off from her just punishment? When has Britain followed the lead of others? Let us remain a law-abiding country where citizens can live and walk abroad in peace and safety.

On Monday, 11 July, within hours of the publication of Mrs Yule's letter, the Home Secretary announced that the execution of Ruth Ellis would go ahead, as planned, on the morning of

POST-MORTEM EXAMINATION.

Name ELLIS, Ruth **Apparent Age** 28 years

At H.M. Prison, Holloway **Date** July 13 1955

EXTERNAL EXAMINATION	
Nourishment	Well nourished. Evidence of proper care and attention. Height - 5ft. 2ins. Weight - 103 lbs.
Marks of Violence, Identification, etc. ...	DEEP IMPRESSIONS AROUND NECK of noose with suspension point about 1 inch in front of the angle of the L.lower jaw. Vital changes locally and in the tissues beneath as a consequence of sudden constriction. No ecchymoses in the face - or, indeed, elsewhere. No marks of restraint.
How long dead	1 hour.
INTERNAL EXAMINATION	
Skull ... ... / Brain Meninges	Fracture-dislocation of the spine at C.2 with a 2 inch gap and transverse separation of the spinal cord at the same level.
Mouth, Tongue, Oesophagus ... ... / Larynx, Trachea, Lungs ...	Fractures of both wings of the hyoid and the R.wing of the thyroid cartilage. Larynx also fractured. Air passages clear and lungs quite free from disease or other change. No engorgement. No asphyxial changes.
Pericardium, Heart and Blood Vessels	No organic disease. No petechiae or other evidence of asphyxial change.
Stomach and Contents ...	Small food residue, and odour of brandy. No disease.
Peritoneum, Intestines, Etc.	Normal.
Liver and Gall Bladder ...	Terminal congestion only.
Spleen	Normal.
Kidneys and Ureters... ...	Slight terminal congestion only.
Bladder, Etc. ... ... / Generative Organs	Lower abdominal operation scar for ectopic pregnancy operation in L.tube, now healed. No pregnancy.
Other Remarks	Deceased was a healthy subject at the time of death. Mark of suspension normally situated and injuries from judicial hanging - to the spinal columnand cord - such as must have caused instant death.
CAUSE OF DEATH ...	Injuries to the central nervous system consequent upon judicial hanging.

Signed [signature] M.D. Lond.

146, Harley St., W.1, and Guy's Hospital (Pathologist)
Reader in Forensic Medicine, London University.

Wednesday, 13 July. Long afterwards, following Lloyd-George's elevation from the Commons to the Lords, he told the lawyer and journalist Fenton Bresler (*see Bibliography*): 'We cannot have people shooting off firearms in the street. This was a public thoroughfare where Ruth Ellis stalked [*sic*] and shot her quarry. And remember that she did not only kill David Blakely; she also injured a passer-by. As long as I was Home Secretary, I was determined to ensure that people could use the streets without fear of a bullet.' And so it seems that Ruth Ellis was hanged, not because she had murdered David Blakely, but because she had inadvertently wounded Gladys Yule (who, incidentally, was not left with 'a partly crippled right hand for life': the injury soon mended).

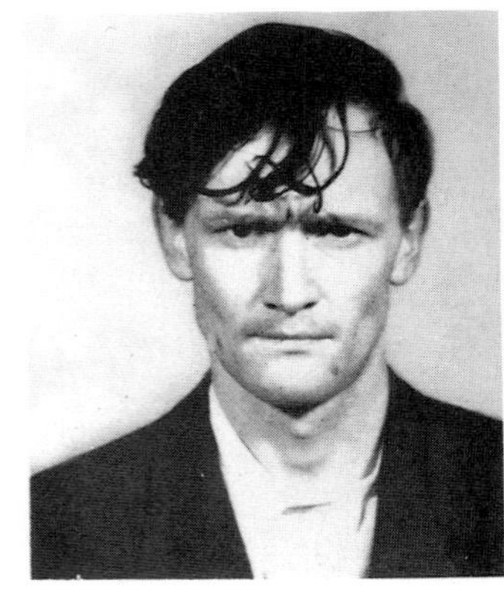

A few weeks after the execution, a National Campaign for the Abolition of Capital Punishment was started by the publisher Victor Gollancz, the writer Arthur Koestler, and Canon John Collins. It received far more public support than the earlier campaign, run by E. Roy Calvert: at its first open meeting, overflowing from Central Hall, Westminster, a collection realized £1100, about twice as much as the Calvert campaign had gathered in its best financial year; by the end of 1955, membership exceeded 16,000.

1956. When, in February, Albert Pierrepoint resigned from the list of executioners, both propagandists against the death penalty and writers for the popular press ascribed his decision to — as one of the latter put it — 'the fact that, following his hanging of Ruth Ellis, he felt he could not go on'. Actually, his resignation was due to a more mundane matter of principle arising from an argument over expenses.

(Above)
John Walby.

(Opposite, above)
Peter Allen.

(Opposite, below)
Albert Pierrepoint, following his retirement.

In March, against the advice of the Conservative Government, Sydney Silverman's Death Penalty (Abolition) Bill was given a second reading in the Commons, the vote being 286–262. The Lords rejected the Bill.

1957. In March, Parliament passed the Homicide Act — often referred to within legal circles as the 'Reggie-cide Act', since Sir Reginald Manningham-Buller, the Attorney-General, was primarily responsible for the compromise legislation. The death penalty was retained for five categories of murder; 'in the course or furtherance of theft; by shooting or by causing an explosion; in the course or for the purpose of resisting or avoiding or preventing a lawful arrest, or of effecting or assisting an escape or rescue from legal custody; any murder of a police officer acting in the execution of his duty or of a person assisting a police officer so acting; in the case of a person who was a

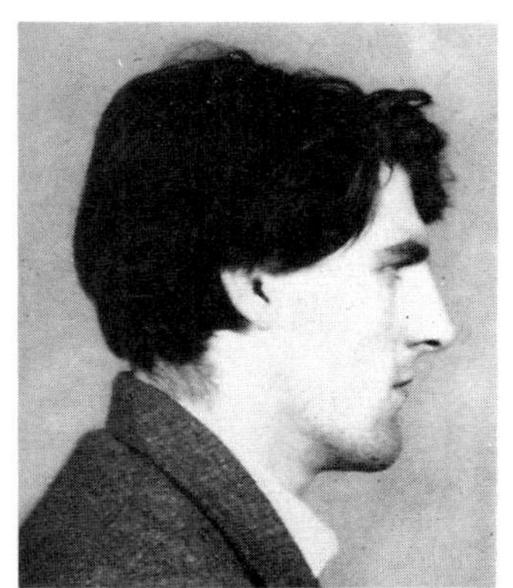

prisoner at the time when he did or was a party to the murder, any murder of a prison officer.' The death penalty also applied to persons convicted of murder on a previous occasion, and to persons convicted on the same indictment of two or more murders done on different occasions.

1964. The last executions in Great Britain were carried out on 13 August, one at Walton Prison, Liverpool, and the other at Strangeways, Manchester, the condemned being, respectively, Peter Allen and John Walby (better known as 'Ginger' Owen Evans), who together had been found guilty of the murder of John West, a van-driver for a firm of launderers in Workington, Cumberland.

On 21 December the Commons gave Sydney Silverman's Murder (Abolition of Death Penalty) Bill a second reading by a majority of 185. The Bill, which suspended capital punishment for all categories of murder for an experimental period of five years, was enacted on 9 November 1965.

1969. On 16 December the Commons voted (343–185) to affirm the resolution to abolish capital punishment for murder, and two days later the resolution was affirmed in the Lords by a majority of 46. Subsequently, the Home Office announced that the gallows at Wandsworth Prison would not be dismantled as the death penalty remained on the statute book for treason, piracy with violence, and setting fire to Her Majesty's ships.

1969 to date. All public opinion polls show that the majority of people favour the return of the death penalty for murder. Efforts by Conservative Members of Parliament to bring in re-introductive legislation (that of 1 April 1987 was the thirteenth) have failed.

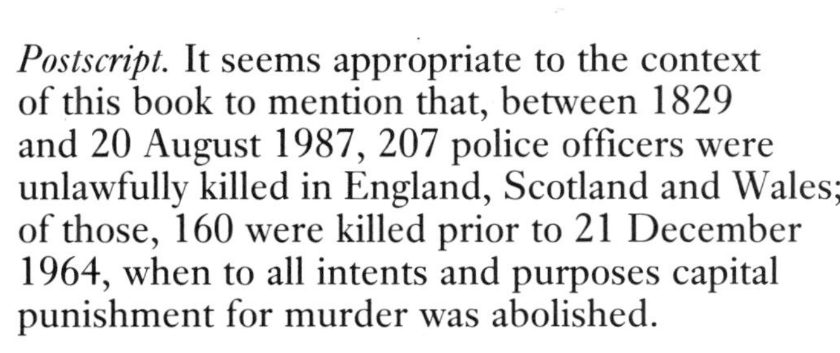

Postscript. It seems appropriate to the context of this book to mention that, between 1829 and 20 August 1987, 207 police officers were unlawfully killed in England, Scotland and Wales; of those, 160 were killed prior to 21 December 1964, when to all intents and purposes capital punishment for murder was abolished.

ELECTRO-MAGNETIC TELEGRAPH, ON THE GREAT WESTERN RAILWAY.

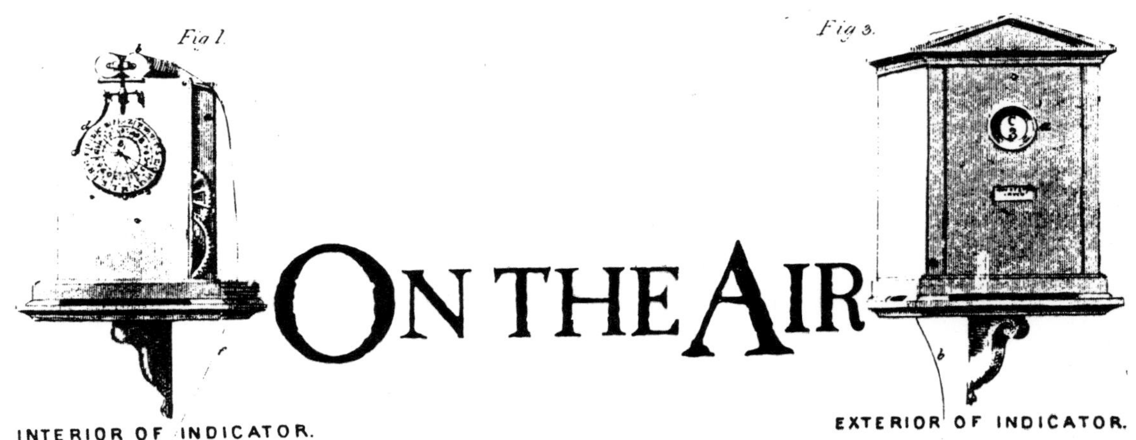

INTERIOR OF INDICATOR.

EXTERIOR OF INDICATOR.

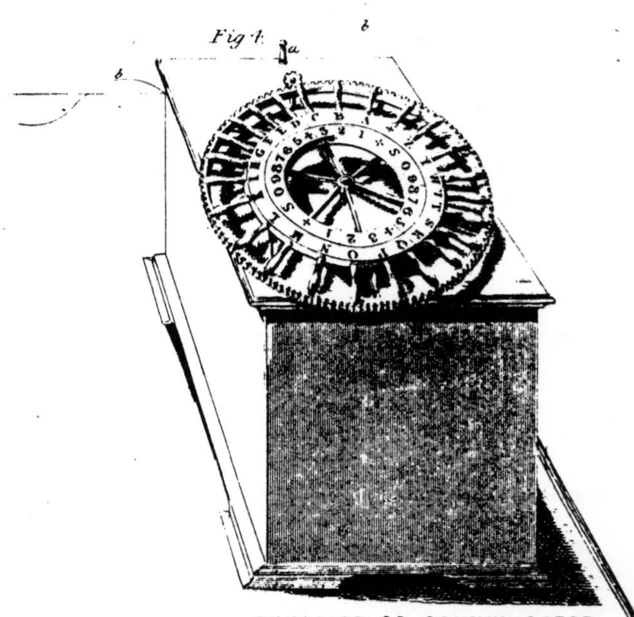

INTERIOR OF COMMUNICATOR.

EXTERIOR OF COMMUNICATOR.

Invented by

PROFESSOR WHEATSTONE.

Unfairly to the memory of the mid-Victorian Mr Justice Maule, who, according to eye-witness accounts of his judicial manner, scarcely ever butted in, the only anecdote anyone knows of him is that, on an occasion when he was fuddled by the haphazard presentation of a case, he interrupted the barrister who was making it, saying, 'I should like to stipulate for some sort of order,' and adding: 'There are plenty of them. There is the chronological, the botanical, the metaphysical — why, even the alphabetical order would be better than no order at all.'

Giving some sort of order to a book about the Black Museum — or rather, about events represented by a selection of its exhibits – is easier said than done. Considering the sheer multitude of represented sins, it would be no more sensible for us to put them, regardless of diversity, into a date-dependent order throughout the book than for someone else to make a single chronology of chalks and cheeses. As for an alphabetical arrangement — well, that seems to be ruled out, if for no other reason than that it would produce a sequence of odd juxtapositions (the oddest of all, perhaps, being the next-door neighbourliness of a mass-murderer and a crook of the smallest fry). Since a botanical order would only work if we restricted our selection of cases to those of murder by the administering of vegetable poisons, belladonna and the like, and a metaphysical one doesn't bear thinking about, we have decided — the previous section having, by its nature, made for impeccable chronological orderliness of many of the Black Museum's remembrances, and the final section being orderly in the sense of discreteness of subject matter — that this section in between will be devoted to murder investigations, landmarks of one kind or another in the first hundred years or so of organized law-enforcement, in which wire or wireless means of communication played a salient or, at any rate, much-publicized part.

The first public telegraph line, which ran for roughly twenty miles alongside the Great Western Railway tracks between the London terminal of Paddington and, to the west, the station at Slough, Buckinghamshire, was opened in 1843. Within two years, that telegraph line was used towards the apprehension of John Tawell on the charge of having murdered Sarah Hart.

Tawell, who invariably wore clothes indicating that he was a Quaker (whether or not he was, in fact, a member of the Society of Friends became a matter of controversy), had served a sentence of transportation to Australia for a crime that does not seem to have been serious, and which certainly did not cause

From the
Illustrated London News,
10 August 1844.

THE ELECTRO-MAGNETIC TELEGRAPH AT SLOUGH, ON THE GREAT WESTERN RAILWAY.

By aid of the extraordinary power of this triumph of science, the auspicious event of her Majesty's accouchement on Tuesday morning, was communicated from Windsor Castle to the metropolis within eleven minutes! The details are as follows:—

"At two minutes past six o'clock, a messenger, mounted upon one of the fleetest horses in the royal stables, was despatched from the Castle to Mr. Howell, the superintendent at the Slough station, with instructions to communicate, by means of the electro-magnetic telegraphic, to the person in attendance at the Telegraph-office, at Paddington, to the effect that the letters, which had been waiting there for several days past, addressed to the Cabinet Ministers and the Great Officers of State, were to be delivered at the residences of the respective parties with-

THE ELECTRIC TELEKGRAPH STATION, AT SLOUGH.

out a moment's delay. The messenger reached the Slough station within 8 minutes of his departure from the Castle, then 10 minutes past 6 o'clock; and although Mr. Russell, the gentleman who has the superintendence of the Telegraph-office, and Mr. Howell, had to be called from their beds, yet such was the admirable nature of the arrangements which had been made, and the extreme rapidity with which they were carried into effect, that within three minutes of the instructions reaching the Slough station, the telegraph was not only at work, but the communication was despatched to Paddington, and an acknowledgment of its receipt returned to Slough; and this was all effected within eleven minutes of the special messenger's departure from the Castle!

"Upon the departure of each of the three special trains conveying the Cabinet Ministers and Great Officers of State, from Paddington, that fact was instantly telegraphed to Slough, so that at that station not an instant was lost upon the arrival of the Ministers, &c., in their proceeding in the Queen's and the Royal Hotel carriages to the royal residence at Windsor."

This telegraph has been constructed for the Great Western Railway by Mr. Cooke, who, instead of laying the conducting wires in iron tubing, has suspended them in the open air from lofty polings, the advantages of which are diminished cost, superior insectation, and facility of repair. The telegraph is available by the public, for the transmission of messages and replies; and the apparatus may be inspected, though at the exhibition charge of 1s. each person.

On the above day, also, were performed some wonders of railway travelling. The journey, from Slough to the Paddington terminus, was accomplished in less time than the distance had ever previously been traversed by a special passenger train on the Great Western line. The eighteen miles and a quarter only occupied fifteen minutes and ten seconds, being at the rate of upwards of seventy miles an hour!

physical harm to the victim or victims; he was qualified as a chemist (or, as that word was spelt in 1845, *chymist*). A contemporary described him as 'a man of about 50 years of age; his appearance is respectable, and the expression of his countenance intelligent, although rendered somewhat disagreeable by a squint'.

His trial, in the assize court of the Buckinghamshire market-town of Aylesbury, was scheduled to start at nine o'clock in the morning of Thursday, 13 March 1845; but, according to the attending reporter for *The Times*,

> so great was the confusion occasioned by the mismanagement of the inferior officers of the court that it was a long time before the proceedings could be carried on. . . . There were three or four testy officials in the hall leading to the staircase [to the court] who seemed to take delight in obstructing the passage of those whom the under-sheriff had already permitted to pass. Ruffianism is not too strong an epithet to apply to the behaviour of these jacks in office, for they were not content with annoying gentlemen, but actually assaulted them. . . . [However,] for the accommodation afforded to the press we have to return our thanks, a place being provided for us in a gallery immediately over the witness-box, where we were secure from interruption by the pressure of a dense and eager audience which thronged every other part of the court.

Contrary to the subsequent stereotyping of early-Victorian prosecutors as being over-zealous from a desire to convict, Tawell's prosecutor, Mr Serjeant Byles, was moderate in his demeanour and strict in regard to the facts. Slightly edited, and with the insertion of some minor details, his opening speech provides a good outline of events that led to Tawell's indictment:

> I rejoice that the prisoner, as the law now stands [under the Trials of Felony Act, 1836], may have the benefit of being defended by counsel.
>
> In cases of this kind, you are not to expect direct and positive evidence. No man who meditates the crime of assassination by poison fails to take some precaution so that, at all events, direct or demonstrative evidence of the fact shall be inaccessible. No eye sees death poured into the cup, save that which is all-seeing and in every place.
>
> Tawell formerly carried on the business of a chymist and druggist. About six years ago, he had the misfortune to lose his first wife. Nine or ten weeks before his wife's death, the deceased, Sarah Hart, then a young woman somewhere about thirty years of age, entered his service. The nature of the acquaintance which subsisted between her

John Tawell.

(Right)
Bath Place, Slough.

and Tawell is indicated by the fact that when she left his service she was in the family way. She lived first after quitting his service, and for about twelve months, as a lodger at 93 Crawford Street, Portman Square, London, where Tawell was in the habit of visiting her. She then lived for a year and three-quarters at 62 Harrow Road, Paddington Green, thence removed to Slough, and for eighteen months previous to her death was living at Bath Place, which consists of four small cottages, forming one detached building, in the district of the town known as Salt Hill. Bath Place stands upon the Great Western Road, about a quarter of a mile beyond the Windmill public house, which is kept by a person called Botham. In the end house, towards London, lived Mrs Mary Ann Ashley, a widow; in the next lived Sarah Hart, with her two children. She was entirely dependent on Tawell for her support, and he was in the habit of visiting her at Bath Place and supplying her with money.

Tawell himself has recently resided at Berkhampstead, to the north-west of London, in circumstances of apparent ease and affluence. He married no long time since a second wife, Sarah Cutforth. Notwithstanding his apparent ease and respectability, he was, at the time of Sarah Hart's death, by no means in such circumstances; a banker's clerk will prove that he had overdrawn his account. It is clear that he was in the constant habit of visiting Sarah Hart, that she was dependent upon him for money, and that he found himself in this position — that the money must be supplied, or that what was secret must become apparent: namely, the nature of his connexion with Sarah Hart.

Tawell subscribed to the Jerusalem Coffee House, Cornhill, London. On New Year's Day of the present year, he was there about noon. He told a waiter that he was going to dine at the west end of town, and desired that his great-coat should be left for him on his return about nine o'clock. He did not proceed to the west end of the town, but to the Paddington station of the Great Western Railway, by the four o'clock train of which railway he proceeded to Slough.

On arriving at Slough, he went to the residence of Sarah Hart, in Bath Place; and after he had been a short time with her she went by his direction to the Windmill public house for a bottle of porter. She was at that moment perfectly well and in good spirits. Having bought the porter, she borrowed a corkscrew, and brought both home with her to Bath Place.

Very shortly after her return, Mrs Ashley, the person who resided in the next house, being seated at work before a candle, heard a noise in the room of Sarah Hart. I should observe that these cottages consist each of two very small rooms on the ground floor. Mrs Ashley heard in her neighbour's apartment a moan or stifled scream. She laid down her work; the noise continued; she became very much alarmed, and, taking up her candle, went to the door, and proceeded down the path leading from the cottage to the road; but before she reached the gate, she saw Tawell approaching the gate which terminated a similar path from the cottage of Sarah Hart. He trembled, appeared greatly agitated, and had much difficulty in opening the gate, which Mrs Ashley, who had reached it by now, assisted him in opening, saying, 'What is the matter with my neighbour? I am afraid she is ill' — the moans of Sarah Hart being distinctly audible. Tawell made no answer, but passed out of the gate and proceeded towards the centre of Slough.

Mrs Ashley then went into the house, and observed in Sarah Hart's room, just before the fireplace, a small table, and on it a bottle of porter open and partly drunk, also two tumblers, one of which was next the window and towards the chair upon which Sarah Hart had apparently been sitting. In one of these tumblers there was froth; in the other there was porter or porter and water, it is not quite certain which. Sarah Hart was lying on the floor; her cap was off, and her hair was hanging down. Her clothes were up to her knees; one stocking was down, and one shoe off. She was still continuing the moaning noise.

Mrs Ashley went up to her and asked her what was the matter, and raised her head up, but Sarah Hart was unable to speak. Mrs Ashley brought in two neighbours, and some water was brought. Eventually, Mr Henry Champneys, a surgeon, was sent for. He felt her pulse and said he thought he could discover one or two beats. She moved her tongue, or jaw, a little. Mr Champneys put his hand under her clothes to feel her heart, but he could discover no pulsation. She was clearly dead.

In the meantime, Tawell was going on quickly towards the railway station. He had come that day from London, and was about to return, and did return; but instead of staying at the station then, he got into an omnibus to go to Eton, which is a few miles south of Slough. Asked by the driver where he desired to be set down in Eton, he replied, 'At Herschel House' [the residence of Sir John Herschel, the astronomer]. 'Oh,' said the driver, 'Herschel House is a long way this side of Eton.' It appears that it is in Slough, a few hundred yards from the station. Tawell, however, rode a short distance, and was set down at Herschel House, where it appears he had no business, for on getting up to the door he proceeded to walk on towards Eton. The omnibus went on in the same direction. What became of him in the interval we do not know, but he certainly went back to the station, and took a place in a first-class carriage for London.

At that time suspicion became attached to him. The Rev. Mr Edward Champneys (a cousin of Mr Champneys the surgeon) was there, and saw him depart on the 7.40 train, which actually left at 7.42. But as soon as he was gone, Mr Champneys communicated his suspicions to the person who conducts the electric telegraph. A signal was made to Paddington Station that a person was in the first-class carriage who ought to be watched. Quick as the train went, the signal was there long before the train arrived at the London terminus. (The message read: 'A murder has just been committed at Salt Hill and the suspected murderer was seen to take a first-class ticket for London by the train which left Slough at 7.42. He is in the garb of a Kwaker [the word 'Quaker' misspelt because the telegraph code did not include the letter Q] with a brown greatcoat which reaches down to his feet. He is in the last compartment of the second first-class carriage.')

A railway policeman, Sergeant William Williams, was on the platform, and as soon as Tawell got out of the carriage, the policeman saw him get into an omnibus, and, putting on a plain coat over his police dress, he stepped on to the rear of the omnibus with the conductor. The omnibus proceeded to the Bank, where Tawell got out, the policeman taking sixpence from him. He went forward to the Wellington statue, turned round, looked back, and then went to the Jerusalem Coffee House, in Cornhill, and enquired for his coat. The waiter gave him the coat, and he then went from Cornhill down Gracechurch Street to London Bridge, and over that to another coffee house in the Borough — the policeman still watching him, and taking care, of course, that he should not be observed. Tawell stayed there about half an hour. He then came out, and retraced his steps over London Bridge, and went down Cannon Street to a lodging house in Scott's Yard, kept by a person by the name of Hughes, who is, I believe, a member of the Society of Friends. The policeman, who is no officer off the railway station, waited half an hour, and, finding that Tawell did not come out of the lodging house, went away.

The next morning, further intelligence was received from Slough, and the policeman, with a London officer, Inspector William Wiggins, of D Division, proceeded to the house in Scott's Yard. He found that Tawell had left the house; and he then went to the Jerusalem Coffee House, where he found Tawell, and said to him, 'I believe you were down at Slough yesterday.'[1] Tawell denied it, saying he knew nobody at Slough. 'You must be mistaken,' said he, 'in the identity; my station in life places me above suspicion.' Inspector Wiggins, however, took him into custody, and took him down to Slough, where he was handed over to the custody of Samuel Perkins, the superintendent of the Eton police. He was searched, and found on his person was £12 10s. in gold, £14 1s. 6d. in silver, some halfpence, and a letter addressed to him from his wife. He slept that night at Perkins's house.

On the next day, at dinner, some conversation took place about Sarah Hart. Tawell said, 'That wretched and unfortunate woman once lived in my service for nearly two years and a half. I suppose you did not know that, Perkins?' Mr Perkins said he had heard so, but was not certain about it. Tawell added, 'She left me about five years ago. She was a good servant when she lived with me. She has often sent to me for money.' He was cautioned to mind what he said, as it would be taken down and used against him as evidence. He replied that he had no objection to that. He was asked if he had the deceased's letters. He said he did not keep letters of that sort. 'I was pestered,' he said, 'with letters from her when I was in London, and I determined to give her no more money. She was a bad woman — a very bad woman. She sent me a letter threatening to do something. She said she would make away with herself if I did not give her any money. I went down to her house and told her I would not give her any more money. She then asked me to give her a drop of porter. She had a glass, and I had a glass. She held in her hand over the glass of stout a very small phial, not bigger than her finger, and said, "I will, I will!" She poured something out of the phial into the stout, and drank part of it and did *so* —' and then Tawell described her manner by signs. He continued, 'She then lay down on the rug, and I walked out. I should not have gone out if I thought she had been in earnest; I certainly should not have left her.'

We will now revert, if you please, to the scene at Salt Hill. By direction of the coroner, a post-mortem examination took place the next day after the death of the woman. The surgeons could not discover any external injury to account for death. They examined the brain; there was no appearance of anything in the brain which could have produced death. In the same manner they examined the lungs, and found nothing but an old adhesion, which is quite consistent with perfect health and is very common. They examined her heart, and found it perfectly healthy; and so were the intestines. There was nothing, so far as they could form an opinion, to show that death had resulted from external injury or from internal causes. In opening the

1. Counsel appears to have paraphrased the inspector's words, making them polite. What Wiggins actually said, it seems, was: 'You're nicked for the Slough job. Get your skates on.'

body, one of the surgeons thought he could smell prussic acid, but the other could not discover anything of the kind. Either it did or it did not exist. But certainly, when they came to examine the stomach, they could discover no smell of prussic acid; but, inasmuch as it appeared to them clearly that the deceased had not died from either external injury or internal causes, they came to the conclusion that she had died by poison of some kind or other; and in order that the contents of the stomach should be known, they took them to a scientific chymist in London who submitted them to a chymical examination.

At the time, the surgeons conjectured that the woman had died through swallowing oxalic acid. Tests for that poison were applied, and none was discoverd. Tests were also applied for sulphuric acid, for opium, for various mineral poisons, and for prussic acid. Sulphate of copper and nitrate of siver were used. The surgeons satisfied themselves on that occasion that prussic acid had been the cause of death. They found prussic acid in the stomach, and it produced what is considered an infallible test of its presence, the 'Prussian blue'. Suffice it to say that, after the stomach had been submitted to the examination of Mr John Thomas Cooper, the chymist, they came to the conclusion that the deceased had died from the effects of prussic acid. At this time it was not known (and it is very important to bear this in mind) that Tawell had had any prussic acid at all. Subsequently, the remainder of the stomach was taken to Mr Cooper, who was now able to say, observing the contents of the two portions of the stomach, that in the stomach there were not fewer than 50 grains of prussic acid, according to the strength of the prussic acid of the *London Pharmacopoeia*. Of all poisons, this is the most volatile, being subject to evaporation most rapidly, and absorbed by the tissues after death. The quantity is equal to one grain of pure prussic acid, which is quite enough to cause death. This poison is so subtle and so energetic that a single drop of the pure acid placed upon the tip of a rod and put into the mouth of any small creature — a bird or a dog — would cause almost instant death. About two-thirds of a grain of pure prussic acid has been known to kill as many as seven adults one after the other. Now, this acid is not sold in its pure state. According to the *London Pharmacopoeia*, there are two grains of pure acid to every 98 grains of water. But a stronger preparation of it, called Scheele's prussic acid, is about two and a half times as strong as that of the *London Pharmacopoeia*.

Owing to the publicity which things of this kind naturally obtain, it was discovered that, on the Wednesday when the alleged murder was committed, Tawell had been to the shop of a chymist at 89 Bishopsgate Street and asked for two drachms of Scheele's prussic acid. He said he wanted it for an external injury. He brought a bottle with him with a glass stopper, but the shopman gave him another bottle, which was labelled for him, and he took it away with him on the day he left London. The cost of the acid was fourpence, and the shopman recorded the transaction in his book at the time. Tawell was again at the chymist's shop on the Thursday, the day after he slept at

Hughes lodging house in Scott's Yard, and he then said he had lost the bottle he had before, and obtained the bottle which he had originally brought and left there.

Those are the material facts with respect to the attempt on the life of the deceased. But there is other evidence, which induces the belief that that was not the first attempt which had been made by Tawell upon the life of the deceased.

Towards the end of September, or the beginning of October last, a person of the name of Charlotte Hoard, who is, I believe, in service with a family in the neighbourhood of Bath Place, was staying with Sarah Hart. It was late in the evening, about seven o'clock, that Tawell then visited the deceased. Mrs Hart, upon that occasion, was perfectly well, and Tawell requested Mrs Hoard to go to Botham's house, the Windmill, at Salt Hill, to purchase a bottle of porter. She did so; and took it home, and left it on the table. Not very long afterwards, Tawell went away. Mrs Hoard heard the front door of Mrs Hart's house shut as he went out. She then saw the deceased. Her cap was untied, and she looked dreadfully ill. She complained of being violently sick, of a severe pain in the head; and she retched and vomited very much. Upon the table 13 sovereigns were lying; and it is a circumstance which ought not to escape attention that she was too ill to see after that money. It was left loose on the table, she being so ill as to be compelled at once to go to bed. She was dreadfully sick in the night. She threw up above a hand-basin full, and was obliged to keep to her bed all day. She complained of great giddiness, and heat in the throat. She attributed these sensations, as did Mrs Hoard, to the porter. She recovered in the course of a short time, and was as well as usual.

Such, then, is the case against the prisoner. He has the right to have the benefit of any doubt — not of capricious doubt, but of any well-founded doubt — and the public have a right to expect, if there is no reasonable doubt, that they will be protected against crimes of this nature, so that they may sit down to their daily meals in peace and safety.

Unexceptionally, John Tawell had *stood* in the dock since the start of the trial; but as soon as Mr Serjeant Byles finished speaking, Mr Fitzroy Kelly, the leading one of Tawell's three counsel, requested that his client be allowed to sit. When the judge, Mr Baron Parke, asked, 'Prisoner, do you wish to sit down?', Tawell replied: 'Yes, I should be much obliged, as I have long had a varicose affection,' and so a chair was placed in the dock for him.

Tawell's reply was soon seen to be part of his defence: he had, so said Mr Kelly, frequently purchased prussic acid, in one form or another, as a treatment for varicose veins. Though Mr Kelly had no difficulty in revealing the inexpertness of the expert medical witnesses for the Crown, he was unable to persuade any of the half-dozen of them to concede that Sarah Hart's death might not have been caused by prussic acid. Therefore, making the best of a bad job, he hammered away at the fact that prussic acid was present in many things that laymen considered inoffensive. In apple-pips, for instance: the remains of masticated apple had been found in the deceased's stomach; also a partly emptied box of pippins in the house at Bath Place. If Sarah has eaten an excessive number of apples, cores and all, she might (said Mr Kelly) have died from apple-pip poisoning.[1] Or perhaps raisins in a cake were the culprits. Mr Kelly's assumptive efforts in that regard were curtailed by the evidence of Mrs Keziah Harding, a washerwoman neighbour of Sarah's. Mrs Harding was doubly destructive to the defence, for she recalled that Tawell had not only been at Bath Place on the day of Sarah's death, but also just two days previously, and went on to say: 'The last time before 30 December, I saw him there on Monday week, when Mrs Hart told me to go out at the back way when he came. I saw a cake in the cupboard. Part of it was eaten before the death of Mrs Hart. I don't know what became of the rest. I sold her the cake. We had it with others from Brentford. I had a bit of that cake. It was a very good cake. I did not suffer any inconvenience from it.' Fruiterers and bakers throughout the land must have taken especial interest in the reports of the proceedings at Aylesbury, dreading the while that Tawell would be acquitted, thus creating slumps in the sale of apples and raisined cakes.

Either Mr Kelly was psychologically unsuited to the task of defending a person on a capital charge or he had the knack of producing thespian tears as easily as if he were turning on a tap. He was moistest while addressing the jury on behalf of Tawell (who, as was so of all defendants, was not permitted to speak from the witness-box: a ban that was not lifted till 1898, with the passing of the Criminal Evidence Act). Indeed, 'tears stood in his eyes' and he 'appeared to be much affected' even before he started his speech by saying that he was 'under a pressure of responsibility that he was scarcely able to bear and that he hoped that the jury would pardon him if, feeling that deeply, he betrayed anything like a momentary weakness'. Mr Kelly chose to read out aloud from a letter that Tawell had received from his wife on the day of Sarah Hart's death. The letter is a fine example of evidence that can be viewed in two opposing ways: so far as Mr Kelly was concerned, 'no man could receive such a

1. Ever afterwards, Fitzroy Kelly was known as 'Apple-pip Kelly'. Within four months of the Tawell trial, he took office as Solicitor-General, and was then knighted; he became Attorney-General in 1858, and eight years later, when he was sixty-nine, he was raised to the bench as Lord Chief Baron of the Exchequer.

letter and do an act that would make his affectionate wife a widow and his children fatherless' — but others must have regarded the letter as a proof that Tawell had the motive of desperation for committing murder. Weeping effusively, Mr Kelly read as follows:

> My only loved one,
>
> My thoughts have been with thee throughout the day, and I can't but hope thou art feeling better than when thou left us. Do, my endeared one, endeavour to keep up thy spirits for my sake. We had no letters by the twopenny post. . . . Sarah Chase called to invite Eliza to dine with her off turkey. Some young men were to be present. She declined the invitation. . . . My poor mind rises and falls as I see how vicissitudes affect thee; and I find it hard work to attain to that wise resignation which becomes us under all the decrees of a wise Providence. I think I could bear up better if the whole burden was on me alone; but that is impossible. I do hope, my dear husband, you will bear up. The year has opened with a lovely day. I hope it is an omen of the future which awaits us. . . . Farewell. Under every circumstance thy beloved wife.

The trial lasted longer than was usual. The first day's proceedings went on till seven in the evening (at which time the judge was forced to adjourn, else participants wanting to return to London for the night would have missed the last train). Day Two began at 8 a.m. and, with a short break for lunch, continued till six, when the only certainly lengthy thing left to be done was the summing-up by the judge. One might have thought that Mr Baron Parke's comment, 'Well, the question now is, can we go any further tonight?', would have cued a unanimous chorus of Noes. However, the members of the jury, though their respective posteriors must have been agonized, said that they would rather sit on — the foreman adding the explanatory complaint that they had not been given beds the previous night. 'The learned Judge expressed his surprise at that, directed the attention of the Under-Sheriff to the subject,' and straightway exited, *en route* to his lodgings. Whether or not the members of the jury were given beds that night does not seem to have been reported. In any event, they were back in their box by 8 a.m. on Friday, shortly before Mr Baron Parke reappeared and, without preamble, began the summation. Unless they were more dog-eared than the reporters, they were not much assisted by the judge's early comments. According to the man from *The Times*,

> There seemed to have been something strangely wrong in the arrangements that had been made for preserving order and regularity

in the Court-house; for notwithstanding the clear and audible manner in which the learned Judge delivers himself, and although we were sitting immediately over the jury, to whom his voice was directed, we were unable to catch little more than the tenour of his address during the first 20 minutes of its duration, owing to the noise which was occasioned by the gradual admission of people from without into the body of the court (who evidently ought to have been admitted, if at all, before the Judge took his seat) — to the coming in and the going out of jurors to and from the side galleries, whose presence was required elsewhere — to the opening and shutting of doors, which called in very distinct, but very disagreeable, tones for the application of a little oil to their hinges — to the coughing of those who had colds, and the unavailing efforts of the crier to procure 'silence' by calling for it.

While the commotion continued, the reporter noted that Tawell

. . . looked more anxious than on the first day . . . and betrayed no little degree of uneasiness. . . . On two or three occasions the prisoner suddenly, and (as far as we could discern at a distance) with considerable irritability, touched the next person immediately before him on the shoulder, in order that an intimation might be made to his solicitor, Mr Bevan, who sat at the table, that he wished to communicate something to him, which he did apparently with great eagerness. . . . His hand trembled whenever he withdrew it from his face, where he held it during the greater part of the Judge's charge, with his forefinger extended on his cheek. Whether this was owing to increased anxiety as the moment that was to seal his fate drew nigh, or to the extreme coldness of the court, the windows of which were covered with a thick frost, we shall not pretend to know.

Mr Baron Parke may, about noon, have had still more to say; but then a sudden silence on his part allowed the foreman of the jury to ask, without being thought rude for interrupting, 'May we retire, my Lord?' — a question that received the perhaps automatic reply of 'Certainly'.

Officers were then sworn, in the customary form, to take charge of the jury, and they retired. During their absence the prisoner remained in the dock, and evinced, in spite of his endeavours to conceal his emotion, intense anxiety, his countenance frequently changing colour.

Present-day critics of what they perceive to be inefficient use of court-time will, even so, feel that there was an excess of such efficiency at the Aylesbury Spring Assizes of 1845:

While the jury of the Tawell trial were out of court, another jury was sworn, and a trial of three men for burglary had commenced and part of the evidence had been taken when, after the elapse of about half an hour, there was a call for silence, and great bustle in the court. The announcement was made by one of the ushers that the jury who had tried the prisoner Tawell had agreed upon their verdict. As the jury-box was occupied, accommodation was made for them in a space between the bar and the counsel's table. When they were so ranged as to be able to face the prisoner, who was placed in front of the dock, and now appeared as agitated as a person who had all along assumed a cool and confident air could consistently be expected to be under the circumstances,

The Clerk of the Indictments, after calling over the names of the jury, asked: 'Gentlemen, are you agreed?'

Foreman: We are.

Clerk: Do you find the prisoner guilty or not guilty?

Foreman (with significant emphasis and in a loud tone): GUILTY.

A cheer and clapping of hands from the spectators in the court immediately followed, the repetition of which was with difficulty stopped.

Clerk: Are you unanimous in your verdict, gentlemen? Is that the verdict of you all?

Foreman: It is.

The prisoner, who merely held down his head, and leaned his hands upon the bar, was then addressed by the Clerk thus:

Clerk: Prisoner, you have been indicted for the wilful murder of Sarah Hart, according to the law of your country, and you have been found guilty by the jury empanelled to try you. What have you now to say that the Court should not pass judgment upon you according to law?

The prisoner still held down his head and made no reply.

Proclamation was then made for silence, and the prisoner was called up for judgment. . . .

The prisoner remained almost unmoved while he listened to his sentence, and descended the trap-door, which leads by a staircase

The Court House, Aylesbury.

Tawell on trial.

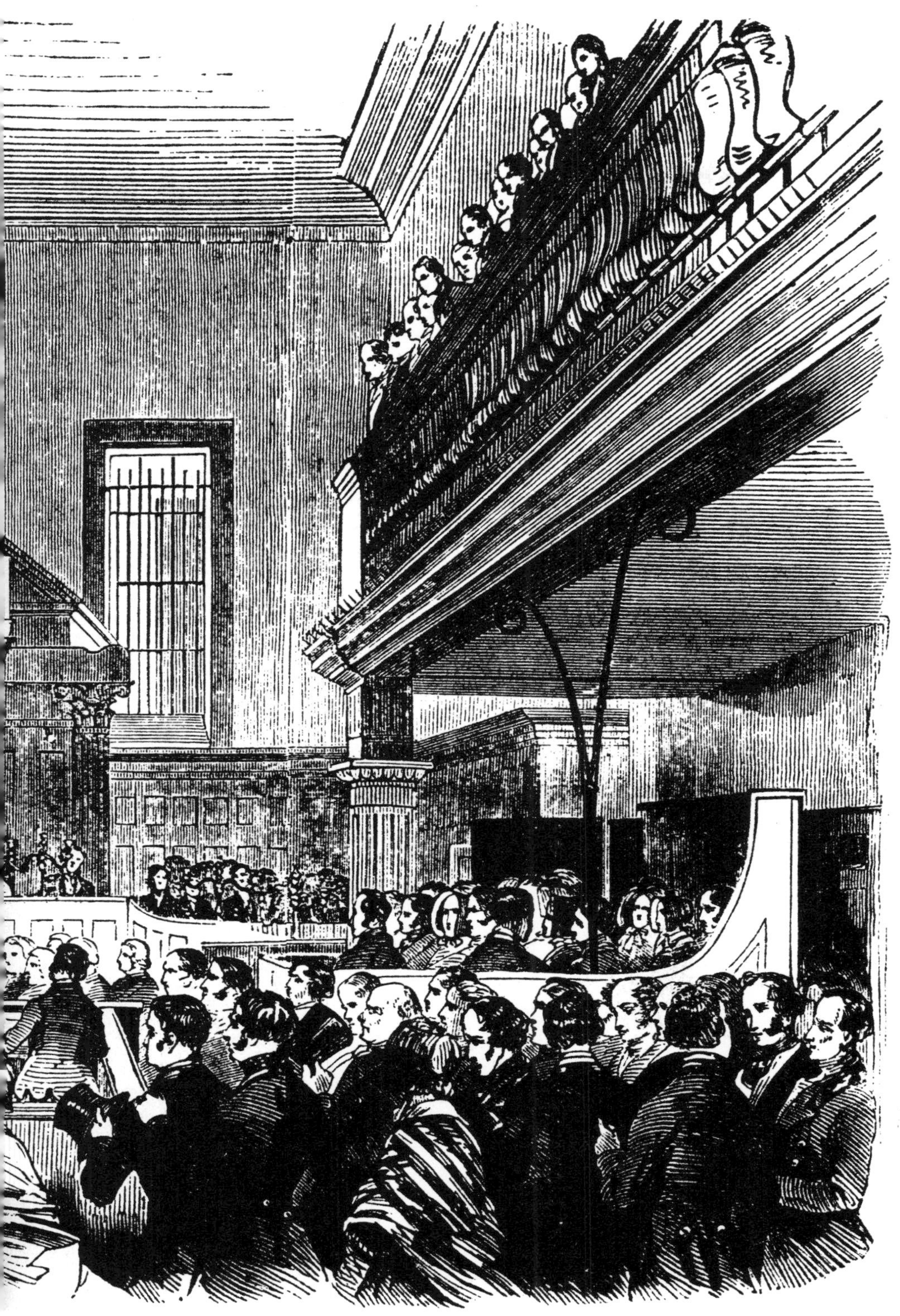

into the gaol, with no more trepidation than he had exhibited at the conclusion of the proceedings on the two previous days.

The verdict was regarded as a just one by the audience and the inhabitants of the town, and the visitors; with the exception of some three or four persons who had the bad taste to make bets, giving odds, that the prisoner would be acquitted.

When the prisoner had been removed to his cell, he gave utterance to lamentations in a low and hurried tone, walking up and down and exclaiming 'Oh dear! Oh dear!' repeatedly. When his dinner was brought, he refused it, saying he could not eat; but he subsequently partook of a beef-steak. He has been removed to the condemned cell, which had been prepared for his reception in anticipation of the verdict. But the prisoner evidently expected a very different one, for on Thursday evening, when it was supposed that the trial would have finished, a carriage was waiting to convey him home to Berkhampstead upon his acquittal. . . .

During his trial the prisoner maintained a bearing approaching almost to levity and impudence. The person who brought him his dinner from the White Hart Inn, next to the Court-house, he invited to come and see him after the trial, observing that he was offering no idle compliment, as he fully anticipated the pleasure of entertaining all his friends, and that he would cordially welcome him among the number.

Several gentlemen were permitted to stand in the dock, which was a capacious one, during the proceedings. On Thursday, during a momentary absence of the Judge, one of them, being near-sighted, raised his eyeglass to look at Tawell, who, when he observed it, immediately went up to the gentleman, and in a pert kind of tone asked, 'What does thee mean by looking at me more than at anybody else!' The gentleman was so taken by surprise at the question that he could make no reply except to stammer out, 'I beg your pardon; I did not wish to hurt your feelings.'

Another incident will also better convey an idea of the man's character than a laboured attempt at description. A prisoner who had been convicted and sentenced to 15 years' transportation came into a room where Tawell was, and while he was crying and groaning bitterly, Tawell began to comfort him by saying that he should not fret, that Sydney was a very nice place, and that in a short time he should get on very well and not be sorry for the change.

The children of Sarah Hart, of which the prisoner is the reputed father, were in the neighbourhood of the court throughout the trial, and would have been called had there been any doubt raised as to the identity of the prisoner. The elder one, a little boy, certainly bears a strong resemblance to him. Perkins, the officer, placed the watch the poor mother wore round the neck of that child this afternoon, and left the two children in care of their deeply afflicted grandmother.

It is stated, and no doubt correctly, that the prisoner's present wife wished to be accommodated with a seat in the court during the trial, but that her friends dissuaded her, and very properly, from availing herself of a favour which would have been granted, but which could only have augmented her sufferings.

On Thursday, while the court adjourned for a quarter of an hour, the prisoner wished to have a glass of brandy and water; the Governor would not accede to his request, but he was allowed a sandwich and a glass of wine, which he swallowed with avidity.

As soon as the result was known, the court was considerably thinned, as well as the town, in a very short time, although some interesting cases remained to be tried at these assizes.

A fortnight later, on Friday, 28 March, John Tawell was put to death. A different reporter for *The Times* was even more dissatisfied with the conduct of that event than the first one had been with the arrangements for the proceedings that had made it legal:

The place of execution was the iron balcony in front of the upper floor of the County Hall [in Aylesbury], before which is a large open space, gradually rising from the level of the building up to the market-house, which is about 300 yards distant from it, thus affording to the spectators all the advantages of an amphitheatre. But the crowd was by no means so great as was expected, there being not more than between 2000 and 3000 persons present. They were chiefly agricultural labourers and a few mechanics. Scarcely a respectably dressed person was mingled in the multitude, and there was so much space that at any time one could, without the slightest difficulty, have walked anywhere.

This may be accounted for by a very general belief that Tawell would not be executed, but that he would be reprieved, and ultimately have the extreme penalty of the law commuted. This opinion appears to have gained great ground, and was founded on a rumour, which I believe to be unfounded, that the prisoner, while in New South Wales under sentence of transportation, was very useful as a spy for the Home Government, and furnished information respecting the conduct not only of condemned but official persons in that colony.

I regret to say that amongst the persons assembled were several women and young children — the former, of course, of a questionable character, and making use of expressions which betrayed the loss of that tenderness of feeling which is one of the chief ornaments of the sex, and the latter so utterly insensible of the awful solemnity of the occasion as to engage in romps and gambols beneath the scaffold.

It may already be thought by readers of this account that, if such was the conduct of the spectators of this awful scene, surely the intended effect of capital punishment was in this instance to a great degree frustrated. Let them read on, and they will have still greater reasons to think so.

In the first place, eight o'clock is the usual hour for the execution of criminals at this place; but it wanted nearly 20 minutes of that hour when the miserable culprit was suddenly thrust out upon the scaffold by the hangman, and the turnkey who accompanied him, and so suddenly and quietly was this done that some minutes elapsed before the greater portion of the multitude was aware that the dreadful operation had commenced.

In the next place, or rather to take up the statement just made, there was nothing at all about the proceeding calculated to give it that effect which it ought to have. The wretched malefactor, on finding himself where he was, stared around with a sort of enquiring look of surprise, and immediately bent to his knees, clasping his hands together, as if desirous of uttering a prayer. Twice he did so, and in the meantime Calcraft, the executioner, drew the cap close over his face, and lower than it was before he unexpectedly made his appearance. It was then that he asked permission to pray, and immediately he knelt down, with his face away from the crowd, and seemed to pray most earnestly. In that posture he remained some minutes, and did not make any attempt to rise until the executioner took hold of his right arm and lifted him up.

Again, when so raised, his lips were seen to move as if ejaculating fervent cries for mercy, his face being uplifted towards the heavens; while, at the same time, the hangman adjusted a rope about the neck of the malefactor, and then deliberately threw the other end of the rope over the cross-beam, an operation that consumed some two or three minutes. The small figure of the criminal as he thus stood under the stalwart executioner produced a contrast, coupled with his meek attitude and air of utter submission, which awakened amongst the assembled multitude generally a feeling of pity and commiseration, and that feeling was greatly heightened by what followed.

Part of a broadsheet.

EXECUTION

OF JOHN TAWELL,

AND FULL CONFESSION, TO HIS WIFE, IN A LETTER

Of the Murder of Sarah Hart.

Aylesbury,
This morning, 8 o'clock.

At an early hour this morning, the sheriffs, with their usual attendants, arrived at the prison, and after partaking of some refreshment, proceeded to the condemned cell, where they found the reverend ordinary engaged in prayer with the wretched culprit.

After the usual formalities had been observed of demanding the delivery of the body of the prisoner into their custody, Tawell was conducted to the press-room, where his irons were struck off. The executioner, with his assistants, then commenced pinioning his arms, which operation they skilfully and quickly despatched. During these awful preparations he sighed deeply, but uttered not a word. At a quarter before 8, the arrangements having been ... the bell of the prison tolling, and the me- ... ned:—

sort of scream, and saw the prisoner coming out of Mrs. Hart's house. I said, I am afraid my neighbour is ill; but the prisoner, who appeared agitat... made no reply. When ... deceased

chemist, and was formerly lecturer on chemical jurisprudence. Mr. Champneys and two other gentlemen called ... and requested ...

ill, and vomitted about a hand-bason full. Deceased laid the blame on the stout.

The jury returned a verdict of ... and the ...

actions. After living 15 years in Sydney, he returned home, where he has been endeavouring to gain admittance as a member of the Society of Friends, to which body he belonged before his transportation, but they would not admit him. During his first wife's illness, the deceased nursed her, whence arose their illicit correspondence

COPY OF VERSES.

GOOD people all of each degree
Attend to what I shall unfold.
It is a dreadful tragedy
Will make your very blood run cold.
Your hearts alas with grief will bleed,
When you this cruel tale shall hear;
There's not been done so vile a deed
Since the days of Courvoisier.

John Tawell is my name 'tis true,
In wealth and splendour once I've dwelt,
A hypocrite I've always been,
Nor meek ey'd mercy never felt.
My first crime was Forgery,
A convict was to Sidney sent,
... ained oh! misery ...

When the fixing of the rope had been properly completed, which occupied but a few minutes, the executioner and the turnkey withdrew into the hall, and the bolts sustaining the platform on which the wretched man stood were instantly pulled back, and he fell; but the length of drop allowed him was so little that he struggled most violently. His whole frame was convulsed; he writhed horribly, and his limbs rose and fell again repeatedly, while he wrung his hands, his arms having been previously pinioned, and continued to wring his hands for several minutes, they being still clasped as though he had not left off praying. It was nearly ten minutes after the rope had been fixed before the contortions which indicated his extreme suffering ceased.

It is not intended to cast blame upon anyone connected with the dreadful fulfilment of this law; but the mechanical arrangements ought to have been so perfect as entirely to prevent the punishment being little more than act of torture to the malefactor, who was so short and small in person that he could scarcely have weighed more than seven or eight stone. He died 'hard' as the phrase is; and his light body dangled in the breeze, backwards and forwards, and round about, a most pitiable and melancholy spectacle.

There was nothing about the execution to give it the force of a warning example to the badly disposed. It took place before the accustomed and expected time; there were no official persons present on the scaffold, except the turnkey and the hangman; neither the sheriff, sub-sheriff, nor chaplain was visible; and below, in the space before the County Hall, there was not even a constable, policeman, or javelin-man. There was no air of authority about the proceedings; nor was there any public display of solemnity suited to it.

The consequence was that the subdued exclamation of the populace, uttered 'more in sorrow than in anger', was, 'Why, they turned him off like a dog!' A just observation; it was truly a hang-dog affair.

Not a hiss, not a groan, not a yell, not any expression of feeling against the unfortunate man, mute or audible, was perceptible amongst the whole multitude, many of whom left the spot immediately, and the rest within a few minutes after the body had been removed.

And the removal of the body was quite consistent with the rest of the revolting exhibition, for it was not cut down, but the turnkey held up the legs while the executioner untied the rope, which was certainly a new one, and probably considered worth saving for some purpose or other.[1]

Tawell wore the dress in which he was tried; at least it appeared

1. Publicly-used hangmen's ropes were often valuable perks for the hangmen who had used them. Though, in 1831, the executioner of John Holloway, the first Brighton 'trunk-murderer' (*see page 40*), was obliged to accept a mere half-crown from a gentleman of Lewes (the scene of the hanging) for the entire rope, only two years before, in Edinburgh, the executioner of William Burke (lately a colleague of William Hare) 'made a killing' from the sale of inch-long snippings of the hemp at half-a-crown apiece.

to be the same to me, but I saw him only from the public street, where all the reporters for the press, after having been rudely repulsed from the door of the prison, were compelled, contrary to all previous experience, to take up their position. And here comes out another strong feature in the most extraordinary conduct of the authorities, who seem to have been actuated by a sort of false respect for the man Tawell or his family. But, whatever their motive may have been, there can be not the slightest doubt that their behaviour neutralised to a great extent the design of public justice.

On my arrival in Aylesbury I heard with astonishment that no reporters would be admitted within the precincts of the gaol on the morning of the execution to witness the conduct of the culprit. As there were other representatives of the London morning newspapers in the town, I had a conference with them, the result of which was that we decided upon sending to the sub-sheriff, Mr Acton Tindall, nephew of the Lord Chief Justice of the Common Pleas — a gentleman who is able completely to appreciate the difficulties which reporters, even under ordinary circumstances, have to battle with — [an] application. . . .

To the letter were appended the signatures of the reporters for *The Times*, *Morning Post* and *Morning Herald* — to whose great surprise the messenger, who had been directed to wait for a reply, returned, saying that Mr Tindal, who is an attorney, and therefore a gentleman by act of Parliament, had sent word that he had no answer to give. A further deliberation took place, and it was believed by the applicants that Mr Tindal could never act so ungentlemanly a part, and that the messenger must have made a mistake. Another note was therefore sent to him, desiring information as to what was his real and correct answer. In the meantime a third person, not regularly connected with the metropolitan press, but who had been in the habit of sending London 'particulars' concerning Tawell since his conviction, waited upon Mr Tindal, and the result of his conference with that sub-official was that while the second note was on its way to him, he despatched an answer, though he had first refused one. . . .

In justice to Mr Tindal it must be stated that he sent a second note, saying that he did not answer the first letter immediately because he 'was just sitting down to dinner after a long day's business' when he received it. But there was no alteration of purpose whatever, and all remonstrances and entreaties were met with a stern denial. Mr Tindal shelters himself under a letter which he received from Mr Darrell, the High-Sheriff, directing that reporters should not be admitted. But Mr Darrell was in London, and ought to have been on the spot to act according to circumstances as they might arise. Mr Darrell at the same time in his letter gave permission to the governor of the gaol to 'exercise his discretion' as to what he would communicate to the reporters of the public press after the execution. Mr Tindal, however, seemed to think he had no discretion at all to exercise, and therefore he rigidly adhered to his 'instructions'. Now, both High and Sub-Sheriff ought to know and feel that such painful exhibitions are intended as public examples, and that any attempt to make the execution of a murderer a private affair is utterly repugnant to the spirit and object of the laws of these realms. Only let those gentlemen carry out their principle, and we may as well have criminals condemned to death strangled in their cells. . . .

It is a common saying that Aylesbury is a hundred years behind any other town in England; the conduct of the authorities upon this occasion goes far to confirm the truth of the observation. It is to be hoped that higher powers will see the necessity of interfering so far as to put an end in future to such silly arrangements which can have no other effect than nullifying the power and design of the law. A public execution is intended to strike awe into the minds of the community at large — it is a public example — it is paid for out of the public purse; and it is meant to be a public good.

All this is frustrated in the proportion that publicity is limited. Reporters do not covet the painful duty of witnessing the last moments of a murderer; but they are the representatives of the public, and it is through them that the great moral lesson which such awful scenes teach is conveyed to the world at large. And why was the absurd exclusion adopted in the present instance? The impression which gains ground is that it was to favour the culprit or his family: but, had he been a poor wretch, without a penny or a friend, no such regulation would have been made.

It will be said that the prisoner made a confession. Who knows that? I have not seen the written statement which, it is said, was presented by the culprit to the chaplain at five o'clock this morning, nor has any other reporter seen it. I made a formal and written application to the Rev. Mr Cox this morning for leave to take a copy of that document, if any such document exists, and the only answer I could obtain was a very brief one: 'I really cannot enter into it. I can say nothing about it — nothing at all.' The reason for this taciturnity on the part of the chaplain is said to be that Tawell requested him 'not to make it public in any way, but that he might disclose the purport of it'. There is a manifest inconsistency in this statement, and doubt is created by it which would never have arisen had reporters been allowed to be present, as on all similar occasions.

The 'purport' of the 'confession' I have only on hearsay authority: that is, from Mr Sheriff, the Governor of the gaol, who did not have it given to him by the executed man; but no doubt he is correct in his account of it. Mr Sheriff states that Tawell in that written statement, which belongs, properly speaking, to the public, and not to the chaplain, confesses that he did poison Sarah Hart by prussic acid, and also that he did on a previous occasion, in September last, attempt to poison her, not by prussic acid, but by a preparation of morphia. The motive, as has been all along supposed, he acknowledges to have been the concealment of his connexion with his devoted victim from his new wife and family, and not on account

THE MURDER AT SALT-HILL.—THE ELECTRO-MAGNETIC TELEGRAPH, AT SLOUGH.

An extraordinary instance of the working of the newly-applied power of electro-magnetism will be found in the details of the "Murder at Salt-Hill," in another portion of our journal. The eventful circumstance is of such interest as to induce us to submit to our readers a series of illustrations of the detailed means by which the intelligence of a suspected person being in a railway train, has been conveyed from Slough to the metropolis, after the train itself had started from the former place. The instrument of this important result is the Electro-Magnetic Telegraph on the Great Western Railway between Paddington and Slough, a distance of eighteen miles; by which any communication can be made from one point to the other in an almost inappreciably short space of time. To Professor Wheatstone and Mr. Cooke are we indebted for this valuable application of electro-magnetism;

THE GREAT WESTERN ELECTRIC TELEGRAPH.

they having made an entirely new arrangement of their telegraph, by it has been greatly simplified, and possesses considerable advantage o former one.

We have already adverted to the performances of this Telegraph, a engraved the exterior of the station at Slough, in which the appa

THE COILED MAGNETS.

worked. We shall now present to our readers the details of such ap before which, however, we shall relate from the evidence on the C Inquest at Salt Hill, the steps which led to the successful employmen novel means of communication.

The Rev. E. T. Champnes, vicar of Upton-cum-Chalvey, examined. ing of the suspicious death of the deceased, and that a person in the

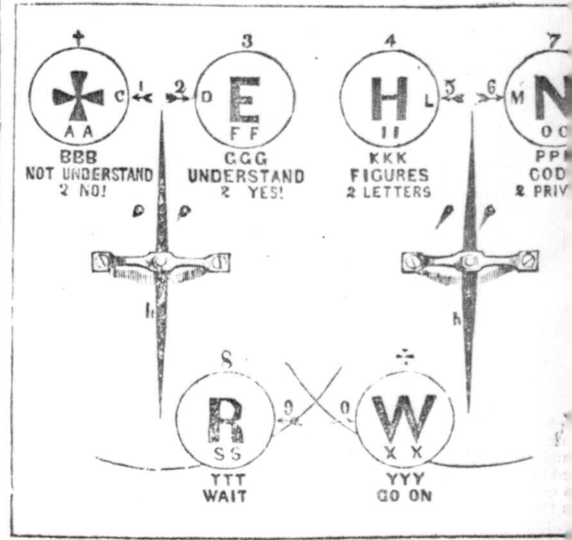

THE INDEX.

aker was the last man who had been seen to leave the house, I pro-
ed to the Slough station, thinking it likely he might proceed to town by
ailway. I saw him pass through the office, when I communicated my
icions to Mr. Howell, the superintendent at the station. He left fo
lon in a first-class carriage. Mr. Howell then sent off a full description
s person, by means of the electric telegraph, to cause him to be watched
e police upon his arrival at Paddington.

. Howell, of the Slough station, deposed as follows :—The prisoner left
wn last night by the 7. 42 train. I despatched orders by the telegraph
ve the prisoner watched on his arrival at Paddington. A few minutes
wards an answer was returned, stating that the suspected party had
ed, and that Sergeant Williams had left the terminus in the same omni-
or the City.

e words of the communication were precisely as follows :—

THE MESSAGE.

*murder has just been committed at Salt Hill, and the suspected murderer
een to take a first-class ticket for London by the train which left Slough
. 42m. p. m. He is in the garb of a Quaker, with a brown great coat on,
reaches nearly down to his feet; he is in the last compartment of the
d first-class carriage.*

THE REPLY.

*e up-train has arrived; and a person answering, in every respect, the
iption given by telegraph came out of the compartment mentioned. I
ed the man out to Sergeant Williams. The man got into a New-road
bus, and Sergeant Williams into the same.*

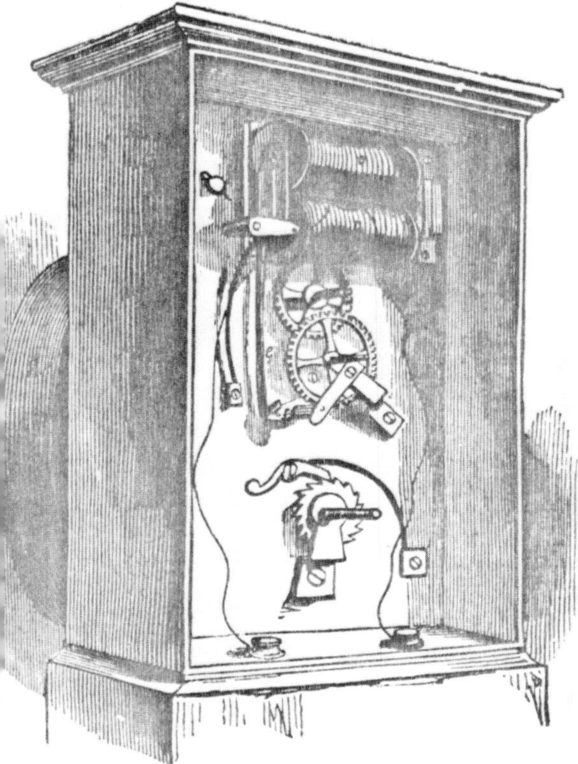

THE STRIKING APPARATUS.

telegraphic apparatus consists of two wires suspended the length of
ne, and attached at either end to the instrument, as seen in Fig. 1, and
ch wire from the instrument, attached to a large metallic surface, im-
d in the earth, for completing the electric circuit. The wire at Padding-
connected with the gas pipe, and that at Slough with the pump-engine.
the instrument is not in motion, the handles, *a a*, are down, as seen in
, and the pointers remain in their vertical position. The handles are
cted by an arrangement of pins and springs, with the battery and other

UNDER THE PATRONAGE

Of the NOBILITY.

INSTANTANEOUS COMMUNICATION,

Between PADDINGTON and SLOUGH, a distance of nearly Twenty Miles, by means of The

ELECTRIC TELEGRAPH

Which may be seen in operation Daily, from Nine in the Morning till Eight in the Evening, at The

GREAT WESTERN RAILWAY,

Paddington Station—and The

TELEGRAPH COTTAGE,

Close to the Slough Station.

Admission. — ONE SHILLING,

Children and Schools Half-Price.

Since this very interesting Exhibition has been opened to the Public, it has been honoured by the visits of His Royal Highness Prince Albert, the Emperor of Russia, the King, and Prince William of Prussia, the Duke de Montpensier, His Royal Highness the Duke of Cambridge, the Duke of Wellington, Sir Robert Peel, the Foreign Ambassadors, and most of the Nobility, &c.

In no way has the Science of Electricity been made so subservient to the uses of man, as in its application to the purposes of Telegraphic Communication, which is now brought to the height of perfection. The working of this beautiful Apparatus is not in the least degree affected by the weather, intelligence can be sent by night equally well as by day; distance is no object; by its extraordinary agency communications can be transmitted, to a distance of a Thousand Miles, in the same space of time, and with the same ease and unerring certainty, as a signal can be sent from London to Slough. According to the best authorities, the Electric Fluid travels at the rate of

280,000 Miles in a Second.

The Electric Telegraph has been adopted by Her Majesty's Government, and the Patentees have just completed a line of communication between London and Portsmouth, agreeably to directions received a short time ago, from

The Right Hon. the Lords of the Admiralty.

In the late trial of John Tawell, at Aylesbury, for the Murder at Salt Hill, near Slough, the Electric Telegraph is frequently mentioned in the evidence, and referred to by Mr. Baron Parke in his summing up. *The Times* Newspaper very justly observes, "That had it not been for the efficient aid of the Electric Telegraph, both at the Paddington and Slough Stations, the greatest difficulty, as well as delay, would have been occasioned in the apprehension of the prisoner." Although the train in which Tawell came to town was within a very short distance of the Paddington Station, before any intelligence was given at the Slough Telegraph Office, nevertheless before the train had actually arrived, not only had a full description of his person and dress been received, but the particular carriage and compartment in which he rode were accurately described, and an officer was in readiness to watch his movements. His subsequent apprehension is so well known, that any further reference to the subject is unnecessary.

The Telegraph Office, at Paddington Station, is at the End of the Up-Train Platform, where a variety of interesting apparatus may be seen in constant operation.

T. HOME, *Licensee.*

S. G. Fairbrother, Printer, 31, Bow Street, Covent Garden.

(Left)
From the Illustrated London News, *11 January 1845.*

(Above)
An advertising leaflet.

of any pecuniary considerations whatever. Singular as it may seem, the love of reputation led him into the commission of the most atrocious of crimes.

The following brief statement of the manner in which Tawell conducted himself yesternight was handed us by Mr Sheriff:

'John Tawell passed the whole night with almost unabated firmness, only giving way to a few tears and emotion occasionally. He listened with becoming attention to many portions of Scripture, and read many himself, joining with propriety in observations arising from them, and not only did he listen to and unite in the prayers which were offered for him, but he several times retired into his sleeping cell, and, falling on his knees, prayed out aloud and most fervently and penitently. His firmness never forsook him to the last.'

Mr Sheriff stated that the prisoner made a hearty meal last night with the chaplain. He took breakfast at three o'clock this morning; after which, he asked of Mr Sheriff if he might go to bed for a short time, desiring, if he fell asleep, not to be allowed to continue in that state after five o'clock. He fell into a profound sleep, which lasted about half an hour. He then awoke, and dressed himself. He desired Mr Sheriff to give a few shillings to some of the prisoners, and made a few trifling memorandums. . . .

The body of the criminal after having been removed from the balcony was immediately buried within the precincts of the gaol. So rapidly was the whole business performed that the wretched man was alive and in apparent health, dead, and buried, all within the space of an hour and a half.

An artist (Mr Ewing, of Nottingham) applied for leave to take a cast of his head, but was peremptorily refused.

Coincidentally, soon after John Tawell's body, still warm, was buried, Her Royal Highness the Grand Duchess Stephanie of Baden, with Her entourage — She and they chaperoned by the Duke of Hamilton — visited the electric-telegraph office at the Paddington terminus of the Great Western Railway, and remained there nearly an hour, during which time, no doubt, the Grand Duchess was given details of how the telegraph had been used towards the apprehension of a murderer. She 'expressed herself greatly pleased with the arrangements for the extraordinary apparatus'.

In his book *Stokers and Pokers* (London, 1849), Sir Francis Head, a former colonial governor, wrote of being in a full compartment of a train travelling from Paddington to Slough shortly after Tawell's execution. For nearly fifteen miles no one said a word; then a respectable-looking man in a corner seat indicated the 'apparently fleeting wires' of the electric telegraph, nodded sagely, and announced: 'Them's the cords that hung John Tawell.'

By Electric Telegraph.

TRIAL

And Sentence of Death

Passed this Day, May 28th, 1856 on

W. PALMER,

FOR THE

Wilful Murder

Of JOHN PARSONS COOK

At Rugeley, Staffordshire.

MONDAY.

The trial of William Palmer was resumed this morning at the Central Criminal Court. Intense interest was felt as to the result of the trial, it being known that Lord Campbell would sum up the evidence, and the probability of the jury returning their verdict almost immediately following its conclusion

Their lordships, Lord Chief Justice Campbell, Mr. Justice Creswell, and Mr Baron Alderson took their seats on the bench precisely at 10 o'clock, accompanied by the Recorder, Deputy-Recorder, and several of the Aldermen. The Earl of Derby and the Right Hon. W, E. Gladstone were also on the bench.

The crown was represented to-day by only Mr. James, Q.C., Mr. Bodkin, and Mr. Huddlestone ; but the four counsel for the prisoner were all present—viz., Mr. Sergeant Shee, Mr. Grove, Q.C., Mr. Kenealey, and Mr. Gray.

On their lordships taking their seats, the prisoner appeared in the dock, and walked to the bar dressed as on each former occasion, in black with black kid gloves Shortly after entering the dock the prisoner seemed to give himself up to inward thought. Suddenly, however, he awoke from this apparent reverie ; the Lord Chief Justice had begun his charge, and it was quite painful to watch the eagerness with which he prisoner devoured every word. He gazed with a fixed look at his lordship, and appeared nervously apprehensive of losing any portion of the address. In this way he eyed the judge with parted lips until his lordship began to read the evidence, and then he seemed to breath freely again and to look on with comparatively calm indifference.

Before Lord Campbell commenced the summing up Mr Serjeant Shee applied to be allowed to put in an acceptance for £500, drawn by Palmer and accepted by Cook, dated Sept. 1855, which was granted.

TUESDAY,

This morning the summing up of the Learned Judge, was again resumed His lordship went carefully through the evidence for the defence commenting on each point that seemed material for or against the prisoner, who maintained the same firmness and composure that he exhibited on the Learned Judge commencing his address : his lordship after carefully revising every particle of the testimony that was urged in favour of the prisoner, concluded by telling the Jury that the case was now in their hands, that they would do their duty without fear or favour and return such a verdict as would satisfy their conscience, their God, and their Country.

The Lord Chief Justice having concluded his summing up, the jury retired to consider their verdict, and after an absence of some time returned with a verdict of **GUILTY.** The colour forsook the countenance of Palmer for an instant, but he did not appear to lose his self-possession ; and during the delivery of the sentence, when there was scarcely a dry eye in the court, and the utterance of the Lord Chief Justice was at times stifled with emotion, the prisoner stood firm and upright in the dock

The execution of the Prisoner is take place in front of Stafford County Gaol.

R. Astill, Printer, Coventry

As this broadsheet shows, in 1856, eleven years after the Tawell case, the electric telegraph was not only a means of transmitting news over long distances (London-Coventry: eighty-odd miles), but was itself still considered sufficiently startling to warrant top billing in big bold print.

Though Dr William Palmer of Rugeley, Staffordshire, had been accused only of the murder by strychnine poisoning of John Parsons Cook, owner of a mare called Polestar that had won a race at Shrewsbury on 13 November 1855, providing him with funds that were desperately needed by Palmer, the latter was (and, despite the literary efforts of Robert Graves, is) thought to have killed at least thirteen others, including an uncle who expired after a 'brandy-drinking match', sundry creditors, and several of his offspring, some of whom were legitimate. The strength of public feeling against him in Staffordshire was so strong that an Act was passed (19 Vict., cap 16, still known as 'Palmer's Act'), allowing trials to be transferred to distant venues.

As soon as he was pronounced guilty by a jury of Londoners, he was returned to Staffordshire for his hanging, which was done in front of the county gaol, before an audience of more than 20,000, on the morning of Saturday, 14 June. Sir Henry Hawkins (known, without reference to Palmer, as 'The Hanging Judge') subsequently heard from Major Talford, the governor of the gaol, 'that Palmer talked freely about his case while awaiting execution; that he said all through the trial he expected an acquittal, and even after the judge's terrible summing up hope did not desert him. "But," he added, "when the jury returned into Court, and I saw the cocked-up nose of the perky little foreman, I knew it was a gooser with me." On the morning of the execution the path from the condemned cell to the gallows was wet and muddy, it having rained during the night, and Palmer minced along like a delicate schoolgirl, picking his way and avoiding the puddles. He was particularly anxious not to get his feet wet.'

Some pillars of Rugeley society, embarrassed by the notoriety that Palmer had brought upon the town, pleaded with the Prime Minister for leave to change its name. 'Certainly,' Palmerston replied, 'why not name it after me?' The idea was dropped.

The murder of Thomas Briggs, which itself was innovative, being the first British railway murder, caused a stir that provoked two other railway innovations: communication cords were eventually fitted in all trains, and for a time, in some carriages without corridors, there were spy-holes in the walls separating compartments from adjoining ones. The latter devices — known, for a reason that will appear, as 'Müller holes' — proved so popular among peeping Toms that communication cords were pulled most often in complaint about their voyeuristic use, and so it was not long before they were plugged up.

It seems surprising that thirty-nine years elapsed between the day in 1825 when a locomotive first plied publicly, from Stockton to Darlington, and the night when murder was first committed on a train running on British rails. Even then, the culprit was not of British nationality. And, as Richard D. Altick has pointed out,[1] there were Continental precedents, one of which had been noted prophesyingly by William Makepeace Thackeray in a 'Roundabout Paper' that appeared in the November 1862 issue of the *Cornhill Magazine*: 'Have you ever entered a first-class railway carriage, where an old gentleman sat alone in a sweet sleep, daintily murdered him, taken his pocket-book, and got out at the next station? You know that this circumstance occurred in France a few months since.' Altick comments:

> Thackeray probably was referring to the second of two such murders which had been committed within a few months of each other in 1860. At 5 a.m. on December 5, a blood-splashed compartment on the train arriving in Paris from Troyes was found to contain the body of M. Poinsot, the presiding judge of the Imperial Court; he had been shot twice and brained, and his watch and chain, wallet, travelling rug, and valise were missing. It was thought that the assailant had escaped when the train slowed at Noisy-le-Sec, just outside the city, to pick up mail bags. The *Sûreté* confidently identified him as a notorious adventurer, army deserter, and suspected Prussian spy named Judd, who a few months earlier had been arrested for a similar exploit, the murder and robbery of a Russian army doctor on a train passing through Alsace. Judd had slipped out of custody soon after his arrest and thus had been free to strike again on the Troyes–Paris run. There was some talk at the time that both homicides, though accompanied by robbery from the person, in reality were somehow connected with espionage. Judd was never re-captured.

In alluding to this French crime in a novel locale, Thackeray seems to be suggesting that, though Britain had so far been free of railway

1. See Bibliography.

carriage murders, there was no reason why she should be permanently immune . . . The isolation of the compartment seemed an open invitation to murder. And so it proved, less than two years after Thackeray's mention of it.

Saturday, 9 July 1864, was a full working day for 69-year-old Thomas Briggs, a widower, who was the chief clerk in the bank of Messrs Robarts & Co. of Lombard Street, in the City of London. He dined with relatives at Peckham, south of the Thames, and, leaving their house at half-past eight, walked to the Old Kent Road, where he boarded a City-bound bus; alighting from it in King William Street, close to his place of employment, he walked a few blocks east and entered the Fenchurch Street Station of the North London Railway in good time to catch the 9.50 all-stops train to Chalk Farm. At the barrier the ticket-collector, who knew Mr Briggs by sight, 'nipped' the return-half of the ticket he had bought that morning at Hackney Wick Station — which was two stops north, a stroll from his house in Clapton Square. Mr Briggs entered one of the first-class compartments that his ticket entitled him to travel in.

The train, which departed near enough on time, reached the next station, Bow, about ten; left Hackney Wick at 10.5; reached Hackney six minutes later. By the sort of coincidence that no self-respecting writer of fiction would let pass, two young men who entered a first-class compartment of the train at Hackney were employed by Messrs Robarts & Co. One of them, Sydney Jones, subsequently recalled: 'On entering, I saw a black bag on the left-hand side, on the seat nearest the door. I put it on the opposite side.' Unless he said more than he was reported as saying, it was as well that his friend and colleague, Henry Vernez, had more to say, which included the following:

> I opened the door of the carriage, which was empty. I and Mr Jones got into it. I sat on the right-hand side going in, and about the centre of the carriage; that is, with my face to the engine. Before the train started, Mr Jones called my attention to something — to some blood on his hand. I immediately called the guard, and the guard got a light. Then we got out. Two other persons besides us, who had got into the carriage, also got out. I saw a stick, hat, and a black bag in the carriage when the guard brought a light. The guard then locked up the carriage, leaving the articles in it. I got into another carriage.

The guard, Benjamin Ames, both amplified and extended the account:

> My attention was called by Mr Vernez to No. 69, first-class, carriage. I noticed something was the matter. . . . On the near-side

> cushion there were marks of blood — that is, the cushion nearest the engine — and on the quarter-lights on the near-side there were marks of blood. The quarter-light is a square of glass that shows light into the carriage. . . . There was a good deal of blood, as there were a great many spots on the cushions. I did not notice any blood on the floor. On the opposite cushion there was a finger mark, as though a person's hand had been wiped there. The blood was in a liquid state when I saw it. There was blood on the glass of the window — blood about the size of a crown piece, and it was trickling down the glass. . . . There were marks of blood upon the hat, which was crumpled up, and also on the stick and the bag. . . . I telegraphed on to Chalk Farm. Mr Greenwood is station-master there. When we arrived at Chalk Farm . . . Mr Greenwood took charge of the hat, stick and bag as lost property.

Meanwhile, back along the line, between the stations of Hackney Wick and Bow, Alfred Ekin, the driver of a south-bound train of empty carriages, noticed 'a black object lying on the six-foot way. . . . We were just entering on the canal bridge when I saw it. I called the attention of the guard to what I saw.' And the guard, William Timms, 'put on the brake and stopped the train as soon as possible. Upon examination, we found the body of a man. He was lying on his back, with his head towards Hackney. He was lying straight, about midway on the six-foot way between the up and down lines.' Timms ran to the edge of the embankment and shouted for help. 'It took four or five of us to carry the man. Several other persons came. I should think there might have been a dozen altogether.' One of the dozen was a beat-policeman, Constable K71 Edward Dougan. He directed the bearing party to follow him to the Milford Castle public house. A doctor who was summoned there found that the man was alive, but unconscious, and that his skull had been fractured by one or more of several wounds to his head, some of which appeared to have been inflicted with a blunt instrument, while others may have resulted from a heavy fall. Either before the doctor's examination or directly afterwards, Constable Dougan searched the man's clothes:

> I found four sovereigns and some keys in the left-hand-side trousers-pocket, and in the vest-pocket a florin and a half of a first-class ticket of the North London Railway. In the right-hand-side trousers-pocket there were ten shillings and sixpence in silver and copper, some more keys, a silver snuff box, and a number of letters and papers, and a silk handkerchief, and a diamond ring on the little finger, which I took away. There was a gold fastening attached to the waistcoat, but I could not undo it. I observed his dress, saw that his shirt was rumpled, and that there was one black stud in the front, which I took away — only one.

It seems probable that the constable exaggerated the contents of the right-hand trousers-pocket; but whether the letters and papers were there or in some other pocket, they provided the man's name and address: *Mr Thomas Briggs, 18 Clapton Square, Hackney, London, E.*

Round midnight, Mr Briggs was carried from the Milford Castle and stretched out in a Black Maria that had been driven from Bow Police Station. Strangely, he was taken, not to a hospital, but to his home. His own doctor was sent for, and concluded that 'it was a hopeless case'. Mr Briggs died the following night, never having regained consciousness.

Long before then, the police had associated his presence between the railway lines with the discoveries in the train compartment, and were treating the case as one of murder. Ostensibly, a police superintendent of the surrounding K Division was in charge of the investigation; in fact it was directed by a Scotland Yard officer named Dick Tanner — at thirty-four, the youngest inspector in the sixteen-strong Detective Department — who had been ordered by Sir Richard Mayne, the Commissioner of the Metropolitan Police, to 'assist Supt. Howie' — and to keep him, Sir Richard, fully informed 'of all actions taken and results of same'. (It seems that the latter instruction, then particular to the Briggs case, was prompted by recent press and partliamentary criticisms of *all* detectives because of blunders by one or two of them, and was the forerunner of a general rule — which still applies — that required detectives dealing with serious crimes to present frequent written reports to their superior officers.)

By Sunday evening the investigators were in possession of a number of facts; they had drawn conclusions from some of those facts, but were puzzled by others. The walking-stick, one of the three articles found in the compartment, was heavily bloodstained at the handle, showing that it had been used as a weapon. Both the stick and the black bag were Mr Briggs's — but the hat, which was low-crowned, of black beaver-skin, was not. The assailant — by mistake, surely — had exchanged his own hat for Mr Briggs's superior one, which was 'a black topper . . . Paris nap of the best quality, with a white silk lining'. The only other possessions of Mr Briggs that appeared to be missing were his gold watch and chain (which must have been jerked from the patent fastener on his waistcoat) and his gold-rimmed spectacles. The likelihood that Mr Briggs, barely conscious, had sought escape from his attacker by jumping from the train, rather than that he had been pushed from it, seemed strengthened by the fact that neither the considerable amount of cash nor his silver snuffbox had been taken from his pockets;

on the other hand, the black bag — in itself attractive plunder, never mind what it might have contained (the contents do not seem to have been mentioned in any reports) — had not been stolen. It is hard to accept the investigators' assumption, based on the walking-stick weapon, that the crime was unpremeditated: if the attacker, underestimating Mr Briggs's power of resistance, had set upon him with his bare hands, Mr Briggs may have retaliated with his stick — only to have it wrested from his grasp and turned against himself with deadly effect.

Mr Briggs was not long dead when the Government and Messrs Robarts each offered a reward of £100 for the discovery of his murderer, and soon afterwards the directors of the North London Railway increased the combined reward to £300 (a sum that would have present-day purchasing power of well over £15,000).

During the next few days, out of a host of applicants there was only one, a jeweller by trade, who was more helpful than hopeful. His name, which was Death, eventually turned out to be as valuable to the investigation as was the information he gave. However, prior to his second, fortuitous contribution, the location of his shop — in Cheapside, a stone's throw from Lombard Street — gave rise to a suspicion, which required a great deal of investigative effort to disprove, that Mr Briggs had been killed by a person presently or till recently a member of his firm. The suspicion must have depended upon a guess that the criminal was a confident actor, for although Messrs Robarts employed no one who was noticably foreign, and never had done, the young man who had visited Mr Death's shop on the morning of Monday, 11 July, had spoken with a strong German accent. He was, Mr Death recalled, 'of sallow complexion and thin in feature'. Unaccountably, there is no sign, either in Mr Death's written statement or in reports of his subsequent spoken testimony, that he was ever asked whether his visitor wore a hat — and, if so, what sort it was. The young man had offered Mr Death a gold albert chain, marred at one end, saying that he wished to exchange it for another, and after some haggling had accepted a chain priced at sixty-five shillings and, making up the difference between that price and Mr Death's valuation of the gold chain, a ring with a white cornelian stone that was priced at five shillings. The young man had seemed in no hurry to complete the transaction; he had waited patiently while Mr Death placed the chain and the ring in green cardboard boxes and wrapped those boxes in brown paper. In the afternoon, Mr Death read his copy of a police notice in regard to the Briggs case that was delivered to all jewellers and pawnbrokers in London, and straightway went to the Wood

Street station of the City Police, taking with him the chain that he had so recently acquired. Within a short while, relatives of Thomas Briggs identified the chain as his.

All at once Mr Death was a celebrity. His name enlivened innumerable headlines, was daubed enticingly on news-vendors' placards, was rhymed with 'traveller's dying *breath*' in broadsheet verses that soon became bar-room songs and children's skipping chants. And yet not until Friday, the fourth day of its renown, did it, let alone any associated hullaballoo, catch the attention of Jonathan Matthews. Or so he said when, late on the following Monday, having done a full stint of cab-driving, he shyly spoke to the police — and when, months afterwards, in the witness-box at the Old Bailey, he was cross-examined as to that assertion, among several others that were almost or quite as hard to credit:

> When did you first hear of the murder? — . . . On the Friday night after Saturday the 9th.
> Do you mean to say that you had not heard of it before? — No, sir.
> Had you been out with your cab? — Yes.
> And did you not hear of the murder? — No.
> Did you go to the cab-stand amongst your fellow cabmen? — Yes, occasionally, when I wanted something to eat.
> And you never heard of it? — No.
> Did you go into a public-house? — I am not a public-house visitor. Perhaps I may go there sometimes.
> There is no harm in going into a public-house to have a glass of ale. Did you go into a public-house for refreshment? — Yes.
> Every day? — Yes, sir. . . .
> Do you buy a daily paper? — Sometimes.
> Did you not see a paper from the 9th until the 14th of July? — Not to bring the murder to my mind.
> Did you not see it in large, conspicuous letters on the newspaper placards . . . ? — No.
> Where do you live? — 68 Earl Street, East Paddington.
> Do you attend the [railway] station? — Yes.
> Do you pass the police station every day . . . ? — I cannot answer.
> And you never saw a placard or a notice in any way? — No; I saw placards, but did not read them.

Having been slow in coming forward, Matthews spun out his statement-making from late on Monday, 18 July, till the following breakfast-time — giving information in dribs and drabs, sometimes contradicting himself, and often professing uncertainty about things that the interviewing policemen, tetchy towards the end, believed he was quite sure about. It may not have been his intention to cause further delay, but that was the effect. The salient details of his statement were as follows:

On Thursday morning (when Mr Death first hit the headlines), Matthews had seen in his house a green cardboard box bearing the gilt-lettered name of Death. (Feeling obliged to explain how it was that he, a paragon of incuriosity, had come to observe that article, he said, 'I noticed it because I put my foot on it.') His wife Eliza had told him that the box had been given to their little girl as a plaything by an acquaintance of theirs, Franz Müller, who had turned up unexpectedly on the Monday afternoon and stayed for three or four hours — during which time he had shown Eliza a chain and a ring with a white cornelian stone, saying that he had received the ring as a present, and had spoken of his intention to seek his fortune in North America; before leaving the house, he had said that he would call again, on Tuesday or Wednesday, for a farewell chat with Jonathan Matthews. He had not kept his promise. (He would have been limited to a comparatively few hours, most of them ungodly, for a return-visit when Matthews was at home — for Matthews, so he stated, plied for hire between nine in the morning and round about midnight.)

Though Matthews was unsure of his own age ('I am thirty-seven or thirty-eight'), he was confident that Franz Müller was twenty-five. Müller, he said, had emigrated to England from Germany soon after completing an apprenticeship to a gunsmith, and, failing to find a job in that trade, had worked menially for tailors — including, latterly, a brother of Eliza Matthews. That was how he had become acquainted with the Matthews family — and indeed had come close to being related to them, for he had courted the eldest Matthews daughter till she, irked by his excessive jealousy, had called the whole thing off.

Jonathan Matthews mentioned that the waistcoat he was wearing had been made for him by Müller, and added, his tone now aggrieved, that the slight garment was Müller's idea of settlement of a debt of ten shillings and sixpence. For once continuing without having been prompted, Matthews recalled that, shortly before Christmas, 'I had a new hat, and Müller came to dine with me on the Sunday after I bought it. He said he would like to have one like it. He asked me what I gave for it, and I said ten and six. I said I would get him one if he wished it. I put the hat on his head and said, "What is too easy for me will suit you".' A week later Matthews handed Müller a hat, virtually a twin of his own, and some weeks later received from him, not cash, but a waistcoat that he didn't really need. He described the hat — or rather, hats. Subsequently he was shown the hat found in the train-compartment, and said that 'it corresponded exactly'.

Some time before Matthews completed his statement, the police interviewed his wife — who, as well as confirming his hearsay-from-her account of Müller's visit on Monday, 11 July, added two important details: one, that as Müller was leaving, she had remarked that his hat had worn well, and he had said, 'It is a different hat' (supposing that the different hat was Mr Briggs's, Eliza's inability to tell a topper from a low-brimmed hat would eventually be explained); two, that he had a slight limp — which he had told Eliza was the result of 'a letter-cart running over his foot on London Bridge', but which the police suspected was a sign that he had injured himself in jumping from a moving train. Having rummaged at the interviewers' request, Eliza produced a photograph of Müller; later in the day it was shown to Mr Death, and he at once recognized Müller as the man who had come to his shop. Also, Eliza told the police that Müller lodged with George Blyth, a messenger, and his wife Ellen at 16 Park Terrace, Old Ford Road — a significant address, for it was roughly halfway between the stations of Bow and Hackney on the North London Railway.

FRANZ MÜLLER, Charged with the Murder of Mr THOMAS BRIGGS, on the 9th July, 1864.

A posse, collectively diffident in view of a concern that Müller might have kept souvenirs of the trade he had been apprenticed to, quickly overcrowded the cottage in Park Terrace. But only the Blyths were there to be surprised. Once most of the posse, disappointed and yet relieved, had departed, some of the remaining officers searched the upstairs back room that Mülller had occupied for seven weeks, while others — Dick Tanner pre-eminent — first of all soothed the Blyths and then coaxed information from them, as follows though not in this order:

Müller, an untroublesome lodger, had endeared himself to the Blyths by his 'kind and humane disposition'. Ellen Blyth's recollections of Saturday, 9 July, and the few days following were partly affirmed and in no way contradicted by her husband:

When Mr Müller went out on the Saturday morning, I did not expect him home at any particular time at night. He had a latch-key. My husband and myself went to bed at eleven o'clock [and] he had not then come home. Next morning, he breakfasted with us, and stopped at home all day. There was nothing different in his manner. In the evening we — my husband, myself and Mr Müller — went out together. On Monday morning he breakfasted with us, and left the house about eight o'clock. He was confidential with us, but I don't know where he was going on the Monday. I saw him next between eight and nine on the same evening [an hour or so after his visit to the Matthews' house in West London]. He spent some time with us, and showed us a gold albert chain. He said nothing about the chain [which he had got from Mr Death that morning]. He remained Tuesday and Wednesday, and left early on the Thursday. I knew of his intention to go to America a fortnight previous to that day. He told us when he left the name of the ship he was going to New York in — the *Victoria.*

Three days later, the Blyths had paid postage-due on an unstamped letter, written by Müller in pencil, that had been posted in the Sussex coastal town of Worthing:

> On the sea, July 16th, in the morning.
>
> Dear friends, I am glad to confess that I cannot have a better time as I have, for the sun shines nice and the wind blows fair as it is at present moment, everything will go well. I cannot write any more only I have no postage, you will be so kind to take that letter in.

The *Victoria*, the police soon learned, had left the London docks on the Thursday, and, having sailed south in the English Channel and then west along the south coast, stopping at several ports to pick up additional passengers, was now well out into the Atlantic, bound for New York. There was no way of knowing how far the winds had taken her; no way of establishing contact. It is reasonable to guess that Dick Tanner, already irritated by Jonathan Matthews, felt like doing him bodily harm for having delayed making his statement for three days — precious ones, it now appeared — from the Friday when he had first heard of Mr Death. If Matthews protested when told that *he* was to make ready for a long sea voyage, Tanner abruptly shut him up. As for Mr Death — when he was invited, not ordered, to take an expenses-paid trip to the New World, he accepted delightedly, after arranging for his brother to mind the shop.

On Wednesday, 20 July, the two witnesses, together with Tanner (bearing a warrant for Müller's arrest, granted by the chief magistrate at Bow Street) and another Yard officer, Detective Sergeant George Clarke, left Liverpool on board the New York & Philadelphia Company's steamship *The City of Manchester*, which was scheduled to arrive at New York a fortnight or so ahead of the *Victoria*. Probably more than any previous publicized event, the 'Müller pursuit' was a godsend to all steamship lines as a generator of advertising, mostly free, of the fact that the mode of propulsion of their vessels beat old-fashioned sails hands-down: an historian of advertising who looked at the newpapers of the summer of 1864 might conclude that they contain the pioneer efforts at what is now termed 'knocking copy'.

The City of Manchester berthed at Manhattan on 5 August. And the American press at once accorded celebrity status to Tanner, Matthews and, especially, Mr Death — not to Sergeant Clarke, who refused even to acknowledge the clamouring reporters, let alone give interviews, as his flattered companions did. While Tanner revelled in being the toast of the town, Clarke did both their jobs: liaising with the British consul and the local police, travelling to New Jersey and there offering a small reward to whoever it was — whether a ship's pilot, a fisherman, a lighthouse-keeper — who made the first sighting of the *Victoria*, and arranging for news of that sighting to be transmitted to police headquarters in Manhattan by the Sandy Hook Telegraph Company. Clarke, like all good detectives, was a firm believer in the proverb that there's many a slip 'twixt the cup and the lip. His main worry was that Müller, somehow apprehending the trap into which he was sailing, would throw himself overboard, either as an act of suicide or with the intention of swimming ashore — an intention which, if fulfilled, might well result in his complete escape, perhaps with the aid of one of the many recruiters to the armies fighting the Civil War, some of whom were criminals themselves, and none of whom was so unbusinesslike as to ask awkward questions of volunteers.

On the morning of 23 August, the Sandy Hook Telegraph Company transmitted the news that the *Victoria* was off the coast of New Jersey. Though the manager of the company had promised Clarke that the message would be sent only to the police headquarters, he had carefully avoided saying that he would not send another message, differently worded but making the same sense, to the newspapers — and so, next morning, when the *Victoria* veered to starboard and sailed into Manhattan's Lower Bay, the shores were crowded with the curious. Fortunately, the wind was in such a direction that the hoots and cheers of those not merely agog did not carry to the vessel. And, though Müller was on deck, he did not make out the meaning of shouts from closer by. To quote George A. Birmingham:[1]

While the *Victoria* was waiting for the pilot to take her into the harbour, a party of excursionists came out and hailed the ship with shouts of 'How are you, Müller the murderer?' It was an American party, but English excursionists would have behaved in exactly the same way. If the mentality of murderers is difficult to understand, that of the crowd, the respectable, middle-class, excursionist crowd, is more puzzling still. Müller did, at all events, get a watch and chain for

1. See Bibliography. 'George A. Birmingham' was the pen-name of the Rev. James Owen Hannay, sometime Chaplain to the Lord Lieutenant of Ireland.

killing Mr Briggs. What gain or pleasure came to the excursionists who hired a steamer and went out to the *Victoria* for the sole purpose of shouting 'Müller the murderer!'?

It may be that weakness from lack of nutrition made Müller oblivious to the shouting of his name. He had not exaggerated his poverty in the unstamped letter he had sent to the Blyths. Having parted with four pounds for the fare, he had been left with just a few pennies to buy food extra to the slight amounts doled out to steerage passengers crammed below the water-line in the *Victoria*. According to H. B. Irving,[1] at least once during the voyage Müller had exhibited his trait of acting without having considered all possible outcomes of the act — in that instance by being quite carried away by the notion that he could fill his belly with free food and be paid for doing so:

> He had no money with him, but tried to raise some by offering to eat 5 lbs of German sausage. He failed in this laudable endeavour, and was compelled to stand porter all round, a penalty he could only fulfil by parting with two of his shirts. . . .
>
> He had behaved fairly well on the voyage out, but had got into trouble once or twice on account of his overbearing manner. On one occasion he received a black eye for calling a fellow-passenger a liar and a robber.

That Dick Tanner's sense of priorities had gone askew is indicated by the fact that, rather than taking part in the event that was the main reason for his being in America — and which he should have spent some of the previous nineteen days making preparation for and looking forward to — he preferred to attend a social event, leaving George Clarke to represent England in the otherwise wholly American arresting-party that boarded the *Victoria* from a pilot boat. Clarke subsequently testified:

> Müller was called to the after part of the ship by the captain. I then seized him by the arm. He said, 'What is the matter?' John Tiernan, an officer of the New York police, replied, 'You are charged with the

1. See Bibliography. H. B. Irving, the elder son of Henry, the first actor-knight, and himself a fine actor, derived enjoyment from studying, writing about and discussing crimes — French ones being his favourites. By hosting a dinner party, attended by other connoisseurs, at his London home in 1903, he unwittingly founded Our Society, sometimes referred to as the 'Crimes Club', the numerically restricted and entirely male membership of which includes lawyers, forensic scientists, crime historians, and actors; the Duke of Edinburgh is patron. At the meetings, which are held two or three times a year, presently at the Imperial Hotel, close to where Irving lived, once dinner is over but not until the waiters have withdrawn, a speaker presents a paper on a particular case or aspect of crime, which is then discussed. There is a New York equivalent, less thriving, of Our Society, called The Society of Connoisseurs in Murder.

murder of Mr Briggs.' I, finding that Tiernan did not recollect the particulars, followed up with 'Yes, on the London railway, between Hackney Wick and Bow, on 9 July.' Müller said, 'I never was on that line.' I do not know whether he said 'that night' or whether he only said 'I never was on that line'. I replied that I was a policeman from London and that Mr Tiernan was a policeman from New York. I then took him down to the saloon, and Mr Tiernan searched him in my presence. He took a key from Müller's waistcoat. I took possession of the key and said, 'What is this the key of?' He said, 'The key of my box.' I said, 'Where is your box?' He replied, 'In my berth.' In consequence of what the captain told me, I went to No. 9 berth and found a large black box, which I brought into the saloon where Müller was standing. He said, 'That is my box.' I unlocked it with the key I had taken from his waistcoat pocket, and in the corner of the box I found a watch. It was sewn up in a piece of leather. I said, 'What is this?' knowing it by the feel to be a watch. He replied, 'It is my watch.' I then took out a hat which was standing in the box and said, 'Is this your hat?' He said, 'Yes.' I said, 'How long have you possessed them?' He said, 'I've had the watch about two years and the hat about twelve months.' I then told him he would have to remain in custody and be taken to New York. I kept him on board all night until Inspector Tanner came on board in the morning, when I gave him over to him.

Clarke's first sight of the hat must have disappointed him, for, compared with the unanimous descriptions of Mr Briggs's missing one, it was slight of height — not a topper at all. But examination of the crown showed that there had once been more of it; and that, though the abbreviating had apparently been intended to remove signs of who had made and sold the hat, and to whom, there remained within the lining the inked letters *d.d.* These had been put there, carefully unobtrusive but telling the hat from others, by a jobbing tailor whose clients included *D*aniel *D*igance, a hatter at the Royal Exchange, close to Lombard Street, who had provided bespoke hats to Mr Briggs for nigh on thirty years.

Müller, his miser's mind swayed by the excellence of the materials of the hat from the sensible thought that he should discard it, had seen the need to make it unincriminating; and that necessity had mothered, not a sartorial invention, but a variation on a long-accepted style of hat, known in the trade as a 'low bell-crown'. Unlike the conventional low bell-crown, which was rounded where the side met the top, the version that Müller had felt impelled to create came to an abrupt conclusion. Within weeks of its being described by reporters of the extradition proceedings, American hatters were offering resemblances of it; within months, English hatters were doing

Murder in the Railway Train.

Listen to my song, and I will not detain you long,
And then I will tell you of what I've heard.
Of a murder that's been done, by some wicked one,
And the place where it all occurred;
Between Stepney and Bow they struck the fatal blow,
To resist he tried all in vain,
Murdered by some prigs was poor Mr Briggs
Whilst riding in a railway train.

Muller is accused, at present we cannot refuse
To believe that he is the very one,
But all his actions, you see, have been so very free,
Ever since the murder it was done;
From his home he never went, but such a happy time he spent,
He never looked troubled on the brain,
If he'd been the guilty man, he would have hid all he can,
From the murder in the railway train.

Muller he did state that he was going to emigrate
Long before this dreadful tragedy;
He often used to talk, about travelling to New York,
In the Victoria, that was going to sea.
Mr. Death, the jeweller, said, he was very much afraid,
He might not know the same man again,
When he heard of the reward, he started out abroad,
About the murder in the railway train.

If it's Muller, we can't deny, on the Cabman keep your eye,
Remember what he said the other day,
That Muller a ticket sold for money, which seems so very funny,
When he had no expenses for to pay.
They say his money he took, and his name entered on the book,
Long before this tragedy he came;
Like Muller's, the Cabman had a hat, and it may be his, perhaps
That was found in the railway train.

Would a murderer have forgot, to have destroyed the jeweller's box,
Or burnt up the sleeve of his coat,
Would he the chain ticket have sold, and himself exposed so bold,
And to all his friends a letter wrote,
Before Muller went away, why did not the cabman say,
And not give him so much start on the main
If the cabman knew—it's very wrong—to keep the secret up so long,
About the murder in the railway train.

When Muller does arrive, we shall not be much surprised,
To hear that that's him on the trial;
Give him time to repent, though he is not innocent,
To hear the evidence give no denial.
Muller's got the watch, you see, so it proves that he is guilty,
But like Townley don't prove that he's insane
For if it should be him, on the gallows let him swing,
For the murder on the railway train.

Now Muller's caught at last, tho' he's been so very fast,
And on him they found the watch and hat,
Tho' across the ocean he did roam, he had better stayed at home,
And hid himself in some little crack,
Tho' he pleads his innocence, but that is all nonsense,
For they'll hang him as sure as he's a man,
For he got up to his rigs, and murdered Mr. Briggs
While riding in a railway train.

London: Printed for the Vendors.

(Opposite)
A verse broadsheet.

likewise. The umlaut-forsaken 'Muller' became, and for decades remained, popular — is now, long anonymous, fashionable among women who hunt foxes for fun.[1]

The extradition proceedings, completed within a few hours, would have been briefer still but for the elongating intervention of a man, allegedly Müller's counsel, whose rantings were not merely beside legal points but far removed from any. George A. Birmingham notes:

> It is here that this case of sordid murder and robbery was, for the first time, but not for the last, elevated into the region of international politics. A certain Mr Chauncey Schaffer was assigned as Counsel to the prisoner to oppose the extradition. Schaffer, one presumes, was a lawyer. He must also, surely, have been a politician. No other kind of man could possibly have made the speech he made before the Court. It abounded in passages of the most glowing purple, which would have drawn frantic plaudits from a crowd of electors anywhere. The amazed Court — it must have been amazed, though the newspapers do not say so — heard about 'the sublime depths of old Niagara', about 'the proud title of Excelsior', presumed to belong to the United States, about 'great argosies, laden with the costliest treasures of the nation, sunk in countless numbers'; about almost anything, in fact, except Müller and the murder of Mr Briggs. . . . The Court kept its head, complimented Mr Schaffer on his eloquence, applied itself to a consideration of the facts, and handed Müller over to the London police.

The English party, with Müller, returned home aboard the steamship *Etna*. Müller is said to have been the most contented of passengers, never showing a sign of sadness at the reason for his being one: compared with the short commons of the *Victoria* and the drab menus in the Tombs Prison in New York, the *Etna*'s fare was respectively sufficient and varied, and Müller tucked into every meal and often requested second helpings. At

1. Whereas the Müller case was a blessing to hatters, the Manning case, fifteen years before, is said to have resulted in the ruination of many manufacturers of black satin, till then the most purchased of materials for female domestic attire. The railway was noticed in that case, too. The Swiss-born Marie Manning (who, posthumously, was a help to Dickens towards his portrayal of Hortense, the evil maid in the novel *Bleak House*) and her husband Fred, a former train-guard, sacked under suspicion of being involved in a bullion theft, were found guilty of having murdered Patrick O'Connor, Marie's erstwhile beau; an editorialist for *The Times*, surer than the jury should have been that Marie was the instigator of the 'transaction', stated that 'the scrip and shares of familiar railway lines' were mixed up with it, and then, even bolder of inference, contended that 'Mrs Manning made haste to slay her man, and realise, since the market was falling'. According to Marie's entry in *The Dictionary of National Biography*, when she, together with Fred, paid the legal penalty outside Horsemonger Lane Gaol on 13 November 1849, she 'wore a black satin dress . . . a fact which caused that material to become unpopular for years'. However, Albert Borowitz, in his book *The Woman Who Murdered Black Satin* (see Bibliography), puts forward strong evidence in contradiction of that title.

the start of the voyage he was lent *Pickwick Papers* from the ship's library, and liked it so much — especially the account of the trial of Bardell v. Pickwick — that he borrowed another book by the same author. Considering the length of the first book, he cannot have started on the second long before 16 September, when the *Etna* docked at Liverpool, and it would be interesting to know whether, perhaps having pocketed the ship's copy (an act that one would expect of him) or acquired another following his consignment to Holloway Prison, London, he followed the tale of *David Copperfield* to its end.

In the weeks before his trial, which began at the Old Bailey on 27 October, all but the *Telegraph* of British papers spoke convincedly of his guilt, and, with *Punch* joining in, scornfully reported that the German press, 'mit vun voice', made him out to be innocent, the victim of a charge trumped up at the behest of English aristocrats who bore a grudge against all Germans; and societies of Germans living in Britain contributed towards the cost of having Müller defended by three barristers, including the expensive 'verdict-getter', Mr Serjeant Parry.

In the absence of any sound evidence telling against the case for the prosecution, Parry did two things that defence lawyers, their predicaments similar, have almost always done, probably will almost always do: he sought to deceive the jury into believing that circumstantial evidence was second-rate (of course, ignoring the fact that as no one had seen Mr Briggs being murdered, the only other type of evidence, termed 'direct', was non-existent in this case) and he tried to give them the impression that testimony that did not help the prosecution was harmful to it, and that any blemish in a witness's character, no matter how slight or long past, was a sure indication that the witness was entirely discreditable. He was most flamboyant in the latter endeavour when Jonathan Matthews, under cross-examination, admitted that, while in his teens, he had 'made a little freak, a spree' — which turned out to mean that he had 'absconded from a situation as conductor of a coach without giving notice', taking with him a box, his own, that because it was secured by his master's sixpenny padlock and contained — singularly unvaluable — one of that gentleman's spurred boots, had resulted (Matthews being unable or unwilling to pay a fine) in his imprisonment for twenty-one days. But the Serjeant's stratagems did not significantly influence the jury, who, at the end of the three-day trial, retired and almost at once returned with the verdict of Guilty. When Müller was asked if he wished to speak, he made no reply; after being sentenced, however, he was understood to say: 'I am perfectly satisfied with my judges and with the jury, but I have been convicted on false evidence, and not a true statement. If the sentence is carried out, I shall die innocent.' Composed till then, he burst into tears, and was still weeping as he was led from the dock, *en route* to a condemned cell in Newgate Prison, next door to the Old Bailey.

There were German efforts to save Müller (one by the King of Prussia, who telegraphed a plea to Queen Victoria); but the execution went ahead in accordance with the convention, established in the period since the Tawell case, that, no matter whether a condemned person was irreligious or of a faith unobservant of Sunday, three such days, but no more, were to elapse between sentencing and hanging. Not until Müller was taken to the scaffold — watched by a vast crowd, hushed while expectant, that not even Queen Victoria would have dared to disappoint — did he accept that he was to die suspended from it. He had believed that, so long as he did not confess, his nationality would protect him. Just before he, inadequately prepared except in Calcraft's mundane ways, was made by the latter to drop, he spoke a few words of German — the tone of which sounded, to those permitted close enough to hear them but not understanding the language, resentful rather than contrite. It was as well that the person to whom he spoke, a priest, was German, else that man's subsequent repeating and translation of the words, which made a confession, would not have been trusted by all — and Müller's name would have been applied, not only to a sort of peep-hole and a sort of hat, but also, among Germans, to a sort of martyrdom.

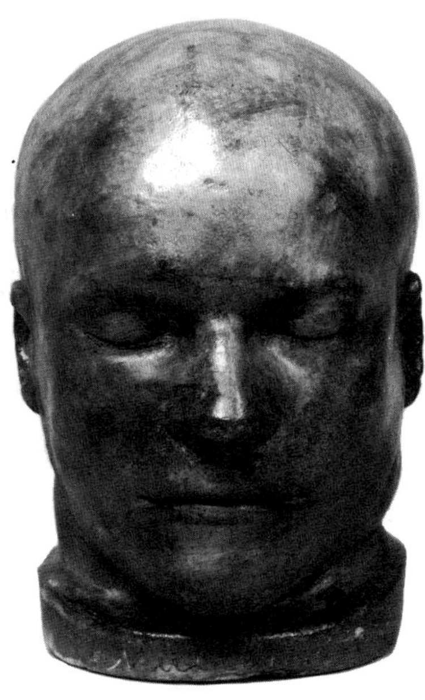

The death-mask of Müller.

Considering the theatricality of the Crippen case, it seems permissible to borrow a theatrical expression and say that if ever a man was 'cast against type' in the rôle of Murderer, that man was Hawley Harvey Crippen — who, quite understandably, preferred to be known to friends (and he gathered many of them) as 'Peter'.

Excepting a few months in 1883, when, at the age of twenty-one, he pottered around various English hospitals in furtherance of his medical studies, he spent the first thirty-five years of his life in America. Soon after graduating from the Homeopathic Hospital College in Cleveland, Ohio, he married Charlotte Bell, a student-nurse of Irish parentage; Charlotte bore him one child, a boy, and was labouring with another when she suddenly died — naturally, according to the death certificate, which ascribed the cause to apoplexy.

Six months later, in July 1892, a nineteen-year-old girl. buxom and dark-featured, came to the Brooklyn surgery where Crippen was acting as locum. He subsequently recalled, rather vaguely: 'I believe she had had a miscarriage, or something of that kind.' She called herself Cora Turner, but her name was really Kunigunde Mackamotzki. Her father, who made a meagre living from a fruit stall in Brooklyn, was Polish, her mother German.

Within a month or so of her first meeting with Crippen, she deserted the married man who was keeping her in an apartment and paying for her singing lessons. She became Mrs Crippen — officially — on the first day of September.

But her name-changing was not yet over. The singing lessons, now paid for by Crippen (who also had to fork out for ornate costumes and bijouterie), were aimed at refining her soprano voice, for she believed that she was destined to be an opera star. 'Cora Motzki' was what she called herself when she turned up for auditions. However, her voice was too small, too quavery on top notes, to impress a single impresario. Though still convinced that, one fine day, her operatic talents would be recognized, she decided to embark on a career as a chantress in vaudeville. Here again, though, none of her auditions led to an engagement. Suspecting that racism was prohibiting her triumphant debut, she concocted the name 'Belle Elmore'. But she never had the thrill of seeing it on a vaudeville poster.

When it eventually became world-famous, for a reason she had not contemplated, that reason had made her unavailable for bookings.

In 1897 the Crippens came to England — he, having forsaken medicine for quackery, to open the London branch of a Philadelphia-based cure-all firm called The Munyon

Homeopathic Home Remedy Co.; she optimistic, because American acts were in vogue, to try her luck on the music-hall stage.

Belle (let us call her that from now on) had high hopes of bringing down 'Number-One' houses in the West End. But it was not to be. After weeks spent traipsing around agents' offices, she made her inaugural appearance, wearing an embroidered gipsyesque gown and presumably singing something matchingly nomadic, at the dingy Marylebone Music Hall. A short while later, the Marylebone closed down; much later still, someone of a humorous disposition contended that the demolition of that theatre was a natural outcome of Belle's appearance there.

Unfair comment. No more so than many other comments on her. Contrary to the view of most crime historians, her singing did not constitute a motive for murdering her. The performer and producer Clarkson Rose saw her at the Dudley Empire, circa 1903:

> The Empire proudly announced that it was the most up-to-date theatre outside London, and it had cost eight thousand pounds. . . . It was there that I first saw that great comedian, George Formby, Senior. On the same programme was Belle Elmore. . . . She wasn't a top-rank artist, but, in her way, not bad — a blowsy, florid type of serio.

An anonymous contributor to a 1910 issue of the stage newspaper, *The Era*, said of her:

> She appeared at the Grand, Clapham, and the Holborn, and also toured the provinces. She last appeared at the Bedford Music Hall [in Camden Town, North London] early in 1907, when she sang a song called 'Down Lovers' Walk' and also a coon song. She wore a short spangled dress. She also sang a costume song called 'The Major' and appeared in a musical duologue entitled 'The Unknown Quantity'. In one of the scenes she had to hold a sheaf of £5 notes. Dr Crippen's desire for realism was so great that he gave her a bundle of genuine notes, which she left on the stage on the first night. Fortunately, they were seen by her leading man.

Her week at the Bedford was in January 1907, during a strike by music-hall artists in aid of higher wages and improved conditions. There is a story that as Belle the Scab was nearing the picket-line around the stage-door, a striker shouted: 'Belle, stay out and help your own people' — only to be told by Marie Lloyd, a fellow-picketer: 'Don't be daft. Let her in, and she'll empty the house.' It seems likely that that tale was the genesis of post-1910 denigrations of Belle's performances by people who had never seen any of them.

She may have believed — shrilly insisted — that she was not a blackleg at the Bedford; that she had not broken ranks. For by then she had — temporarily, she stressed — given up the stage: English audiences were not yet ready for her; until tastes altered for the better, she would hang about the outskirts of show business, keeping up with the news and gossip by reading all the theatrical magazines, currying favour with stars at social gatherings, and doing good as the honorary treasurer of the charitable Music Hall Ladies' Guild. Her circle of friends widened: openly so far as the music-hall ladies were concerned — discreetly, even stealthily, in the case of certain gentlemen who enjoyed the pleasure of her company tête-à-tête. Her longest-running extra-marital relationship was with Bruce Miller, an American ex-pugilist, moderately musical and adroitly ambidextrous, who toured the halls as a one-man band.

Belle acquired the nickname of 'the bird of paradise', which probably meant one thing to her lady-friends, impressed by her fine clothes and expensive-looking accessories, and quite another to her gentlemen callers. Some of the friends who had encountered her husband had a nickname for him, too: they referred to him as 'the shrimp'. Clarkson Rose:

> I met Dr Crippen once or twice; he was a quiet, meticulously mannered little man — a great frequenter of the music-halls, and, in fact, attended professionally several variety artists, and somehow I don't think he would have minded the fact that his name was to become a rather macabre music-hall joke. For years after his death, many comedians, in sketches or otherwise, used the slogan, 'Crippen was innocent!' It was a sort of pay-off to an outrageous happening or situation, as, for instance, one well-known comic, discussing in his patter his discomforts as a lodger, ending up by saying, 'Cor blimey! You ought to see the landlady — what a face — Crippen was innocent!'

The actor-manager Seymour Hicks would recall:

> I knew Crippen personally but not well. On the first occasion that I met him I spent half an hour in his company at the Vaudeville Club.... I am bound to say that I never hope to have the privilege of drinking with a milder-looking or more gentle little murderer. Crippen was short, slightly built, of pale complexion and was possessed of fair hair, a quantity of which had played truant. The most noticeable thing about him was his eyes. They bulged considerably and appeared to be closely related to some kind of ophthalmic goitre. Added to this, as they were weak and watery he

(Opposite)
Belle Elmore.

Dr Crippen.

was obliged to wear spectacles with lenses of more than ordinary thickness, which so magnified his pupils that in looking at him I was by no means sure I was not talking to a bream or mullet or some other open-eyed and equally intelligent deep-sea fish. He spoke with a slight American accent. I fancy I should have forgotten him altogether had it not been that on this particular afternoon he presented the acquaintance who had introduced us with one of Munyon's Remedies, assuring him that it would instantly relieve the acute toothache from which he was suffering. . . .

He numbered among his friends many music-hall artists, and it was Marie Lloyd, that Queen of music-hall comediennes, who nicknamed him 'the half-crown king'. It appears he was always short of this particular coin of the realm and made a habit of borrowing it whenever possible. His usual procedure was to invite a friend to have a drink with him and then, finding to his dismay that he had come out without any money, say, 'I'm so sorry. Would you mind lending me half-a-crown?' Not only did two-and-sixpence enable thirst to be quenched but the change found a home in the 'Doctor's' pocket.

Crippen's career as a puffer and purveyor of quack remedies was patently unsuccessful. He augmented his salary from 'Professor' Munyon by moonlighting as 'consultant physician' to other swindlers, running his own con-the-deaf mail-order firm, The Aural Remedies Company, and being the sleeping partner of a dentist in a 'painless extraction' business. 'Anything for a quiet life' seems to sum up his attitude towards Belle, who over the years became more domineering, quarrelsome and complaining; somehow or other he managed to buy her jewels (never emeralds, since she was superstitious of the colour green) and to pay her dressmakers' and vintners' bills.

From 1902, or thereabouts, he made excuses for coming home late from the office. Towards the end of the previous year, he had been hired on a freelance basis by the Drouet Institute for the Deaf, a mail-order company that was criminal in its quackery, and there he had got to know a typist who had tinkered with her given name of Ethel Neave to make it Ethel Le Neve. He had fallen in love with her — and she, though junior to him by twenty-one years, had reciprocated.

'Large grey or blue eyes, good teeth, nice looking, rather long straight nose (good shape), medium build, pleasant, lady-like appearance; quiet, subdued manner.' That was the description of Ethel that, some years later, would be circulated by Scotland Yard to police forces throughout the world.

In September 1905 the Crippens moved to the district of Holloway, just north of Camden Town: to 39 Hilldrop

Crescent, a semi-detached dwelling of three storeys and a basement, on which they had negotiated annual rent of £52 10s. 0d. It has been suggested that the decision to move from a one-bedroom flat off Tottenham Court Road to a house was taken by Crippen because Ethel, by now his mistress, was disconsolate at the thought of him sleeping with Belle. If that is right, then he over-reacted, for 39 Hilldrop Crescent — an address that would become, for a while, as famous as 10 Downing Street — was far too large for a childless couple who did not intend to employ living-in servants. More likely, the decision was Belle's — another of her several extravagances, this one meant to impress colleagues in the Music Hall Ladies' Guild. She took charge of the decorating. As she was now using peroxide to turn her raven tresses blonde, and wanted a fitting background, she arranged for the whole place — apart from the basement — to be papered or painted in various shades of pink.

Ethel Le Neve.

The Crippens had been residing in Hilldrop Crescent for just over a year when Belle decided to take in paying guests. Crippen had no say in the matter, but it was he who bore the brunt of looking after the lodgers. Now he had to be up at six each morning to fetch coal from the basement, light the fire in the kitchen-range, lay the table for breakfast, give Belle coffee in bed, clean the lodgers' boots, and deal with other chores before leaving for work.

But by the end of 1909 the last of the lodgers had departed. Perhaps Belle had felt that the sound of them moving about was a distraction to the gentlemen who came to her pink paradise in the afternoons; or that people invited to supper-parties — she gave at least one each week — would think of her as a common-or-garden landlady rather than as a 'resting artiste'.

Belle's best friends were the Martinettis: Paul, the famed pantomimist, and his wife Clara. They came to supper on Monday, 31 January 1910, and played whist with the Crippens till after one o'clock the next morning. When they were leaving, Belle started to follow them down the steps from the front door, but was stopped by the thoughtful Clara, who cautioned her: 'You'll catch your death.'

The Martinettis were the last outsiders to see Belle Elmore alive or — complete in all respects — dead.

For reasons that will become apparent, one may surmise that Tuesday, 1 February, was a busy day for Crippen. The following day certainly was. In the morning of that Wednesday, when Ethel Le Neve popped into the offices of the Aural Remedies Company, she found that he had already come and gone, leaving for her attention a note, two letters, and a package. The note began, 'B.E. has gone to America,' and went on to ask

Ethel to deliver the letters and the package to Melinda May, the secretary of the Music Hall Ladies' Guild. At lunch-time Ethel did as she had been asked.

Both letters were in Crippen's hand, apparently dictated to him by Belle, in too much of a hurry to write them herself. One of the letters was to Melinda May, explaining that 'illness of a near relative has called me to America on only a few hours' notice,' and tendering her resignation as treasurer of the Guild; the letter ended, 'Now goodbye, with love hastily. Yours Belle Elmore, p.p. H.H.C.' The other letter, more formal, was to the committee of the Guild, and the package contained the bank-books that Belle had used as treasurer.

That afternoon Ethel visited Crippen at 39 Hilldrop Crescent. He invited her to take her pick of Belle's jewellery, and when she had done so, left her alone in the house while he went off to pawn the rest. In his first-thing-in-the-morning note, he had said that they could have 'a pleasant little evening'; but it turned out to be a pleasant *night*, for Ethel slept with him at Hilldrop Crescent for the first time. She did not move in till a month or so later.

By then, the leading lights of the Music Hall Ladies' Guild were gossiping. They had been surprised by Belle's sudden departure — but when Crippen had turned up, with Ethel on his arm, at a ball to raise funds for the Music Hall Artists' Railway Association, they had grown suspicious. Because, you see, they had recognised the jewellery adorning Ethel — one piece in particular, a 'rising sun' diamond-brooch — as Belle's.

In the middle of March, Crippen, perturbed by the wagging tongues, embarked on a plan aimed at stilling them. First, he told the Martinettis that he had received letters from relatives of Belle, saying that she was 'dangerously ill with pleuro-pneumonia'; less than a fortnight later, he inserted an obituary notice in *The Era*: 'ELMORE — March 23, in California, U.S.A., Miss Belle Elmore (Mrs H. H. Crippen).' Then, sanguine that his plan had succeeded, he took Ethel to France for a week's holiday: a pre-marital honeymoon, one might say.

But far from putting an end to the matter, the obituary notice spurred the ladies to make inquiries in America. Eventually — in June — word came back that, according to Californian death records, no one named Belle Elmore or Mrs Hawley Harvey Crippen had died in the state that year.

Enter Lil Nash, half of a song-and-dance act called the Hawthorne Sisters. She and her American-born husband Fred, himself a music-hall turn, had been friendly with Belle for some years. Another of the Nashes' social acquaintances was Superintendent Frank Froest of Scotland Yard. They voiced their suspicions to the Superintendent, and the latter, after taking written statements from them, scribbled a memo: 'Have the doctor seen and shaken up by a Chief Inspector.'

Walter Dew was the officer given the assignment. He did not hasten to carry it out. A full week passed before he visited Crippen at his office. Crippen at once admitted that the whole story of Belle's death back home was untrue: she had left him to live with another man, he knew not whom, and to avoid scandal he had invented the tale of the trip to America, the illness, the death. He accompanied Dew and other officers to 39 Hilldrop Crescent, showed them round the place, from attic to basement, and wished them farewell. Dew considered that the investigation was closed.

All unwittingly, however, he had succeeded in 'shaking up' Crippen. When, for no particular reason, he visited Crippen's office on the following Monday, he was told that the doctor had gone away. Thinking that that was odd, he decided that he had better double-check. Returning to Hilldrop Crescent, he made a 'thorough' search of the house, lasting till the Tuesday evening; he found nothing at all suspicious. But on the third day, 13 July, while prodding the cellar-floor with a poker, Dew observed that one of the bricks was loose. He prised the brick away, lifted surrounding ones, and scrabbled at the earth. The sight and smell of what he found caused him to summon medico-legal experts.

They shovelled out Dew's discovery and, after a fairly cursory examination of it in a mortuary, reported that it consisted mainly of human flesh from which the bones had been filleted; there was no sign of the head, or of the organs that would have established gender. Further examination revealed tufts of blonde hair, dark at the roots (three of the tufts were clasped by Hinde's metal hair-curlers); also, on a morsel of abdominal skin, a scar that might have been left by an operation that Belle Elmore had undergone shortly before her marriage, and which she had delighted in chatting about to her friends in the Music Hall Ladies' Guild. Chemical analysis revealed the presence of a narcotic poison, hyoscine, in the remains. That those remains were of Belle Elmore — or rather, *not* of someone who had died and to some extent been buried in the cellar prior to September 1905, when the Crippens had moved into the house — seemed to be proved by a label on the collar of part of a pyjama jacket: 'Shirtmakers, Jones Brothers (Holloway) Limited, Holloway, N.' Jones Brothers had not become a limited company till 190*6* — and, according to the chief buyer, the sort of pyjamas represented by the fragment unearthed in the cellar had not been stocked till 190*8*.

Long before all of the above facts were gathered, a warrant was issued for the arrest of Crippen; and of Ethel Le Neve, who had disappeared at the same time. The case made — or was made into — front-page news. **WANTED FOR MURDER AND MUTILATION,** screamed the headlines, repeating the words on the police notice.

By the time that notice was issued, the wanted couple were in a small hotel in the Belgian port of Antwerp, waiting to depart for Quebec on a Canadian-Pacific liner, the s.s. *Montrose*. When registering for the voyage, Crippen had called himself Mr Robinson; had said that his companion was his son, Master Robinson. Adding a theatrical touch that Belle might, just might, have applauded, Ethel was to travel at half-fare, posing as a lad.

In conventional garb, and with her brunette hair coiffured and her cheeks rouged, Ethel Le Neve was a fairly attractive young woman — but when dressed in male clothes, including a Homburg hat to hide her chignon, she looked like an extraordinarily pretty boy. As she strolled on the deck of the *Montrose* with Crippen (who, additional to his alias, had shaved off his moustache and was managing without spectacles), she was very eye-catching indeed. And made more so by the fact that as the trousers of her juvenile suit, untailored to her hips, had split as she walked up the gangway at Antwerp, they were now assisted towards decency by several blanket-pins.

The ship was only two days out of port when its captain, Henry Kendall, became convinced that Mr and Master Robinson were none other than the 'London cellar-murder fugitive and friend' whose portraits he had seen, time and again, in British and Belgian papers. And so he ordered the Marconi operator, Llewellyn Jones, to send a message to the Canadian Pacific office in Liverpool. He did not realize it, but he was making history: this was the first time that wireless telegraphy was used in a murder hunt.[1]

The message was passed on to Scotland Yard — to Chief Inspector Walter Dew. Next morning Dew set off from Liverpool on the s.s. *Laurentic*, a vessel whose sailing time to Quebec was seven days, compared with the eleven of the *Montrose*. By then Captain Kendall had agreed terms with

1. Henry Kendall had been present during a previous maritime-wireless 'first'. In 1900, when the s.s. *Lake Champlain* became the first British ocean-going vessel to be fitted with Guglielmo Marconi's apparatus, Kendall was one of the ship's officers. To prove that the apparatus worked, Marconi himself sent a message to the *Lake Champlain* when it was off the South of Ireland, and Kendall was in the wireless room at that pre-arranged time.

METROPOLITAN POLICE

MURDER

AND MUTILATION.

Portraits, Description and Specimen of Handwriting of HAWLEY HARVEY CRIPPEN, alias Peter Crippen, alias Franckel; and ETHEL CLARA LE NEVE, alias Mrs. Crippen, and Neave.

Wanted for the Murder of CORA CRIPPEN, otherwise Belle Elmore; Kunigunde Mackamotzki; Marsangar and Turner, on, or about, 2nd February last.

Description of Crippen. Age 50, height 5 ft. 3 or 4, complexion fresh, hair light brown, inclined sandy, scanty, bald on top, rather long scanty moustache, somewhat straggly, eyes grey, bridge of nose rather flat, false teeth, medium build, throws his feet outwards when walking. May be clean shaven or wearing a beard and gold rimmed spectacles, and may possibly assume a wig.

Sometimes wears a jacket suit, and at other times frock coat and silk hat. May be dressed in a brown jacket suit, brown hat and stand up collar (size 15).

Somewhat slovenly appearance, wears his hat rather at back of head

Very plausible and quiet spoken, remarkably cool and collected demeanour.

Speaks French and probably German. Carries Firearms.

An American citizen, and by profession a Doctor.

Has lived in New York, Philadelphia, St. Louis, Detroit, Michigan, Coldwater, and other parts of America.

May obtain a position as assistant to a doctor or eye specialist, or may practise as an eye specialist, Dentist, or open a business for the treatment of deafness, advertising freely.

Has represented Munyon's Remedies, in various cities in America.

Description of Le Neve alias Neave.—A shorthand writer and typist, age 27, height 5 ft. 5, complexion pale, hair light brown (may dye same), large grey or blue eyes, good teeth, nice looking, rather long straight nose (good shape), medium build, pleasant, lady-like appearance. Quiet, subdued manner, talks quietly, looks intently when in conversation. A native of London.

Dresses well, but quietly, and may wear a blue serge costume (coat reaching to hips) trimmed heavy braid, about ¼ inch wide, round edge, over shoulders and pockets. Three large braid buttons down front, about size of a florin, three small ones on each pocket, two on each cuff, several rows of stitching round bottom of skirt; or a light grey shadow-stripe costume, same style as above, but trimmed grey moire silk instead of braid, and two rows of silk round bottom of skirt; or a white princess robe with gold sequins; or a mole coloured striped costume with black moire silk collar; or a dark vieuxrose cloth costume, trimmed black velvet collar; or a light heliotrope dress.

May have in her possession and endeavour to dispose of same:—a round gold brooch, with points radiating zig-zag from centre, each point about an inch long, diamond in centre, each point set brilliants, the brooch in all being slightly larger than a half-crown; and two single stone diamond rings, and a diamond and sapphire (or ruby) ring, stones rather large.

Absconded 9th inst, and may have left, or will endeavour to leave the country.

Please cause every enquiry at Shipping Offices, Hotels, and other likely places and cause ships to be watched

Information to be given to the Metropolitan Police Office, New Scotland Yard, London S.W., or at any Police Station

E. R. HENRY,
The Commissioner of Police of the Metropolis

Metropolitan Police Office,
New Scotland Yard *16th July 1910*

British and North American newspapers (users of wireless since 1898) for his provision of daily communiqués on his observations of and conversations with 'the Robinsons'. A quaint situation, this: while Crippen and Ethel developed health-looking blushes from the ozone and ate like troopers at the captain's table, never for a moment thinking that their covers had been blown, millions of newspaper readers were aware of how they had overtly occupied themselves so far during the voyage. The 'world interest' in the fugitives was treated by the popular press as if it were almost as newsworthy as they were: special editions of British papers contained reports of how North American papers were printing special editions; depending on geographical location, headlines

Captain Kendall.

announced, **QUEBEC AGOG, EXCITEMENT IN NEW YORK, LONDON AT FEVER-PITCH.** As well as the map-patched news-stories sparked off by Captain Kendall's brief wireless messages, there were articles that, with the Marconi publicists' unattributed help, made news of wireless itself — such articles exemplified by the following extracts from one that appeared in the London *Daily Mail* on 30 July, towards the end of the seven days' wonder:

PURSUIT BY WIRELESS. LONG ARM OF THE LAW.

Wireless telegraphy is bound to play an important part in the tracking down of criminals in the future. Its value has been demonstrated in the past few days. The suspect fugitive flying to another continent no longer finds immunity in mid-ocean. The very air around him may be quivering with accusatory messages which have apparently come up out of the void.

'Wireless' has proved itself of use in procuring help in disaster and now appears likely to prove its value in helping justice. It will be as effective in gripping criminals as it has been in saving threatened men. How it carries the long arm of the law into lonely waters is an interesting process.

THE MAGIC CABIN.

Each ship has on its upper deck a little cabin for the operator, a tiny square erection, wherein two young men take turns by day and night waiting and watching for any word that may come rushing to them from unseen sources behind the horizon. The little cabin, crowded with apparatus, is like a magician's cave. All kinds of appliances are stacked within it. Printed telegraph forms are scattered at one end of the instrument table. The operator on duty is wearing a telephone headgear, with receivers over his ears.

Suddenly there comes to him a low musical note. It is the first indication of a Morse code message. It begins with two or three letters signifying the identity of the ship which is calling. He signals back the letter 'K', which means that he is ready to take the communication.

As he replies the cabin is transformed. A vivid electric spark throws a weird bluish light over the operator and his machinery. The young man on duty, with a pencil, writes out slowly the message as it arrives. The message may mean suspicion by the authorities of a man aboard the ship. It is hurried to the captain. It may mean that a confederate on shore has transmitted a word of warning to a criminal among the passengers. Again the message is hurried to the captain. In either case the man in question is placed under immediate, though unobtrusive, surveillance. Strict secrecy is observed. None of the passengers know what has been transmitted

A CHAIN OF MESSAGES.

The difficulty in pursuing criminals by 'wireless' is that of getting quick communication between ship and shore. A vessel such as the Montrose throws out her wireless message in a circle all around her, 150 miles in every direction. Should a wireless station on land be within 150 miles of her the messages can be transmitted direct. But should the distance be greater, say 500 miles, the Montrose or any similar ship would have to wait till some part of her 150 miles radius struck that of another ship equipped with a 'wireless'. This second ship might be nearer land or might be possessed of wireless power with a greater radius, thus enabling her with her higher masts and greater length to out-distance in telegraphing a ship like the Montrose. The Lusitania, for instance, can send messages 300 and sometimes 400 miles. Most of the great liners could keep up direct communication at a distance of 250 miles from the shore station. Ploughing through the sea the ships carry with them a circle of communication, the extent of which varies with their power. It is easily seen therefore that it is far more difficult to get links with a chain of smaller ships than where large ships are available.

Perhaps a steamer like the Montrose with an urgent message to deliver gets in touch with a great liner behind her. The liner flings out the message to the extremity of her power, and it projects far beyond the range of the Montrose ahead. It is taken by another ship, which in turn sends it forward for other ships to pick up. So it proceeds across the ocean till it reaches land.

But the fleeing criminal must not think that the ship he is in is prevented from receiving news of him because she happens to have a range of only a few hundreds of miles for sending messages. It is a characteristic of 'wireless' that it can be received by ships at a far greater distance than it can be transmitted by them. The result is that steamers a thousand miles from Poldhu are daily receiving messages to which they can make no direct reply to the Cornish coast.

Helping to make the story the greatest circulation-booster since Mafeking, there was all the excitement of a race. Bookmakers did a roaring trade in wagers on whether or not the *Laurentic* would reach Quebec ahead of the *Montrose*, and, if the *Laurentic* won, the winning distance and the time to spare. Meanwhile, songs were hastily cobbled — one a parody of 'Has Anybody Here Seen Kelly?':

Has anybody here seen Crippen,
C R I double-P E N?
Has anybody here seen Crippen? —
Seek him up and down.
He's done a bunk to Ca–na–dah
And left his wife in a coal-cellar.
Has anybody here seen Crippen,
Crippen from Camden Town?

SUNDAY EVENING EDITION

VOL. 136—No. 3,484 [ESTAB. 1843.] LONDON, SUNDAY, JULY 31, 1910. 16 PAGES. PRICE ONE PENNY.

CONTAINS MORE NEWS THAN ANY OTHER PAPER.

CRIPPEN'S LIFE AT SEA.

CAPTAIN KENDALL DESCRIBES HIS TERROR AND MISS LE NEVE'S MISERY.

THE HUNTED MAN WITH REVOLVER IN READINESS.

(*"News of the World" Special.*)

Steadily the Montrose draws near to the consummation of one of the most dramatic scenes ever enacted on board ship. Within a few hours the Montrose will be off Father Point, Rimouski, and there Inspector Dew will come face to face with Hawley Harvey Crippen and Ethel Clara Le Neve. There a famous masquerade will end for the masqueraders, and for their fellow-passengers, who will learn for the first time that the reticent middle-aged man and his effeminate "son" stand in a very different relationship; that they are bound together by what would be called a more tender tie if it were not for the accusing spectre risen up from the cellar of Hilldrop-crescent. By wireless messages from Captain H. G. Kendall, of the Montrose, an account has come to hand of the life of his notorious passengers. The man was nervous, ill-at-ease, silent. The woman was all the time on the verge of hysterics. So abject was her terror that tears were seen in her eyes as she watched the man who had reduced her to straits so desperate. Captain Kendall describes Crippen as having shaved off his moustache and altered his appearance in various ways. He passed himself off as a merchant, his "son" as a young student. But under the habiliments of the young student, the ship's officers soon discerned the figure and bearing, the walk and manners of a girl. Once the girl's disguise had been seen through, suspicion was, of course, aroused, and the identification of the pair was soon established as the result of careful observation. Capt. Kendall says the pair have no idea they have been discovered. The advent of the police officers will, therefore, come as a complete and staggering surprise. Meanwhile, Inspector Dew has landed at Father Point. There he awaits the coming of his quarry. The prisoners will be taken to Quebec, and may be either deported forthwith as undesirable aliens, or extradited in the ordinary course.

CRIPPEN AS HE APPEARS WITHOUT A MOUSTACHE.

WIRELESS MESSAGES.

GIRL'S LOVE BETRAYS.

CAPTAIN KENDALL TELLS HOW HE KNEW LE NEVE.

It was a love-passage between the runaway from Hilldrop-crescent and his female companion which first aroused Captain Kendall's suspicions. Standing on the bridge he saw the pair sitting apart sheltered by a boat. Some sign of endearment passed between the pair. It was only a trifle. But the shrewd skipper knew that boys did not treat their fathers with such effeminate tenderness. What followed on that indiscreet sign of affection is told in the following wireless messages to the "Montreal Star," the Central News, and Reuter from Captain Kendall:—

SPECIAL TELEGRAMS.

Father Point (Quebec), July 30.

I have just received the following special wireless message from Captain Kendall, of the Montrose, despatched when the vessel was off Heath Point this morning:—

Off Heath Point, 7 a.m., July 30.

I feel quite convinced of the identity of the suspected pair, who booked at Antwerp as Mr. John Robinson and his son.

The man answers exactly to the description of Crippen as received from the police.

The "son" can also be easily identified as Miss Le Neve.

The man is showing extreme nervousness in nearing land. He fears apparently that he is suspected of being Crippen.

The girl is pale and worried-looking.

The man spends sleepless nights.

Both keep in their room almost entirely.

All arrangements for effecting arrest have been made. We expect to reach Father Point early on Sunday.

We had only been at sea a couple of hours when

MY SUSPICIONS WERE AROUSED

as to the younger passenger's disguise.

The "son" was observed to treat the "father" with extraordinary signs of endearment.

This was so unusual as between men as to excite suspicion.

Careful watch was in consequence kept, and suspicion was strengthened that young Robinson was a girl.

The clues were numerous. The "boy's" attire was ill-fitting, revealing a figure of feminine proportions.

The hands and feet were those of a woman.

I spoke with the supposed boy. The voice and demeanour convinced me that Master Robinson was playing a part.

Crippen was ill at ease. He did not wish his companion to speak apart. Nor did she desire to make acquaintances.

Our observations were made so guardedly and rationally that, even after we had discovered everything, Crippen was satisfied with his disguise.

During their absence from their stateroom their belongings were inspected.

They had next to no luggage.

The woman's belongings left scarcely a doubt as to her sex. During meal time these were examined at leisure.

When suspicion had become certainty watch was kept night and day.

Throughout the night the couple lay awake, speaking in subdued voices.

In the morning Crippen looked haggard and wretched. The girl kept to her cabin as much as possible.

When spoken to about his wretched looks as he paced the deck, Crippen complained that

HIS BOY'S HEALTH

troubled him.

As the Montrose drew nearer land his nervousness increased.

Fearing lest he should attempt suicide watch was never relaxed.

He never went unarmed. A revolver was always in his hip-pocket.

He seemed to find some comfort in the growth of his beard. He kept his moustache shaved.

Crippen and the girl read a great deal throughout the voyage. It was perhaps an excuse for evading the attentions of loquacious passengers.

CRIPPEN COMPLAINS OF INSOMNIA.

Montreal, July 30.

The Montreal "Star," in a further lengthy wireless message from Captain Kendall, of the Montrose, gives other interesting details. He says:—

Crippen came on deck early this morning while we were passing Belle Isle. He was looking worried, and continued pacing the deck about two hours.

Le Neve seems very depressed, and even tearful. She kept her room practically all day yesterday.

There is no proof that either Crippen or Le Neve suspects they are being watched.

Crippen complains of insomnia, and looks very haggard.

When the couple were lunching the first day out their hats were hanging up outside the dining saloon, and I noticed that the "boy's" was several sizes too large.

Later I saw Le Neve with coat and waistcoat off, and I noticed that the trousers were attached at the waist by means of a safety-pin. Crippen carries a revolver; surely a suspicious circumstance. —Central News.

Father Point, July 30 (Later.)

The wireless telegraph operator on board the Montrose telegraphed at seven o'clock this morning, when the ship was abreast of Health Point:

Crippen and Le Neve have become more retiring than ever.

The couple have not been arrested, and they still have no suspicions of the observation that was being kept on them.—Reuter.

CANNOT BE PARTED.

CRIPPEN AND MISS LE NEVE INSEPARABLE ON SHIP.

The world-wide curiosity as to whether Crippen was really aboard the Montrose was earlier satisfied with the following despatch from Captain Kendall:—

"Doctor Crippen wanted London for murder of Belle Elmore, actress, aboard." —Reuter.

A further wireless message despatched from Point Amour, amplified this to the extent of stating that Miss Le Neve was also on board, and that their identity had been established "beyond all doubt." Following up this came the captain's account of the disguise which had been adopted by Crippen, as follows:—

Montreal, July 29.—Captain Kendall, of the Montrose, has supplied by wireless exclusively to the "Montreal Star" the following very interesting statement regarding his two passengers, in whom so much interest is taken:—

I am confident they are Crippen and Le Neve. The man continues to shave his upper lip, and is growing a beard.

Crippen has no suspicion his identity is suspected, and the passengers also are ignorant of the remarkable situation in which they are unconsciously acting a part.

Le Neve refrains from talking. They have no baggage with them.

The couple cannot be parted, and are very reticent.

The man has evidently travelled much. He is generally busy reading books, and appears to be very sleepless.

The first clue as to the identity of the couple was obtained two hours after we left Antwerp.

The man says he is taking the boy to California for his health. He spends much of his time in his room.

THE ORDER OF RELEASE.

With acknowledgments to the picture by Sir John Millais, P.R.A.

MR. LLEWELLYN JONES, THE MARCONI OPERATOR.

The boy appears bright at times, but shows signs of worry. The man looked as a merchant; the boy as a student.—Central News.

SLEEPLESS NIGHTS.

HUNTED MAN UNABLE TO OBTAIN RESPITE FROM FEAR.

Later came the following:—

New York, July 29.—Another wireless message has been received from Captain Kendall, of the Montrose, in which he says:

During the voyage Crippen showed unmistakable signs of extreme nervousness.

Miss Le Neve was alternately gay and sad.

One of the most noticeable traits in the dispositions of Crippen and Miss Le Neve has been their obvious disinclination to mingle with the other passengers.

At times they have appeared to be labouring under anxiety, and have conversed together in subdued tones during the night hours.

From this it has been remarked that Crippen and his companion have been obtaining but little sleep.

Miss Le Neve is dressed in a grey suit, and when on deck wears a brown hat.

Not only has Crippen's moustache gone and a fortnight's growth of beard appeared, but prominent eyebrows are displayed. His elaborate waistcoats have been replaced by a soberer kind, more befitting the dress of a merchant.

Crippen explains his occasionally worried expression of face by telling the solicitous passengers that he is anxious about his son's breakdown—caused by overwork at his studies.

At times Miss Le Neve was observed to be watching Crippen with tearful eyes.—Exchange.

PLANS FOR ARREST.

DETECTIVES IN DISGUISE.

SURPRISES IN STORE FOR THE UNSUSPECTING FUGITIVE.

When the Montrose reaches Father Point to-day the passenger who will watch the approach of the Customs boat with the greatest eagerness will be Crippen, with his "son" at his side. As stated by Captain Kendall, he is in complete ignorance of all that has happened in the last ten days, and in the happy delusion that no one has recognised him or his companion on the Montrose, he will be anxious to get hold of a newspaper to learn, if possible, if he has succeeded in throwing the police off his scent. Cool, clever, and resourceful though he is, the "Dr." would be more than flesh and blood if he were not anxious as to the result of this first communication with land since July 20. He will suffer more than a slight uneasiness at the thought that the information of his flight from Antwerp may have been flashed across the ocean, either by cable or wireless, while the Montrose has been slowly making her way to the Gulf of St. Lawrence. As he leans over the side of the vessel among the other passengers he will, therefore, be keenly on the look-out for any sign of danger to himself in the visit of the Customs boat. The sight of a police uniform would instantly startle him into fears for his safety, and he has, as we know, a revolver in his pocket. Crippen will, however, see no police in uniform when the boat swings round to the side of the Montrose. He will see the Customs officers and one or two assistants in their usual innocent garb. Among those assistants will be a couple of Canadian police officers and Inspector Dew, who, as stated, landed on Friday, the Laurentic, in which he made the voyage, having easily outdistanced the Montrose. Mr. Dew will be so disguised that "his own mother would not recognise him." He will take care, also, not to force himself on the attention of Crippen till the proper moment. Arrangements have been made with Captain Kendall as to the manner in which the location of Crippen and his companion will be pointed out when once the police are on board. The captain will be careful not to lose sight of the suspects when the Montrose comes to anchor, and he will be able to indicate at once where they are. Inspector Dew will choose an opportunity of identifying Crippen without revealing himself too prominently, and if he gives to the Canadian police the signal that he is the man wanted, the arrest will be made at once. From the moment Crippen is arrested until Quebec is reached, he will be watched night and day by police officers, lest he should attempt suicide. The authorisation given to Detective Gavreau, of the Canadian police, who will be actually in charge of the fugitives, reads:—"If sure of your people, make the arrest, and keep the prisoners in separate cabins, and make certain that no chance is given either of committing suicide."

INSP. DEW'S RECEPTION.

THE FIRST PASSENGER TO LAND AT FATHER POINT FOR MANY YEARS.

The following cable was received from Reuter's correspondent at Father Point yesterday, describing the arrival of Inspector Dew:—

"At half-past three, a cloud of smoke on the eastern horizon betokened the approach of the Laurentic. All was astir in this spot beloved of summer visitors, and the home of pilots.

"The Government tug Eureka was almost uncomfortably crowded with newspaper men, artists, and other privileged persons. The Laurentic towered high above the little tug, and her sides were lined with passengers, evidently curious to know the reason of the invasion from the shore.

"Among those on board the Eureka was the inspecting medical officer of the Immigration Department, who was specially commissioned to board the Laurentic here, in order to enable Inspector Dew to land.

"The regulations are that no passengers shall be allowed to go on shore from incoming steamers until their arrival at the quarantine station at Grosse Isle.

"The doctor had not been many minutes on the Laurentic when Inspector Dew came down the gangway wearing a heavy tweed overcoat and a cloth cap.

"He found himself the centre of attraction on the tug, and had to face a regular battery of cameras.

"The pressmen crowded round the inspector to interview him, but he would only say that he had nothing to communicate.

"On landing Inspector Dew was driven to the house of Chief Constable McCarthy, where he will remain until the arrival of the Montrose, which, it is now stated, will get in this morning.

"The Laurentic will be detained at Grosse Isle, on account of the outbreak of measles on board reported by the ship's physician."

Inspector Dew, according to the correspondent, is the first passenger to land at Father Point for many years.

"A TOUGH PROPOSITION."

Already Inspector Dew is proving himself a "tough proposition" to the American and Canadian reporters, who are used to the less reserved methods of their own police. The special correspondent of the Central News at Father Point says Inspector Dew "has brought the silence, as well as the science, of Scotland Yard with him, and his manner towards pressmen is decidedly frosty. Two correspondents secured rooms in the hotel where he is staying, but no sooner did the fact become known to Mr. Dew than he went to the proprietor, and announced that if they remained there he should depart elsewhere. The pressmen went. Mr Dew last night paid visits to the Marconi and telegraph stations."

COURSE OF ACTION.

PROBABLE EXCLUSION OF THE DOCTOR AS AN "UNDESIRABLE" IMMIGRANT.

Rimouski, July 30.—At seven o'clock this morning the Montrose was reported off East Point, 280 miles distant. This should mean her arrival at Father Point at five o'clock to-morrow (Sunday morning), or noon at Greenwich.

As some doubt exists as to the legal position of Dr. Crippen and Miss Le Neve, the opinion was obtained to-day of Judge Chauvreau. He expressed the belief that, in view of the circumstances of the case, the procedure to be adopted will be that

MISS LE NEVE AS SHE NOW APPEARS.

Inspector Dew will give such information as will enable the immigration authorities to reject Dr. Crippen on his arrival at Quebec as an "undesirable."

This course obviates the possibility of legal complications, as immediately upon the order for their deportation being made, the two prisoners can be placed in charge of Inspector Dew for return to England by the next steamer.

In the course of conversation last night Inspector Dew mentioned his interview with Dr. Crippen on the day before the latter's disappearance, and recalled how in reply to his enquiry where Mrs. Crippen had been cremated, Dr. Crippen replied that owing to family jars his wife had taken her departure for California, where she intended to join some of her friends.

The local detectives who have been detailed to assist Inspector Dew in the arrest state that they have every reason to believe

(*Continued on page 3*).

ALIEN'S SECRET HOARD.

An inquest has been held on the body of a Roumanian named Maurice Gold, 60, who was found dead in bed at his lodgings in Bennett-street, St. Pancras. Medical evidence showed death to be due to heart failure while suffering from bronchitis and heart disease. A constable stated that in an old bag under the man's bed were found five £5 Bank of England notes, one French note for fifty francs, and a Post Office bankbook showing £50 balance.—Mr. Schroder stated that many people preferred to leave their money unprotected, thinking that it

STOP PRESS

CRIPPEN ARRESTED

DRAMATIC SCENE ABOARD THE MONTROSE.

FUGITIVES TAKEN INTO CUSTODY AT END OF VOYAGE.

Father Point (Rimouski), July 31. Crippen and Le Neve have both been identified and arrested.—Reuter.

INSPECTOR DEW BOARDS LINER

Father Point, July 31.

By special arrangement Inspector Dew this morning boarded the steamer Montrose from a rowing boat leaving the numerous newspaper correspondents to follow in the Government tender Eureka.

The object of this proceeding was to enable the detective to make the arrest without perviously arousing the suspicions of "Dr." Crippen and Miss Le Neve.—Reuter.

Mr. Dew was disguised as a pilot.—Central News.

FINAL PLANS FOR ARREST.

HOOTS FROM LINER SIGNAL CRIPPEN'S SEIZURE.

Earlier came tidings of the plans finally made for the arrest as follows:—

Father Point, July 31.

After eight hours' interruption, indirect communication with the Montrose via Fame Point and Clark City was restored at eight o'clock this evening.

At 12.30, when the Montrose was 70 miles east of Fame Point, Captain Kendall telegraphed that the position was unchanged.

Later he informed Inspector Dew that the suspects were becoming increasingly nervous.

Late last night Inspector Dew informed the pressmen that, owing to the necessity for the absence of any fuss in connection with the identification of the suspects, he and the Canadian police would get out in a small boat as soon as the Montrose arrived.

When the police had completed that business, the vessel would give two hoots as a signal that the tender might bring the pressmen aboard.—Central News.

EMERGED FROM FOG.

WATCHERS IN EARLY HOURS DESCRY MONTROSE APPROACH.

Another message describes the long and weary vigil kept ashore by the army of policemen and pressmen, and now the liner at length loomed in sight, emerging from the fog that had hung over the great river.

Father Point, July 31, 8 a.m.—The dense fog which set in at half past eleven last night began to lift at a quarter to eight this morning. Above the roar of the Father Point foghorn was heard a steamer's whistle, and the watchers on the shore took this as an indication of the proximity of the Montrose. If the fog continues to lift it is expected that the vessel will be off Father Point soon after eight o'clock.—Reuter.

TO THE MONTROSE.

HAND OF THE LAW ON MAN FROM HILLDROP-CRESCENT.

At 8 a.m. the Montrose had hove in sight. Fifteen minutes later the beginning of the end had come, so far as Crippen's flight were concerned.

Father Point, July 31, 8.15 a.m.—The tender has left to meet the Montrose, which has been sighted in the Gulf. The weather is very foggy.—Reuter.

ON THE WAY TO QUEBEC

FIRST STAGE IN TRIAL OF CRIPPEN FOR HIS LIFE.

Following upon this message came the wireless telegram stating that the deed was done; that "Robinson's" nervousness was fully justified by his real character. Inspector Dew at once identified the "merchant" from Antwerp as Dr. Hawley Harvey Crippen, "the man wanted," and his companion as the typist, Miss Le Neve, and the Canadian officers at once acted upon the warrants in their possession. Inspector Dew at once informed his authorities, who issued the following official message:—

Scotland Yard at four o'clock this afternoon received official intimation from Chief Inspector Dew that:

"Crippen and Le Neve had been identified and arrested;

"And that they were now on their way to Quebec."

CRIPPEN AND WIRELESS ROMANCE.

A scientific interest attaches to the arrests. The long arm of the law has been lengthened by the Marconigram, and the captures now effected will long be remembered in connection with the development of wireless telegraphy.

EXCURSIONIST CUT TO [illegible]

At Chapel-en-le-Frith, James Thomas Burton, of Barnley, met with a terrible death early yesterday morning. He was on an excursion train which had stopped, and he alighted. In attempting to board the train while moving he fell, and, slipping underneath, was run over. His mangled remains were picked up and placed in the waiting room. A coroner's

THE OCEAN CHASE SHOWING THE POSITIONS OF THE TWO BOATS EACH DAY.

No.

THE WESTERN UNION TELEGRAPH COMPANY.

THE LARGEST TELEGRAPHIC SYSTEM IN EXISTENCE.

DIRECT ROUTE FOR ALL PARTS OF THE UNITED STATES. CANADA, CENTRAL AMERICA, WEST INDIES, SOUTH AMERICA, & VIA THE PACIFIC CABLE TO AUSTRALIA, NEW ZEALAND, FANNING, FIJI AND NORFOLK ISLANDS.

ATLANTIC CABLES direct to CANADA and to NEW YORK CITY.

DIRECT WIRES TO ALL THE PRINCIPAL CITIES.

No.	Service Instructions.	Time Received.
4228	Col	8.46
	Handed in at	No. of Words.
	Montrose via Father Point Que	10

WESTERN UNION TELEGRAPH Co. 31 JUL 1910 EFFINGHAM HOUSE, ARUNDEL ST, STRAND, W.C.

CABLE OFFICE: EFFINGHAM HOUSE, ARUNDEL ST, STRAND. Telephone No. 1113 Gerrard.

To Handcuffs Ldn Eng

Crippen and Leneve arrested wire later

Dew

The public are requested to hand in their replies at the Company's Stations, where free receipts are given for the amounts charged.

CABLE ADDRESSES ARE REGISTERED FREE OF CHARGE.

No inquiry respecting this Message can be attended to without the production of this Paper.

Punters who had backed the odds-on favourite, the *Laurentic*, collected their winnings on 31 July; the 'winning-distance bets' were null and void, for the race ended just before Quebec, at a place called Father Point. Walter Dew, disguised as a ship's pilot, boarded the *Montrose*, took one look at the clean-shaven and unbespectacled 'Mr Robinson', and uttered the polite but implication-laden words: 'Good morning, Dr Crippen.' Ethel was lying on her bunk at the time; she was reading a romantic novel entitled *Audrey's Recompense*. A few minutes later, Dew and some Canadian policemen entered the cabin without knocking, so startling Ethel that, having emitted a scream, she fainted.

Following extradition proceedings in Quebec, the couple were brought back to England. Crippen's main concern was that Ethel ('wifie,' he called her, while her pet-name for him was 'hub') should get off scot-free. The slender chance he had of escaping the gallows was scuppered by two lawyers: his solicitor, a rascal named Alfred Newton, gave more thought to the selling of phony 'Crippen confessions' than to the saving of his client's life; and Richard Muir, the leading Crown counsel, ensured that by the time that Crippen was tried in October 1910, virtually every component of the case for the prosecution was secure.

(Below)
From the originals of drawings made during the committal proceedings by William Harrison.

(Below, left)
A photograph of 39 Hilldrop Crescent taken in November 1910, and showing its new tenant, a musical-hall artist named Sandy McNab, in the doorway.

39
DR CRIPPEN
LISTENS TO THE EVIDENCE
MISS
LE NEVE

The demand for tickets for the 'show' at the Central Criminal Court (on this occasion true to its unofficial title of 'Theatre Royal, Old Bailey') far outstripped supply. During the entire limited run — of five days, as it turned out — the forensic equivalent of a House-Full board was on display at the gallery entrance. Dramatists and stage performers loomed large among the spectators, and on one of the mornings the actress Phyllis Dare, recently dubbed 'The Belle of Mayfair', sat beside the judge, the Sword of Justice seeming to be an additional and excessive pin in her picture-hat. *The Times* thundered:

> A Criminal Court is not a show room, nor is such a trial of the nature of a *matinée*; the Old Bailey is not a place to which fashionable ladies may fitly go in search of the latest sensation, where actors may hope to pick up suggestions as to a striking gesture or a novel expression, and where descriptive writers may look for good copy.

Four days after Crippen was sentenced to death, Ethel was tried as an accessory and acquitted. A month or so later, on the morning of Crippen's execution at Pentonville Gaol, she again set sail for North America; this time, while being dressed aptly to her sex, she masqueraded as 'Miss Allen'.

She was fairly well provided for. As well as being Crippen's sole legatee, she had received payments from popular papers for publicized-as-exclusive stories, for snaps of herself in her *Montrose* outfit, and for the right to publish some of her lover's letters to her from the condemned cell.

She stayed in New York for a few days, then travelled to Toronto, where she reverted to earning her living as a typist. Shortly before Crippen's death, he had asked her to assume his name, and she had promised to. Presumably because she decided that calling herself 'Ethel Crippen' would be a contradiction in terms of her desire to escape from her past, she compromised by taking Crippen's middle name, so becoming Ethel *Harvey*. Returning to England, to London, in 1916, she became a typist in the offices of Hampton's furniture store in Trafalgar Square. Stanley Smith, a bookkeeper at Hampton's, shyly courted her, plucked up courage to propose marriage, and was accepted. The couple rented a house at Croydon, on the southern outskirts of the metropolis, and in time were blessed with children, a son and a daughter. Years passed: the children married . . . Stanley died from a heart attack before reaching retirement-age . . . in 1943 Ethel became eligible for an old-age pension from the State. In the summer of 1967 she was taken into hospital, terminally ill.

Nearly fifty-seven years before, her letters to Crippen had, at his request, been buried with him. Legend has it that Ethel's last request was that a locket holding a faded likeness of 'Dearest Hub' should be placed close to her heart before the coffin was closed.

The legend provides such a fitting end to the story that it seems a shame to say that it is untrue. In 1985 Ethel's children were traced. They had looked after her in her waning years, putting up with her frequent bouts of cantankerousness; they remembered her as an ordinary little woman — practical, undemonstrative, and scornful of romance. Till they were traced, they were unaware that their mother had once been known as Ethel Le Neve — that for a few months, three-quarters of a century before, she had been perhaps the most famous woman in the world.

Ethel was always good at keeping secrets.

Mrs Ethel Smith.

The tall chair, of the sort associated with Dickensian clerks, stands in a shadowed corner of the Black Museum. It is not there to be sat upon; indeed, any visitor who, tired towards the end of a tour, thought of using the chair as a resting-place would, coming closer to it, change his mind — perhaps because of the grubbiness of the struts, but certainly because of the gaping hole where the raffia seat used to be.

The insufficient chair is a memento of what the press would have called The Furnace Murder Case even if the name of the murderer had not made that title entirely apt. The case is not among those that the Metropolitan Police look back upon with pride. Mistakes were made; lessons were learned from them.

Shortly before eight o'clock on the evening of Tuesday, 3 January 1933, firemen were called to a builder's yard in Hawley Crescent, Camden Town, where a large shed was ablaze. By the time the fire-engine arrived, men living near the yard had broken down the two doors of the shed — one leading into a storage room, the other into an office — and dowsed the flames. Firemen, masked against the pitch-black, acrid smoke, entered the office, which was by far the worst affected of the rooms. There, seated on a tall chair by an equally tall home-made table, was a dead body. When the body was dragged into the yard, it was seen to be male. Little more could be said of it — not by the firemen, at any rate — for the flames had licked the hair from the head, the features from the face; much of the clothing had been burnt away, and parts of the rest were fused with the melted skin of the torso and arms. After the body had been removed to St Pancras Mortuary a pencilled note was found pinned to a table in the storage room. The note read: 'Goodbye to all. No work, no money. Sam J. Furnace.'

The young detective assigned to investigate the incident must have thought it odd that Sam J. Furnace had left an apparent suicide-note in a shed that, so it seemed, he had intended should be burnt to the ground, with himself part of the debris. But the detective never thought, not for a moment, that any other aspect of the incident was at all peculiar. Having ascertained that the yard was rented as the premises of a small building firm, and that the proprietor of that firm, Samuel James Furnace, aged forty-two, was extremely hard up, at his wits' end to know how he could support his wife and two children, let alone pay off sundry creditors, the detective concluded that the body found in the shed was that of Furnace. As a matter of routine, he arranged for a man who lodged at the Furnaces' house off Haverstock Hill to view the remains — and, without wondering at the lodger's positiveness, accepted his positive identification of them as those of his 'old friend

(Overleaf)
The scene of the fire.

Sam'. The divisional police-surgeon, as uninquiring as the detective, glanced at the remains and stated that death was due to burning.

That would probably have been the end of the matter had not Bentley Purchase, the coroner for St Pancras, questioned the notion that a man who had decided to burn himself to death would start the fire, seat himself — and remain seated. Purchase went to the mortuary and, remedying one of the police surgeon's several omissions, turned the body face-downward. There was a bullet-hole near the top of the lumbar region.

Consequent to Purchase's observation, the remnants of the dead man's clothing were examined. Among other charred and waterlogged items that came to light were a wallet, empty of cash but containing bits of correspondence on which the name 'Spatchett' appeared, and a Post Office savings book, made out to a Mr W. Spatchett. The investigators soon linked those finds with a missing-person report concerning Walter Spatchett, a 28-year-old collector of rents for a firm of estate managers in Camden Town, who had not been seen since the late afternoon of Monday, 2 January. Spatchett's employers had, over the past few months, given odd jobs to Samuel Furnace, and thus Spatchett and Furnace had become friends — and thus Spatchett had joined the list of Furnace's creditors. When last seen, in the vicinity of Hawley Crescent, he was carrying afternoon takings of about thirty-five pounds. Any doubt that the dead body was his was dispelled by his dentist, who, having been brought to the mortuary, looked for and at once recognized a misshapen tooth in the upper jaw.

Meanwhile, the police gathered further information about Samuel Furnace: for instance, that shortly after the Great War he had served as an auxiliary policeman — a Black and Tan — in the south of Ireland, and that he had never returned the Webley revolver that was issued to him; late in December 1932, he had scraped together money for the renewal of his life-insurance — the policy for which would have become null and void if he had committed suicide prior to midnight on New Year's Eve.

The first official press-release on the murder case made no mention of murder: Furnace, who was described, was said to be 'wanted to be interviewed' only in regard to the fire. But, that discreet wording having been ignored by the press, subsequent 'wanted notices' — a series of them — were topped with the word MURDER in the biggest and boldest of type. The search for Furnace — referred to in newpaper headlines as 'History's Greatest Manhunt' — illustrates the fact that, although the police are dependent upon public co-operation, a surfeit of it in

& SHOWROOMS
HENLY HOUSE
EUSTON ROAD
Phone Mus 7734
WORKS

METROPOLITAN POLICE.

MURDER

WANTED

For the wilful murder of **Walter Spatchett,** whose dead body was found on the 3rd January, 1933, in a shed at the rear of 30, Hawley Crescent, Camden Town, London, occupied as an office by the wanted man.

SAMUEL JAMES FURNACE, born 1890, about 6 feet, well built and set up, complexion fair, hair fair (thin in front), eyes hazel, full face, square jaw, gunshot wounds on left leg and both arms, long scar on right bicep shewing marks of 13 stitches, 1 tooth missing in front upper jaw which may be replaced by false tooth. When last seen on the 7th January, 1933, was wearing a brown suit, black shoes, light trench coat with sliding belt, brown and red check lining edged with brown leatherette binding. He has also a brown overcoat, a grey soft felt hat and a bluish coloured cap. Possesses a fair sum of money. In possession of a revolver. He has passed in the name of Raymond Rogers but might assume any other name.

He might seek employment in the building and decorating trade as a foreman or workman, or in the mercantile marine as a steward or seaman and may take lodgings at a boarding house, apartment house, coffee house, cottage, or any place taking male lodgers.

A warrant for his arrest has been issued and extradition will be applied for.

Any person having knowledge of his whereabouts is requested to inform the nearest Police Station at once.

Metropolitan Police Office
New Scotland Yard S.W.1.
[illegible] January, 193[illegible]

TRENCHARD,
The Commissioner of Police of the Metropolis.

Printed by the Receiver for the Metropolitan Police District, New Scotland Yard, London, S.W.1 [illegible]

a particular case can cause an investigation to go galloping off in all directions. It appears that the high-ranking Scotland Yard detective in overall charge of the Furnace case was, on the one hand, dogmatic in his assumptions from certain items of information regarding the fugitive's whereabouts, and, on the other, not strict enough in ensuring that each of his helpers knew what the rest had done and were doing, thereby avoiding duplication of effort — and, even more important, increasing the likelihood that numbers of 'leads' from diverse sources would be linked, making a sum greater than the parts.

On Friday, the second full day of the search, the police learned that, about the time of the discovery of the fire, Furnace (calling himself Roy Rogers) had booked into a lodging house in Camden Town; he had stayed there two nights, till Thursday morning, when he had told the landlady that he needed to go to the Essex town of Southend-on-Sea, but that he would return; during the afternoon the landlady had received a telegram that was marked as having been handed in at the main post office in Southend: 'BROTHER ILL RE-LET ROOM RETURNING MONDAY — R. ROGERS.' Following a telephone call from Lord Trenchard, the Commissioner of the Metropolitan Police, to the Chief Constable of Essex, road-blocks were set up around Southend, and the railway station and the sea-front patrolled, while officers, most of them brought in from other parts of the county, visited hotels and guest-houses in the town. This operation was halted by the senior Scotland Yard detective directly after it was learned that Furnace had stayed at a guest-house near the railway station from late on Thursday but had left, in great haste, at midday on Saturday. The detective's unbudgable assumption — which indicates that he was not entirely confident of the Essex Constabulary's cordoning — was that Furnace had not only fled from the guest-house but also from the town. He was by now suffering from influenza, and so it may be that his mind was deliriously confused towards the certainty that Furnace was no longer in Southend by the continuing stream of reported sightings of him in other places: on each day since the manhunt had become front-page news, Scotland Yard had received more than a hundred such communications — from as far north as Aberdeen, as far south as the Isle of Wight; and latterly, after publications of details of the crime and the search in foreign papers, from places in Europe. Or perhaps the detective had some excellent reason for believing an anonymous tip-off that Furnace, back in London after his stay in Southend, intended to drive to the south coast, there to board a vessel bound for France. On Sunday, but only after Lord Trenchard had given his approval, the Metropolitan

Police mounted the most extensive stop-and-identify operation in its history: while officers on foot and in wireless-cars combed Camden Town, many more were stationed at road-blocks in a quarter-circle around the southern suburbs of the capital. A dozen Furnace look-alikes, unable at once to establish their respective identities, were held until they were able to do so — but when, late at night, the operation was called off, the real Samuel Furnace was still at large.

The BBC had been in existence for ten years (the 'C' originally standing for Company, but since 1927 for Corporation). There is uncertainty as to whether, during that decade, the police had ever requested the broadcasting of an appeal for assistance in a murder case — and, for that matter, as to whether the BBC had ever offered to help in that way. The first time that such an appeal was broadcast was on the evening of Monday, 9 January 1933, when, as part of a regular news-bulletin, an announcer spoke of Samuel Furnace, saying that he was 'wanted for wilful murder' and reading out a description of him before asking 'any person having knowledge of his whereabouts [to] inform the police at once'.

After the broadcast the daily volume of reported sightings almost doubled; there was an even greater upsurge of offers of co-operation from people who claimed to be supernaturally gifted as fugitive-finders, and a still greater increase in the number of catch-me-if-you-can messages — some from almost sane people who thought it rather fun to pretend that they were Furnace, some from people who, despite overwhelming evidence to the contrary, were quite convinced that they were.

On the second Saturday morning, Charles Tuckfield visited the police station in Kentish Town, North London, that was being used as 'search headquarters'. He gained the distinct impression that, though he should not have been expected, the detectives were waiting for him. Explaining that Furnace was his brother-in-law, he handed over a letter that he had received earlier that day — and gained the distinct impression that the detectives were already aware of its contents. The envelope was post-marked 'SOUTHEND'. The letter read as follows:

Dear Charlie,

Just a line to you in hope that I shall be able to see a friend before I end it all.

I am writing to you because I know they will watch May [Furnace's wife] for a long time.

I am at Southend, quite near the station, making out I have been ill with the 'flu, so have been able to stay in all the week.

I am far from well through want of sleep. I don't think I have slept one hour since the accident happened. I will tell you all about it when I see you.

Now, what I want you to do is not for me, but for May and the kiddies. My days are numbered. I want you to come down Sunday, on your own, please. Catch the 10.35 from Harringay Park [close to Tuckfield's home]: that gets you down in Southend at 12.8. Come out of the station, walk straight across the road, and down the opposite road; walk down on the left side.

I will see you. I am not giving my address in case you are followed. Just walk slowly down.

If you come will you bring me 15½ shirt and two collars — any colour will do. Also one pair of socks, dark ones, and one comb. I think that is all now. Don't let anyone know, only Nell [Tuckfield's wife]. If possible say you have to work or something.

Best of luck. Mine is gone.

H. FARMER

On the Sunday, having been instructed by the detectives to do exactly as Furnace, alias Farmer, had asked, Tuckfield walked along Whitegate Road, Southend — two blocks from the road in which Furnace had lodged at the start of his stay in that town. A sheet of paper bearing the name SAM appeared at the ground-floor window of No. 11 — and disappeared as soon as Tuckfield hurried towards the house. He remained inside for an hour and a half.

During that time, detectives gathered at both ends of the road; and soon after one of them, posing as a busker, had wandered past the house, slyly examining it as he played *Roses Are Blooming in Picardy* on a borrowed fiddle, several of those at the railway-station end crept through the front gardens and gained access to No. 9 — the residents of which, once recovered from the shock of being outnumbered by armed detectives, told them that No. 11 was occupied by Mrs Charlotte Shaw, an elderly widow who took in paying guests.

A few minutes after Charles Tuckfield had left No. 11 by the front door, a posse of detectives entered through the kitchen. As soon as Mrs Shaw had meekly done as she was told, which was to push open the door of the front room, say 'Did you call?' and, without waiting for a reply, step aside, the detectives rushed into that room — so much to the astonishment of Samuel Furnace, who was sitting in an armchair by the fire, that he let fall, among other things, a cigarette that he had been smoking and a copy of the *Sunday People* in which he had been reading about himself.

He was hastily searched and found to be unarmed. A detective fetched him his overcoat and, after checking that the pockets were empty, told him to put it on. Handcuffed, he was driven back to London. During the journey he admitted to the shooting of Walter Spatchett but insisted that his revolver had gone off by accident; as the car passed along Camden Road he indicated a stretch of the Regent's Canal, saying that he had thrown the gun there (it was subsequently fished up). In a written statement he made at Kentish Town Police Station, he said that, following the 'accidental' shooting in his office on the night of Monday, 2 January, 'I realised my position and lost my head': he wrapped tarpaulin around his friend's body, bundled it between the legs of the work-table, and went home: next day he worked in the office until his employees, three men and a boy, had left, and then methodically carried out a sequence of tasks that culminated in the touching of a lighted match to paraffin oil.

After he had signed the not entirely credible statement, he turned down the offer of a meal; all he wanted, he said, was 'a spot of shut-eye'. Ever since his enforced departure from Southend, he had kept his overcoat on. He was still wearing it when he was locked in cell No. 3.

Throughout the night, a police-constable periodically peered through the judas-hole in the door of the cell. Furnace always appeared to be sound asleep. But when, at seven o'clock in the morning, the constable made his final inspection prior to going off duty, he saw Furnace standing by the far wall — saw that he had ripped the lining from the bottom hem of his coat and was holding a small green bottle. By the time the constable entered the cell, Furnace was spreadeagled on the stone floor. He was screaming — but trying desperately not to scream, for that increased the searing pain in his throat. The bottle was lying in a corner. It had contained hydrochloric acid. He had bought the acid — generally called spirits of salts — on Twelfth Night, soon after his arrival in Southend.

He was rushed to St Pancras Hospital. A doctor there realized at once that there was no way of saving him — that the only hope for him was that his suffering, eased by morphine, would soon be over. It lasted till the early hours of the next day.

Two inquests followed. At the end of one of them, the jury brought in the verdict that Samuel Furnace had committed suicide; the other resulted in the verdict that Walter Spatchett had been wilfully murdered by Furnace. Both hearings were conducted by Bentley Purchase — which, poetically speaking, was proper, considering that if he had not been perplexed by a report that a man had sat down to his own burning, there might well have been just one inquest, to all intents and purposes on somebody who was quite healthy at the time.

THE DAILY MIRROR, Monday, January 16, 1933.

Daily Mirror

THE DAILY PICTURE NEWSPAPER WITH THE LARGEST NET SALE

No. 9,094 Registered at the G.P.O. as a Newspaper. MONDAY, JANUARY 16, 1933 One Penny

NEW TEST SENSATION —Page 3

WIRELESS PAGE 20 AMUSEMENTS PAGE 20

FIRESIDE ARREST OF FURNACE

Exclusive "Daily Mirror" Story of His Life in Hiding at a Southend Boarding House

CHARGED WITH MURDER AFTER SEARCH THAT LASTED ELEVEN DAYS

After one of the sternest and most far-flung man-hunts on record, Samuel James Furnace, the Chalk Farm builder, was arrested yesterday while seated by the fireside in a Southend boarding-house.

He had been in the house for nine out of the eleven days on which the police were searching for him. His landlady, Mrs. Charlotte Susan Shaw, a widow of sixty, thought he was recovering from the 'flu.

Furnace, who was brought handcuffed to London last night, was charged with the murder on January 3 of Walter Spatchett, the young rent collector, whose charred body was found in a shed used by Furnace as an office at the back of a house in Hawley-crescent, Chalk Farm, N.W. Furnace will appear at Marylebone Police Court this morning.

"MR. FARMER OF LONDON"

Landlady Tells How She Nursed a Supposed Invalid

(EXCLUSIVE)

When a *Daily Mirror* reporter talked to Mrs. Shaw last night he foun l her still bewildered by the swift turn of the days events.

"The whole thing has been a terrible shock to me," she said. "Furnace had been so exceptionally pleasant all the time he had been at my house. I thought he was an invalid and I had treated him as one, and did my best to look after him.

"He came to my house a week last Saturday. He seemed a quiet, presentable sort of man, and when he asked me for a room I had no hesitation in letting one to him.

"He told me then that he was convalescent. 'I am just getting over a severe attack of influenza, Mrs. Shaw,' he said, 'and the doctor has sent me down here to recuperate.'

Wrapped in Blankets

"At the time he was looking pale, though not noticeably so, but as the days went on he seemed to get worse.

All the time he was with me he only left his room twice. On each occasion it was in the morning, and then he went out of doors, but only for fifteen or twenty minutes.

"As time went on he seemed to get more ill and I became very sorry for him. On several occasions I took him tempting foods and tried to persuade him to eat, and more than once I wrapped him round with blankets and urged him to keep himself warm.

(Continued on page 2)

Mrs. Shaw, landlady of the boarding-house in which Furnace was found. She states that she looked after him "like a mother."

The boarding-house where Furnace was living for the past week. He stayed indoors, saying he was unwell.

Samuel Furnace.

An aerial view of Southend-on-Sea, showing: (A to B) Whitegate-road, where Furnace was found and arrested, (C) the L.M.S. railway station, (D) Alexandra-street, in which the police station is situated, (E) the beginning of High-street and (F) the pier.

Walter Spatchett, victim of the Chalk Farm blazing shed tragedy. Furnace has been charged with his murder.

MARKS OF CAIN

(Opposite)
Alfred Stratton's right thumbprint (see page 178).

Lives of great crooks all remind us,
We may do a stretch of time;
And, departing, leave behind us
Fingerprints on the tracks of crime.

A parody (circa 1910) of a stanza from Longfellow's *'A Psalm of Life'*

Of the sciences that, often or occasionally, are turned to forensic ends,[1] dactylography, the study of fingerprints, is unique in the sense that it is carried out by policemen or by auxiliary workers who have been trained and who are supervised by members of the police force.

Though there is argument, unlikely ever to be resolved, as to who among the Victorian pioneers of fingerprinting deserves the title of founding father, there is no doubt at all that it was Edward Henry who, by incorporating ideas that he could call his own with some that he had cribbed, came up with the first practical system of telling one digital impression from others. It has been suggested that Henry was fortunate in that he did right things at the right times, but the same could be said of most great innovators: chance favours the prepared mind.

Born in 1850, the son of a doctor, he completed his education at University College, London, and then joined the Indian civil service as an assistant magistrate-collector, and worked his way up until, in 1891, he was appointed inspector-general of police in Bengal. His predecessor had instituted a method of registering and identifying habitual criminals that was a variation on the 'anthropometric system' devised by the French criminologist Alphonse Bertillon — a system that relied upon (*a*) the recording of measurements of bony structures in the body, (*b*) the production of a *portrait parlé*, that being a pair of photographs, full-face and profile, which were cut into sections and mounted so that particular

1. The sciences range from Anatomy to Zoology, with few of the intervening initial-letters excepted. (X is represented by Xylography, the study of the structure of wood — which was employed, most famously, in America in 1934, towards the solution of the kidnapping and murder, nearly three years before, of Charles Lindbergh, Jr., the infant son of the fêted aviator. Following the discovery of evidence against a German-born carpenter, Bruno Hauptmann, a 'wood technologist' named Arthur Koehler, who had been working on the case almost from its beginning, proved that sections of a home-made ladder used in the kidnapping had been cut from the attic-floor of Hauptmann's home in the Bronx, New York City. Hauptmann was convicted on 13 February 1935 and, after a series of appeals, executed on 3 April 1936.)

In Britain, much of the extra-medical scientific investigation of crime is conducted within the ten forensic science laboratories, of which the largest is that of the Metropolitan Police. Founded in 1935, at the Hendon police training

features could be studied. Within a few months of his appointment, Henry modified the method he had inherited; still not satisfied, he made further modifications — and then, influenced by recently published articles and books on fingerprints (many of those works discussing the subject in the context of ethnology or of Darwinian theories of evolution), and perhaps having read press reports that convicts in Argentina were being fingerprinted, he instructed that record cards were to include left-thumb impressions (that digit chosen both because of its size and in the belief that, as most people were right-handed, its ridges were likely to be relatively unworn). While on leave in England in 1894, he gathered information on developments in the fields of data-collection and identification, and he returned to Calcutta with the determination to supplant *bertillonage* with a fingerprinting system. Over the next couple of years, with considerable help from native police officers, he devised a classification of the 'arch', 'loop' and 'whorl' patterns of prints, and then applied for an independent committee to inquire into the relative merits of the existing system and his proposed fingerprints-only one. The committee's recommendations were entirely in his favour, and, as a result, the Government of India directed that the 'Henry system' be adopted throughout the country. By the end of the second year of the period of transition, Henry was able to report considerable success.

Meanwhile, in England, there was growing criticism of the *bertillonage*/fingerprints method used in the Anthropometric Office at Scotland Yard. Towards the end of 1899, the Home Secretary appointed a committee, chaired by Lord Belper, 'to examine the working of the method of Identification of Criminals by Measurement and Finger Prints, and the administrative arrangements for carrying on the system'. Shortly after the committee began hearing evidence, Henry travelled to England — ostensibly for the sole purpose of

---

college, the Metropolitan Police Forensic Science Laboratory was moved to Whitehall in 1948, to Holborn in 1965, and to its present location in Lambeth, south of the Thames, in 1974. The Director is responsible to the Commissioner through the Assistant Commissioner (Specialist Operations); operationally, the laboratory communicates directly with officers of both the Metropolitan and the City of London forces who submit material to it. The two hundred or more scientists, all civilian, are divided into four sections: *General & Administration*, which includes departments of ballistics and of questioned documents. *Chemistry I* — 'general chemistry' (examination of contact-traces of, for instance, paint and tool-marks); 'physics and metallurgy' (chiefly concerned with traffic accidents); fire investigation. *Chemistry II*: among other responsibilities, analysis of drugs and toxic substances; the use of magnifying/analysing electron microscopy equipment on behalf of Locard's Law — that the slightest contact between two objects caused an exchange of material between them — and for the examination of gunshot

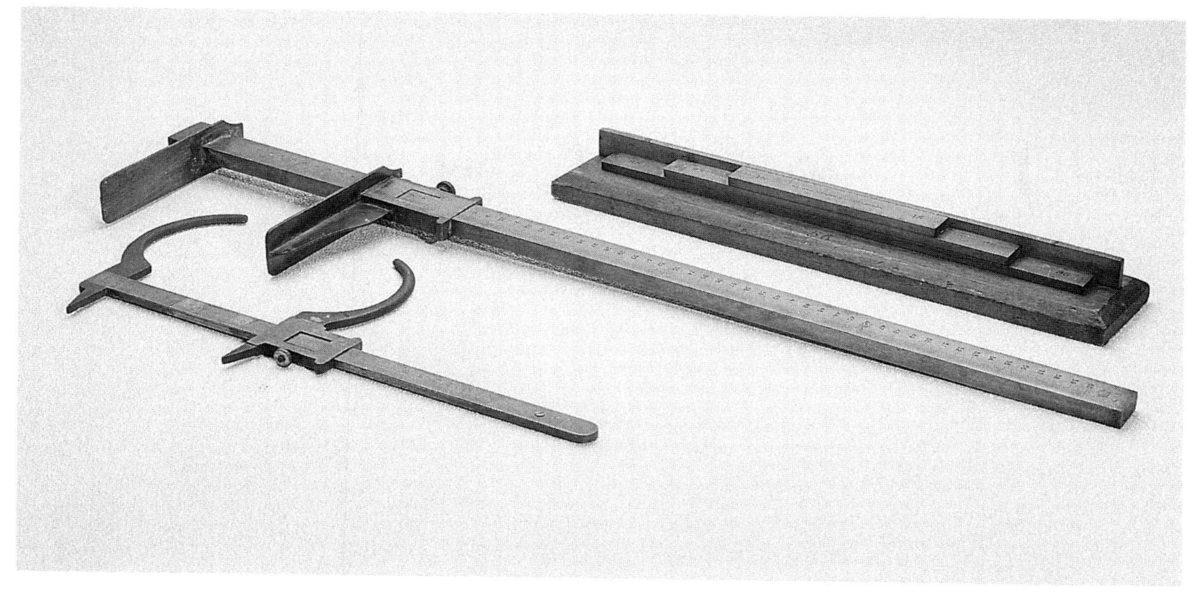

'Anthropometric system' callipers, for measuring bony parts.

addressing the British Association for the Advancement of Science on the subject of 'Finger Prints and the Detection of Crime in India' — and, at the personal invitation of Lord Belper, gave the committee an account of his system; early in the following year each member received an advance copy of a book, *Classification and Uses of Finger Prints*, which Henry had written at the request of the Government of India. In December the committee issued its report. Unobtrusive in the centre of the last, long paragraph — which was made long by the insistence, over and over again, that the existing system was not to be discarded unless and until a replacement was shown to be more efficient — was the recommendation that 'active steps should be taken towards the immediate introduction of the Henry System'.

The decision to implement that recommendation was taken early in 1901 — at exactly the right time so far as Henry was

---

residues; research and development. *Biology*: again with Locard in mind, the largest sections seek to find and classify textile fibres, fragments of vegetation, etc., and — usually in regard to offences against the person — to establish the grouping of blood (by the use of immunological techniques and biochemical phenotyping of enzymes and proteins, such grouping is becoming more and more accurate; at present, six groupings of semen are possible, and three of saliva).

The laboratory deals with around 30,000 cases each year.

There is a 'police liaison' group, headed by a detective chief superintendent; those members working in the laboratory are responsible for receiving material, checking that it is correctly described and that nothing unnecessary has been sent, explaining the scientists' requirements to investigating officers and the needs of the investigators to the scientists, keeping track of exhibits, arranging for court appearances; those members acting as scenes-of-crime officers are responsible for collecting physical evidence, packing it, and forwarding it to their colleagues at the laboratory.

A 'Spy' cartoon of Edward Henry; from Vanity Fair, *5 October 1905.*

concerned. Robert Anderson, the Assistant Commissioner of the Metropolitan Police responsible for the CID, was due to retire. Henry applied for the job, and was accepted. On 1 July, within a few weeks of his arrival, he set up a Fingerprint Branch, staffing it with three detectives from the Anthropometric Office: Inspector Charles Stedman, Sergeant Charles Stockley Collins and Constable Frederick Hunt. By the end of the year, nearly a hundred identifications had been made: more than had been achieved by the Anthropometric Office in a similar period — and, individually, with far greater speed. The Home Office was encouraged to extend, in stages, the registration of criminals beyond those with one or more previous convictions, eventually to include anyone sentenced to a term of imprisonment of more than a month without the option of paying a fine.

In his published memoirs[1] (*see Bibliography*), Melville MacNaghten, the old-Etonian Chief Constable of the CID, recalls that, in 1902,

> as the first Derby Day drew nigh after our 'fingerprints' were in full swing, it was feared that we should not be able to fully utilise them on that occasion, inasmusch as offenders were taken in up till six or seven in the evening, and were dealt with summarily by the Petty Sessional Court at nine-thirty the next morning. Scotland Yard, however, determined not to be beaten in the matter; experts were sent to Epsom and then and there took the finger-prints of fifty-four men who were arrested for various offences on Derby Day. These impressions were taken up to the finger-print department that night. Two officers, who had been kept on reserve duty for that purpose, examined them, with the result that twenty-nine of these men were found to be old offenders. Their records and photographs were taken down to Epsom early the following morning by a chief inspector. When the 'arrests' appeared before the justices at half-past nine, they were confronted with a record of their previous convictions, with the result that they received summonses twice as long as would otherwise have been awarded.
>
> The first prisoner on this occasion gave his name as Green of Gloucester, and assured the interrogating magistrate that he had never been in trouble before, and that a racecourse was, up to this time, an unknown world to him. But up jumped the Chief Inspector, in answer to a question as to whether 'anything was known', and begged their worships to look at the papers and photograph, which proved the innocent to be Benjamin Brown of Birmingham, with some ten convictions to his discredit. 'Bless the finger-prints,' said Benjamin, with an oath; 'I knew they'd do me in!'

1. The book is dedicated to Henry: 'The best all-round policeman of the twentieth century — a man to whom London owes more than it knows.'

In 1902 the Fingerprint Branch, its staff increased to about a dozen, made 1722 identifications. The success of the Henry system was apparent. And in the short time that Henry had been at the Yard, his qualities as a leader, as an administrator, had been recognized: of those many detectives who had queried his appointment, only a few, they so devoted to their prejudices that they could no no more than rearrange them, continued to mutter that he was 'a policeman *only* at the fingertips'. In March 1903, upon the retirement of Colonel Sir Edward Bradford (who had himself served in India for many years prior to his becoming Commissioner in 1890), Henry was appointed as his successor. Ever afterwards, however — and notwithstanding the fact that he was created a baronet following his resignation in 1918 — he was referred to as 'Mr Fingerprints', a nickname that did not displease him.

Among the first to suffer at the hands of the fingerprint detectives, the brothers Fox deserve a mention — and perhaps some sympathy. If their brotherhood had been a mite less apparent, they would have found it difficult, neither being bright, to get away with the most rudimentary of illegal acts; but by making use of their evident brotherhood, they had enjoyed an uninterrupted prosperity that was the envy of other partners in crime. The Foxes, as you will have gathered, were identical twins: what was more, their voices were of similar timbre — and, just to add to the confusion, though one was named Ebenezer Albert, and the other plain Albert, they were both known as Albert. They worked as a team — but never together. Turn and turn about, while one carried out a theft, making sure that he was seen with the swag, the other advertised his own presence in some fairly faraway place; the thief ran towards his brother, but hid before reaching him — at about which time the brother started sauntering, and continued to saunter till the person or persons who had witnessed the thief's getaway 'recognized' him and effected his apprehension . . . for a crime that his advertised alibi proved he couldn't have committed. If, as sometimes happened, the thief-brother was subsequently apprehended, he added a neat touch to the scheme of rôle-reversal by insisting that the alibi claimed by his brother was actually *his* — and since there was no doubt that only one of the brothers could have committed the crime, the police, not knowing which was which, but knowing that they couldn't bring one charge against both of them, were obliged to let both of them off scot-free. The long-running doubles act soon ran into trouble after the introduction of the Henry system. As the

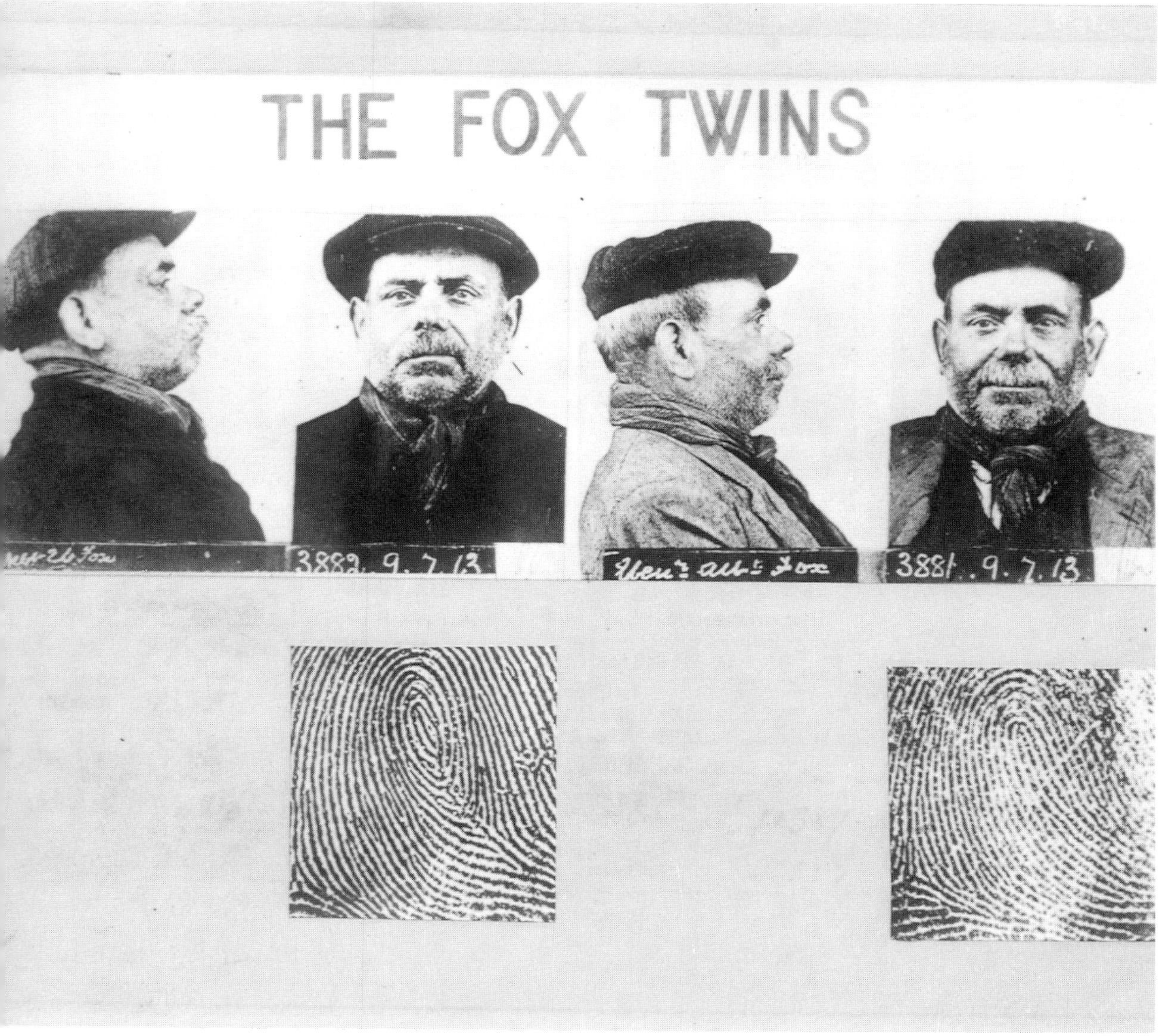

THE FOX TWINS

peas-in-a-pod duality of Albert and Albert stopped short at their wrists, 'dabs'[1] left by one or other of them at the scene of a crime — or at the scene of an alibi — were all that were needed to tell them apart. Either the Foxes' twinship was shown to be only skin-deep by their respective efforts, whenever just one of them was arrested, to 'shop' the other, or their attachment was such as to make concurrent imprisonment seem preferable to separation.

1. A colloquialism coined some time before 1926, when it was mentioned by Netley Lucas in his book *London and Its Criminals*.

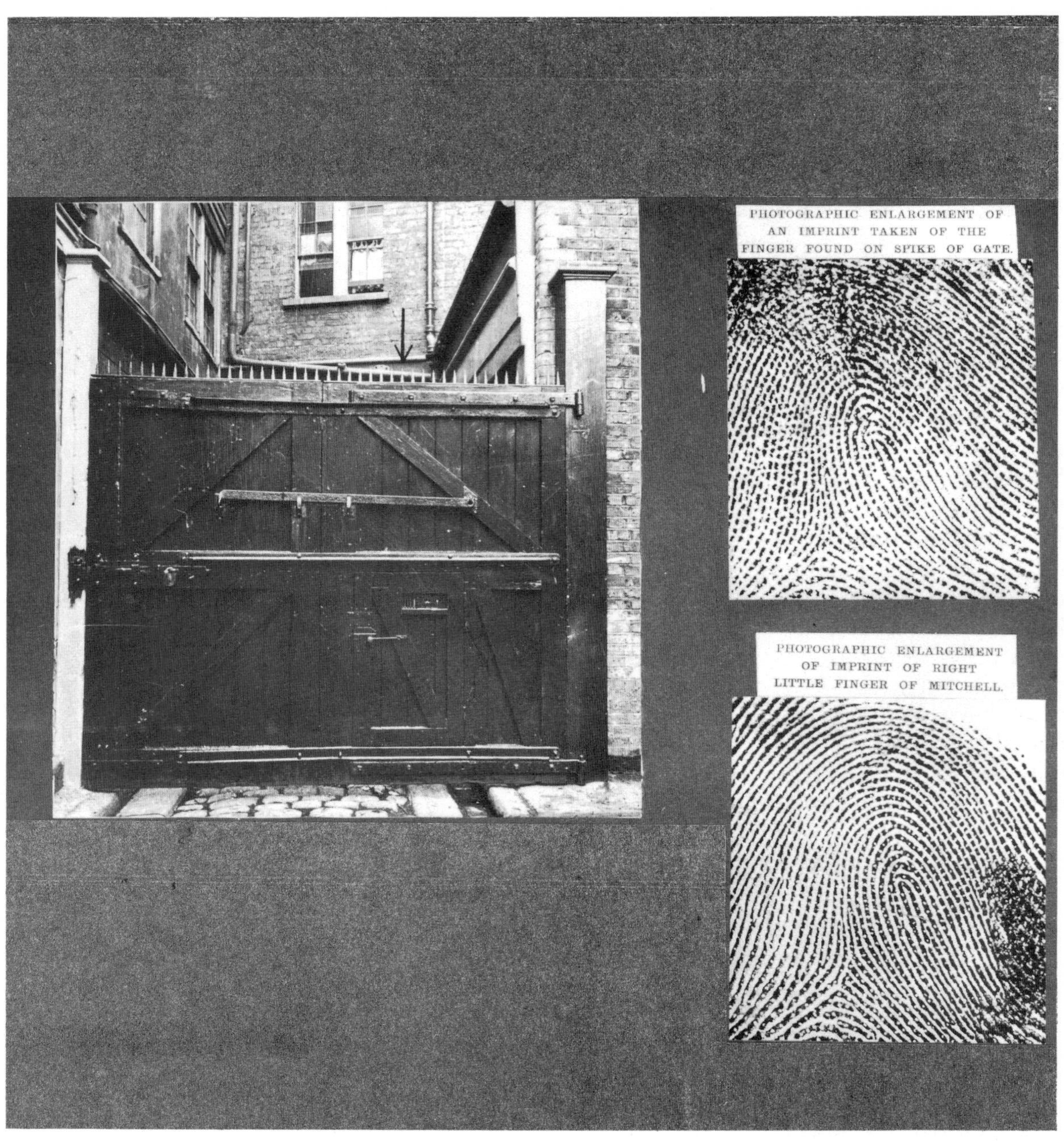
PHOTOGRAPHIC ENLARGEMENT OF AN IMPRINT TAKEN OF THE FINGER FOUND ON SPIKE OF GATE.
PHOTOGRAPHIC ENLARGEMENT OF IMPRINT OF RIGHT LITTLE FINGER OF MITCHELL.

The gate in Clerkenwell; the spike on which the finger was impaled is arrowed.

The first time (though, as will appear, not the last) that fingerprint officers were requested to examine the bodily parts of a person who was not present followed a break-in at a crockery warehouse in Clerkenwell. A police constable whose beat included the lane at the rear of the premises was surprised, and no doubt disgusted, by the sight of a finger impaled thimble-like on one of the spikes along the top of the wooden gate leading to the yard. Forcing himself to look closer, the constable observed that the finger was encircled by a gold ring. He climbed to the top of the gate and, peering at the ground inside the yard, saw an additional slight piece of the finger and a sprinkling of bloodstains. The signs, taken together, showed that a man had scaled the gate and, while grasping the spike, lost his balance; his ring had caught on the spike, causing his finger to be jerked off as he fell in the yard. The evidence was delivered to the Fingerprint Branch, and after a lengthy search through the record cards the ridges on the finger were found to match the impression of the right little finger of a versatile crook who went by several aliases but whose real name appeared to be George Mitchell. A month after the break-in, a detective of L Division arrested two men on suspicion of pickpocketing in a crowd at a tramstop by the Elephant & Castle public house in South Lambeth Place. One of the men was Mitchell. Waving a heavily bandaged right hand, he complained, 'How the — could I pick pockets with a hand like this?' A moment later he wished he had kept his mouth shut, his hand out of sight — for the detective, recalling a notice in the *Police Gazette*,[1] said, 'I don't know about that, but I reckon you've lost a finger. The blokes at the Yard are looking after it for you.' Subsequently Mitchell was charged under the Prevention of Crimes Act, and sentenced to twelve months' hard labour. The police had reason to believe that the ring on the dismembered finger was stolen property; but, feeling that it had caused Mitchell trouble enough, they decided not to pursue the matter.

1. The blind Sir John Fielding, who became the Bow Street Magistrate when his half-brother Henry (novelist as well as magistrate) died in 1754, founded three publications: the *Quarterly Pursuit*, which listed criminals wanted in London; the *Weekly Pursuit*, its contents similar, which was distributed among magistrates; the *Extraordinary Pursuit*, an occasional supplement which gave details of extraordinary criminals. In 1786 the *Quarterly* and *Extraordinary* publications were merged, to become *Public Hue and Cry*. In 1878, when Howard Vincent became head of the Metropolitan CID, he remodelled this publication, chiefly by including illustrations, and retitled it *Police Gazette, or Hue and Cry*. That publication was — and, the 'Hue and Cry' sub-title a thing of the past, is — for police use only. An early issue outlined the contents:

'. . . the substance of all information received in cases of felonies and misdemeanours of an aggravated nature, and against receivers of stolen goods, reputed thieves, and offenders escaped from custody, with the time, place, and every particular circumstance marking the offence. The names of persons charged, who are known but not in custody, and of those who are not known, their appearance, dress, and every other mark of identity that can be described. The names of accomplices, and accessories, with every other particular that may lead to their apprehension. The names of all persons brought before the magistrates charged with any of the offences mentioned, and whether committed for trial, re-examination, or how otherwise disposed of. Also a description of property that has been stolen, and particulars of stolen horses, with as much particularity as can be given, with every circumstance that may be useful for the purpose of tracing and recovering it.'

Fingerprint evidence was first presented at a British murder trial in 1905.

Early in the morning of 27 March of that year, which was a Monday, an elderly couple, Thomas and Ann Farrow, were battered to death in the 'colour and oil store' in Deptford High Street, South-East London, which they had managed, living upstairs, for a quarter of a century. A cashbox in which the Farrows had kept the takings from one Monday to the next was lying empty on the floor in the bedroom; also on the floor were the tray of the box, a sixpenny piece, and a penny. Two masks made from old black stockings were found in the kitchen.

The investigation was led by Detective Inspector Frederick Fox, with Melville MacNaghten holding a 'watching brief'. The most valuable information obtained on the first day came from a milkman and his eleven-year-old mate, who, between them, provided descriptions of two men they had seen leaving

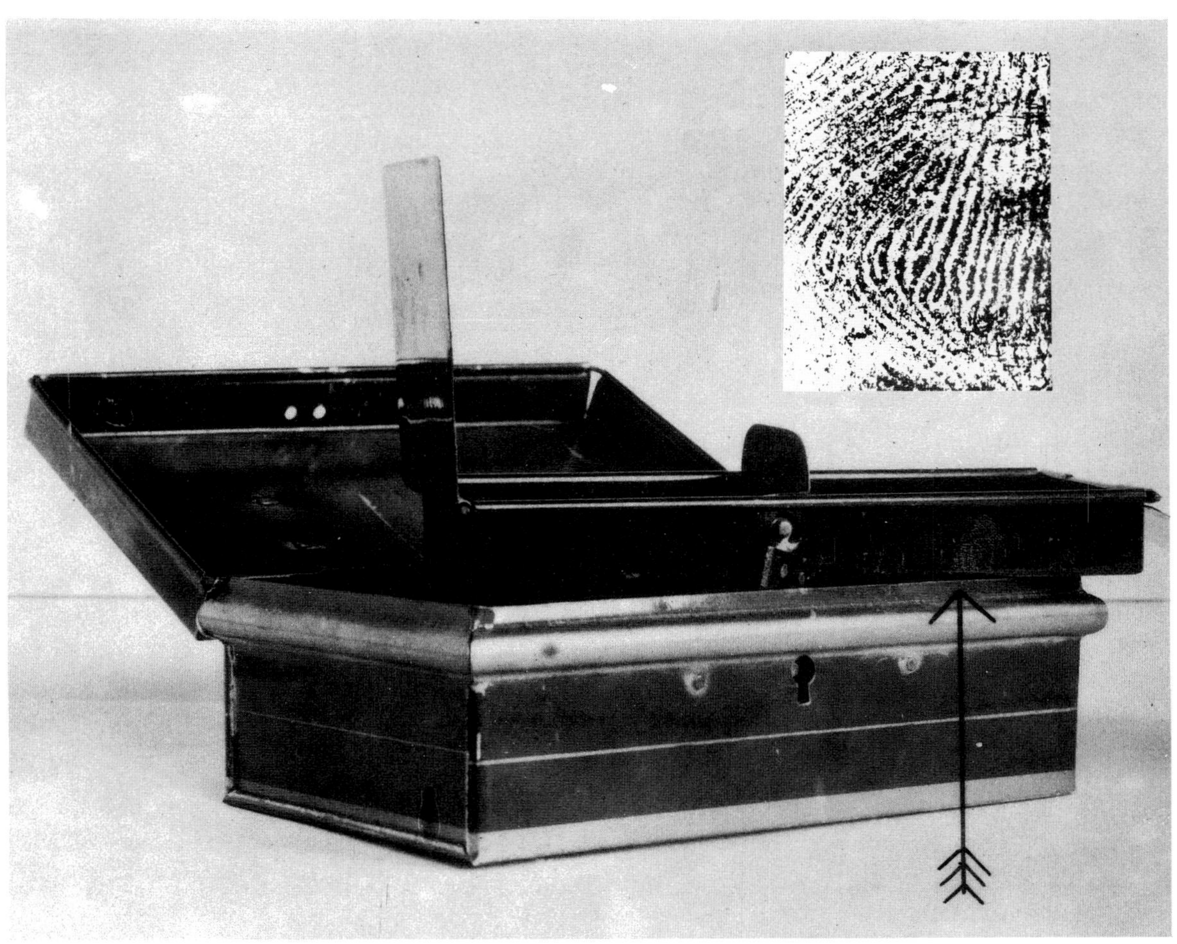

the shop at about 7.15 on the Monday morning. On Wednesday, going by gossip overheard in a café in Deptford, the police interviewed a professional boxer, who reluctantly admitted that he was 'a bit suspicious' of two brothers, Alfred and Albert Stratton. The local police knew the brothers as 'hooligans', and suspected them of being house-breakers. Their descriptions tallied in some respects with those given by the milkman and his mate.

The last known address of Alfred, who was twenty-two, was a lodging house in Deptford; the landlady had not seen him since the evening of the murders. She recalled that, one or two weeks before, she had been 'unable to oblige him' when he asked for an old pair of stockings. Shortly afterwards, when turning up the flock-mattress on his bed, she had noticed some stocking-tops tucked between the mattress and the frame. Albert, who was twenty, was also missing from *his* last known address — that being another lodging house in Deptford, where he had shared a room with a young woman. She recalled that on the morning of the murders she had asked him why his trousers smelt oily, and he had explained that he had spilt some paraffin while filling a lamp; later that day she had seen him spreading black polish on his brown boots; on the Tuesday, she had asked him what had become of his overcoat, and he had said that he had given it to a needy friend.

The cashbox and, in a separate bag, its tray had been sent to the Fingerprint Branch. Before suspicion fell on the Strattons, the impression of a sweaty or oily thumbrint on the tray had been isolated from the prints of the Farrows, the owner of the shop, and the first policeman on the scene, and an enlarged photograph taken of it. A search through the record cards failed to reveal a matching thumbprint.

At the end of the week the Strattons were still at large. If Inspector Fox had had his way, the hunt for them would have been reported in the press; however, Melville MacNaghten, fearing that the case against them was good only in parts, and that a much-publicized hunt might be followed by a much-publicized dismissal of charges in a magistrate's court, insisted that a softlee-softlee approach was to be employed. On Saturday afternoon, acting on information that the Strattons were football-fans, plain-clothes policemen mingled with the crowds at grounds close to Deptford; neither of the brothers was noticed. But because the hunt lacked the customary appearances of being one, the Strattons were lulled into a false sense of security. On Sunday night, Alfred, in celebratory mood, went to a public house where he was known, bought drinks all round for those who knew him, and

From an original drawing made during the trial by William Harrison.

was arrested before he had taken the first sip from his own glass. Next morning, Albert was arrested while strolling towards a different public house.

Stockley Collins, recently promoted to the rank of detective inspector, travelled to the police station in Greenwich where the brothers were held, and compared their thumbprints with the photograph of the print on the tray of the cash-box. There was no doubt that that print was of Alfred's right thumb.

Despite an attempt by the Strattons' solicitor to delay the trial, mainly on the ground that he needed time to assemble a rebuttal of the fingerprint evidence, the brothers appeared in the dock of No. 1 Court, Old Bailey, on Friday, 5 May. The prosecution was led by the Treasury Counsel, Richard Muir, who had not needed to bone up on the science of dactylography: in September 1902, after being given a crash-course by Stockley Collins, he had presented the first case in which the

Crown relied upon fingerprint evidence from the scene of a crime; the defendant, Harry Jackson, was found guilty of having burgled a house on Denmark Hill (a couple of miles west of Deptford), and was sentenced to seven years' penal servitude.

As the milkman and his mate had been unable to identify the Strattons, the prosecution could only succeed if the jury accepted that the thumbprint could not have been left on the tray of the cash-box by anyone other than Alfred; the case against Albert was basically one of guilt by association. Muir's examination of Collins was chiefly intended to make the jury confident of the uniqueness of prints. Collins said that he had found twelve 'points of agreement' between Alfred's thumbprint and that on the tray; the most he had ever found in impressions made by different digits was three. He pointed out the matching characteristics on greatly enlarged photographs.

Alfred's counsel called to the witness-box a man named John Garson, an expert on *bertillonage* who had acted as 'scientific adviser' to the Anthropometric Office until it was replaced by the Fingerprint Branch. He stated that, in his opinion, the evidence given by Collins was open to doubt. Cross-examined by Muir, he admitted that he had no experience of the Henry system — but then said that he was *certain* that the thumbprint on the tray had not been made by either of the Strattons. Muir, his tone contemptuous, read from two letters that Garson had written on the same day following the committal proceedings: one was to the defence solicitor, the other to the Director of Public Prosecutions, and both contained an offer from Garson to give 'expert' evidence at the trial. The judge, the monocled Mr Justice Channell, thereupon declared that Garson was 'an absolutely untrustworthy witness'; and when defence counsel, re-examining, gave Garson cues so that he might try to explain away his duplicity, the judge snapped: 'Is there not a limit to whitewashing this . . . er . . . gentleman?'

The jury retired at 8 p.m. on the second day of the trial. More than two hours elapsed before they filed back into the box, and the foreman, a fishmonger named Graves, announced verdicts of Guilty against both of the Strattons.

It seems likely that the younger of them would have been reprieved but for some indiscreet remarks he made to a gaoler during an adjournment of the committal proceedings. In the course of a bitter tirade against Alfred, he virtually confessed that he had taken part in the robbery and murders.

The executions were carried out on 23 May. There had been double-executions of brothers in the long-distant past, but this occasion was made especial by the fact that the hangmen, John and William Billington, were similarly related.

Stockley Collins.

The bridge over Gardenholme Linn.

The Ruxton case was the first in which fingerprinting was successfully used to identify a murder victim. Understandably, perhaps, the prosecuting lawyers in the case decided to keep quiet about that; they were sure of the quality of the evidence, but worried that their leading opponent, Norman Birkett, a brilliant manipulator of juries, might cast doubt upon it, simply — for him — by using words like 'untried', 'new-fangled', and 'incredible'. Few of the many retrospective accounts of the case contain more than passing reference to the fingerprint evidence, and hardly any of those speak of it as being an inaugural landmark in crime detection.

On 29 September 1935, a Sunday, a nature-loving young woman holidaying at Moffat, in the Scottish shire of Dumfries, walked to Gallows Hill, just to the north of the town, and then east for a couple of miles to the bridge on the Edinburgh-Carlisle road that spans Gardenholme Linn, a stream running into the river Annan. Her appreciation of the scenery was curtailed by her observation of a ragged parcel lying in the

ravine. She tutted at litter-louts in general — but a moment later let out a yelp of horror as she realized that an object poking from the parcel was a human arm. Without more ado, she ran back to Moffat.

Soon afterwards, the local constable cycled to the bridge and, having clambered down the embankment, found not only the parcel that had given the young woman such a nasty turn but three others. The parcels, all with inside wrappings of newspaper, their outer covering either torn sheets or old clothing, contained an assortment of human remains. Over the next few days, mainly as the result of a police search but also by sightseers' serendipity, other parcels of a similar nature and some unwrapped pieces of flesh were discovered downstream. The subsequent nicknaming of the ravine as the Devil's Beef-Tub was almost justified, considering that seventy separate pieces and parts came to light.

They were taken to the dissection room at the University of Glasgow, there to be scrutinized by pathologists (who soon concluded that they were the incomplete remains of at least two women) and then examined and the bony parts measured by an anatomist (who established that the pathologists' 'at least' could be deleted). While the anatomist was still at work on his jigsaw task, an odontologist took casts of the teeth in the mutilated heads, and an entomologist pored over the maggots: his opinion as to their age did not contradict the police belief that the parcels had been made up no earlier than 15 September (for the most recent of the newspapers forming the inner wrappings was of that date) and that they had been deposited on or after 17 or 18 September (for there had been heavy rainstorms during those days, lifting the level of the stream: presumably the parcels, thrown into the stream, had been left on the banks when the flood abated).

One of the newspapers dated 15 September was the *Sunday Graphic*: a 'slip' edition — with a complete sheet devoted to the Morecambe Carnival — that had been distributed only in the area around Morecambe, the English seaside resort about a hundred miles south of Moffat.

The county town of Lancaster was within that distribution area.

Probably the only Indian living and working in Lancaster in 1935 was a doctor named Buck Ruxton, who ran a general practice on the ground floor of his home, 2 Dalton Square, in the centre of the town. Ruxton, who was thirty-six, had settled in Lancaster five years before. His common-law wife Isabella, a British woman who had once been officially married to a Dutchman, had borne Ruxton three children, whose nursemaid was a young local woman named Mary Rogerson. On 17 September Mary Rogerson's parents had informed the police that she was missing; the police do not seem to have taken any action — not even after they heard rumours that Mrs Ruxton was also missing. But when the Chief Constable of Dumfries, seeing a newspaper account of an interview with the parents, telephoned Captain Vann, his opposite number in Lancaster, inquiries were begun. When interviewed, Dr Ruxton claimed that Mary Rogerson had gone away to Scotland, and that his wife had left him for another man.

The police already knew that the doctor had a fiery temper and was extremely jealous of his wife, for they had twice been called to 2 Dalton Square by neighbours, alarmed by the sound of his shouting and screaming, and they had received reports of his 'acting like a madman . . . looking like a person about to have a fit, and then bursting into tears' and of threats he had made against men whom he suspected of 'carrying on' with Isabella.

A patient of the doctor stated that, on Sunday, 15 September, he had asked her to help him in the house, explaining that he had decorators coming in and that he could not manage on his own as he had cut his hand; the woman had found the place in such a mess — the carpets taken up, straw protruding from beneath the locked doors of the Ruxtons' bedrooms, the bath stained a dirty yellow — that she had insisted that she could not cope without the assistance of her husband, and Ruxton had agreed to pay them both for several days' work.

Articles of clothing found in the ravine — a blouse and a baby's woollen romper-suit — were tentatively connected with the Ruxton household.

(The strangest item of evidence among the remains was a Cyclops eye: two eyes fused into one. The scientists in Glasgow were unable to say whether it was of human or of animal origin; clearly, though, it was not a component of either of the bodies. The fact that the eye was less putrefied than the rest of the soft tissues suggested that it had been preserved as an ophthalmic exhibit. Ruxton had been interested in ophthalmology at one time, and he may well have obtained the eye as a specimen for study. When the case was over, a literary researcher noted a 'supernatural clue' in Thomas De Quincey's *The English Mail-Coach*, written more than a hundred years before, which contained the passage: 'But what was Cyclops doing here? Had the medical men recommended northern air, or how? I collected, from such explanations as he volunteered, that he had an interest at stake in some suit-at-law now pending at Lancaster.')

Ruxton was arrested on 13 October. Immediately afterwards, and for a period of nearly a fortnight, policemen and scientists

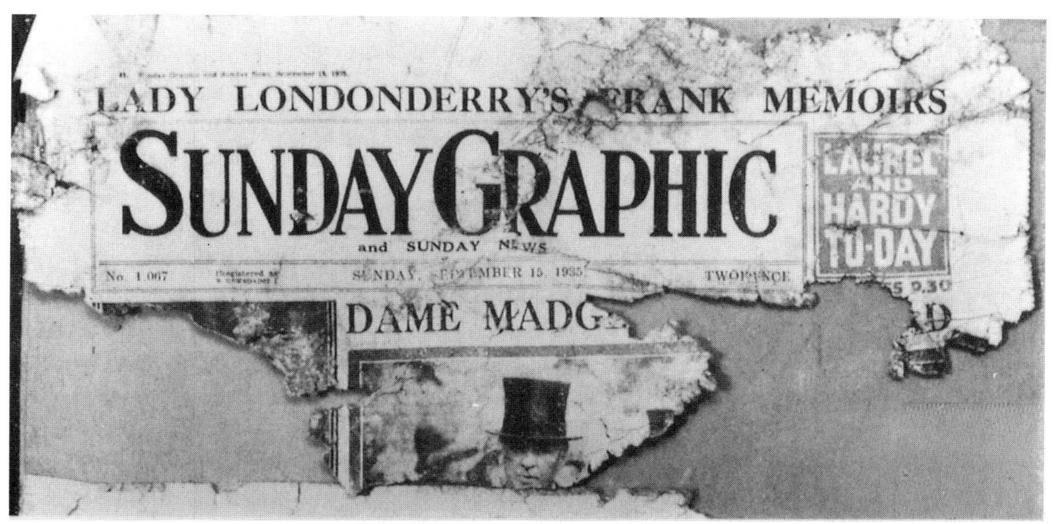

LADY LONDONDERRY'S FRANK MEMOIRS

SUNDAY GRAPHIC

and SUNDAY NEWS

No. 1,067 SUNDAY, SEPTEMBER 15, 1935 TWOPENCE

LAUREL AND HARDY TO-DAY

DAME MADG

Page 2 SUNDAY GRAPHIC and SUNDAY NEWS September 15, 1935

"Knife" Storm Hits a Town

Farm Buildings Wrecked: Trees Torn Down

"UNCANNY"

From Our Own Correspondent

DAL DEAD

SUNDAY GRAPHIC

and SUNDAY NEWS

SUNDAY SEPTEMBER 15, 1935

GENASPRIN

NEW 6d SIZE

AMBE'S CARNIVAL QUEEN CROWNED

TO-DAY
LIVE GHOST
"VANESSA"
CINEMA
HAYES
TO-DAY
VANESSA

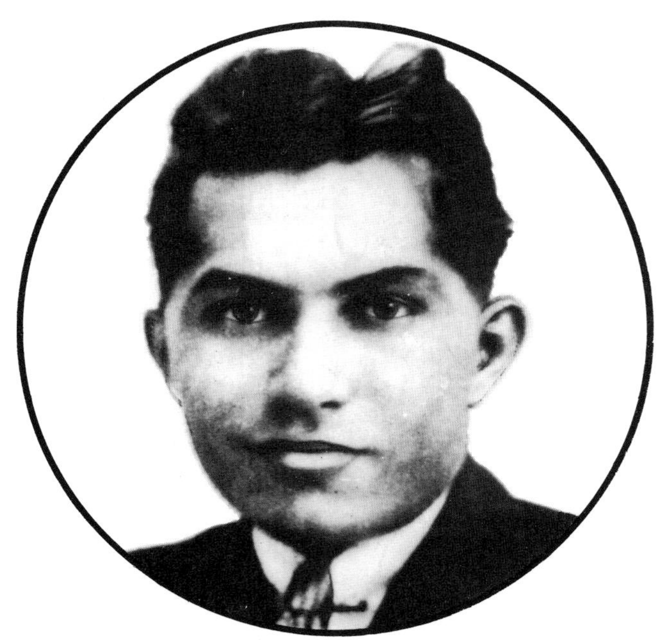

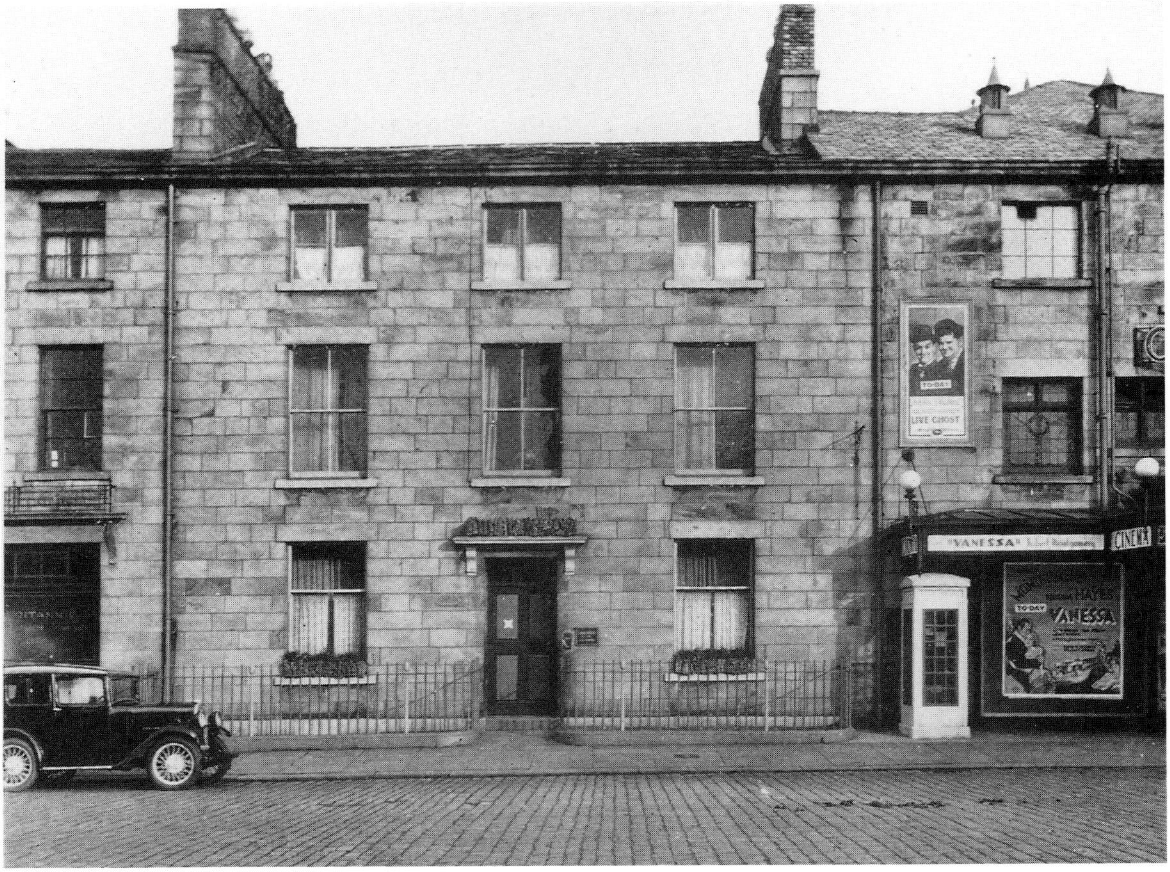

examined every nook and cranny of 2 Dalton Square. Portraits of Mrs Ruxton and Mary Rogerson were sent to Glasgow, where, after painstaking work by a specialist photographer and members of the anatomical departments of both Glasgow and Edinburgh Universities, 'double-exposure' photographs were developed, showing that each of the faces corresponded with each of the skulls; the scientists also reckoned that the bodies matched those of the missing women in terms of age, height and physique. In addition to that positive evidence, the location of mutilated areas of the bodies provided equally convincing 'negative evidence' — which would be outlined by the leading prosecutor at the trial as follows:

(Opposite, above)
Dr Buck Ruxton.

(Opposite, below)
2 Dalton Square, Lancaster.

> There were certain peculiarities about both women . . . and if these marks were left after death, anyone would be able to identify these persons. Mary Rogerson had what is commonly called a glide in one eye; the eyes had been removed. She had had certain teeth drawn by a dentist, a fact which could have been identified by the dentist; more extractions had been made on the body, and these had been made about the time of her death. . . . She had a very bad birthmark on her right arm, a very noticeable mark; the flesh on that forearm had been cut away. . . . She had freckles on her face; the skin had been removed. . . . She had had an operation for appendicitis; all that part of her body has never been found. . . .
>
> Now, with regard to the other body, which we say is that of Mrs Ruxton, Mrs Ruxton had brownish hair with a patch of grey hair on the top of her head; that head had been scalped. . . . She had a prominent bridge to her nose; the nose had been cut off. . . . Her legs were almost the same thickness down to the ankles; the flesh round the ankles had been cut away so that you could not tell the shape of her legs. Her toes had been humped; and these had been cut off.

The clinching evidence that one of the bodies was that of Mary Rogerson was found by Detective-Lieutenant Bertie Hammond, the officer in charge of the fingerprint department of the City of Glasgow Police. Prior to Ruxton's arrest, the hands in the collection of pieces that were then known only as 'Body No. 1' or, unofficially, as 'the young one', had been soaked in hot water so as to remove most of the post-mortem wrinkling; afterwards, impressions of the fingertips and the palms had been taken and all parts of the hands photographed. As soon as Ruxton was in custody, Hammond started dusting for fingerprints in the house — a task that occupied him for eleven days. Returning to Glasgow, he spent several more days comparing the photographs of fingerprints in the house with those from the dismembered hands, eventually concluding that, of the 'house prints', three palmar impressions and thirty-one

(Right)
Mrs Ruxton.

(Far right)
The skull of 'Body No. 2'.

(Below)
The above photographs superimposed.

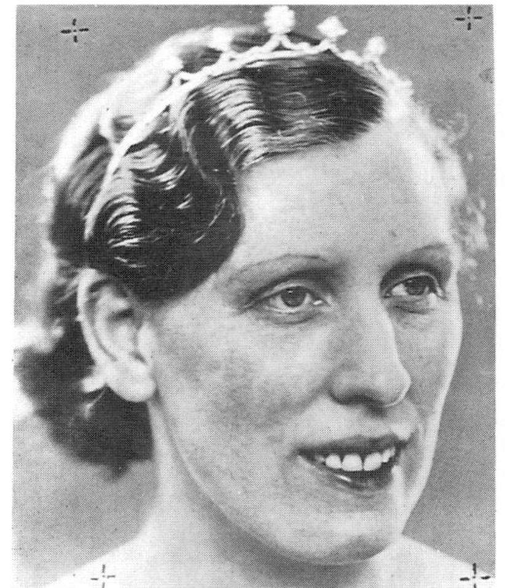

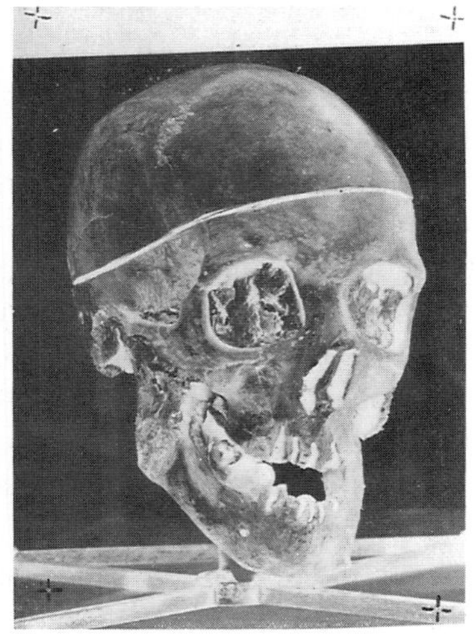

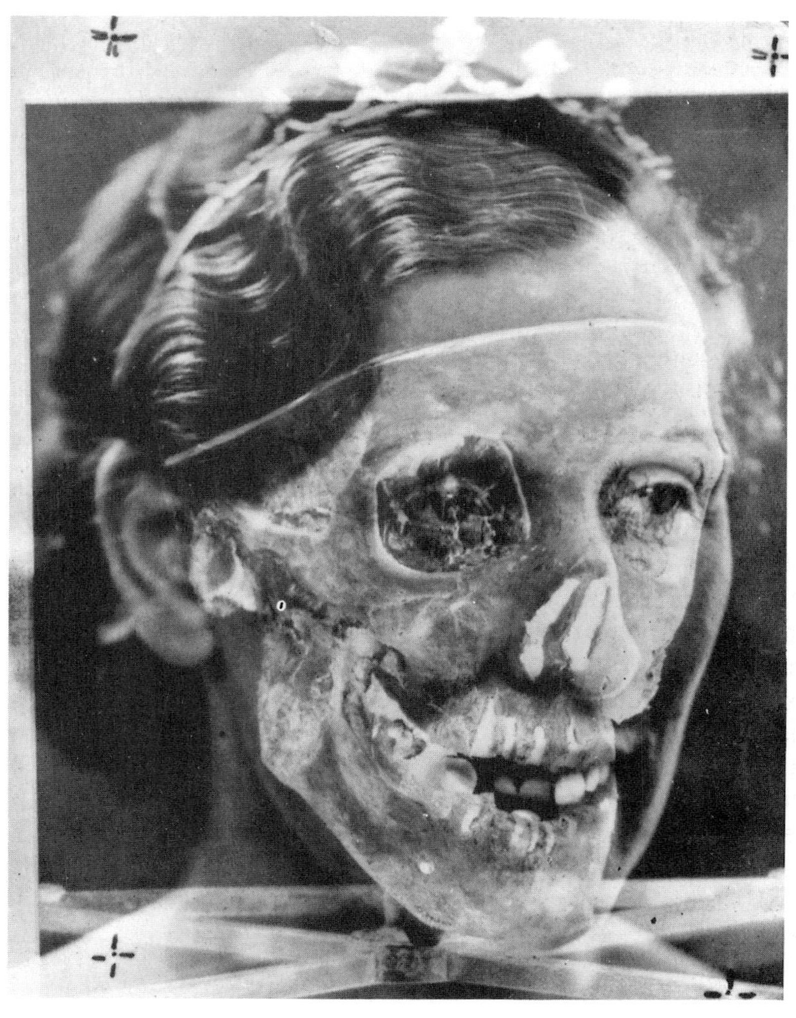

fingerprints had been made by the left hand of Body No. 1 — that of Mary Rogerson. The number of 'points of agreement' ranged from eight to twenty-two.

Although the epidermis had been shed from the right hand, Hammond found that the dermis of the thumb matched two 'house prints', one of which showed eight 'points of agreement' and the other sixteen. The Director of Public Prosecutions, after speaking to fingerprint experts at Scotland Yard, arranged for Hammond to come to London — for no other purpose, apparently, than to tell him that he was not to refer to his examination of the right-hand prints when giving evidence at the committal proceedings or the trial, as it was considered 'too controversial'. The meeting, attended by several Metropolitan Police detectives, including Superintendent Harry Battley, was made stormy by Hammond's protests at the order that he was to exclude evidence that he considered (in hindsight, rightly) to be perfectly valid. According to his subsequent recollection, Battley contended that it was not possible to prove that dermal prints were the same as those in the top layer of skin — and he retorted,

> in no uncertain manner, that it would be a bad job for the fingerprint system if, on the removal of the outer skin, the underskin showed a different pattern of ridges. . . . Superintendent Battley asked me what I would do if he sent an officer to rebut the evidence. I told him not to send anyone but to come himself. I should have an answer to his rebutting evidence. Superintendent Battley was very annoyed that an officer from Scotland should be in 'on the case', as he expressed it, 'of the century'.

One feels sorry for Bertie Hammond, not merely because he was denied the kudos that should have resulted from the evidence he gave on 11 March 1936, when he appeared as the final prosecution witness at Ruxton's trial in the High Court of Justice in Manchester, but because, as he was prevented from speaking of his achievement in obtaining dermal fingerprints, most historians of the forensic sciences credit that 'first' to an American detective of the 1940s. It is hard to understand why Hammond, upon his return to Glasgow from the meeting at the DPP's office, did not ask one of the pathologists working on the case to help him disprove Battley's contention that dermal prints differed from epidermal ones: the casualty departments of Glasgow hospitals could have provided any number of dismembered fingers (most of them lopped by razor-blades during fights between the city's rival gangs), and it would have been a simple surgical task to shave a random selection of them.

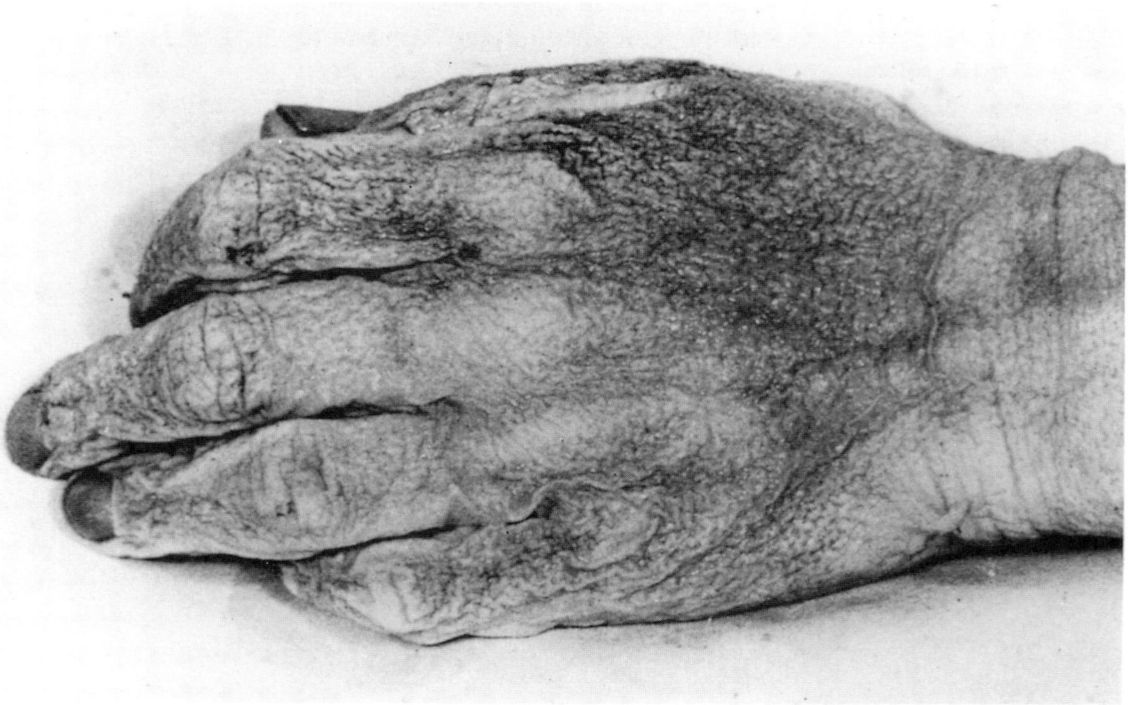

(Above)
The left hand of 'Body No. 1'.

(Below). Left:
a print found at 2 Dalton Square.

Right:
a print from the left hand of 'Body No. 1'.

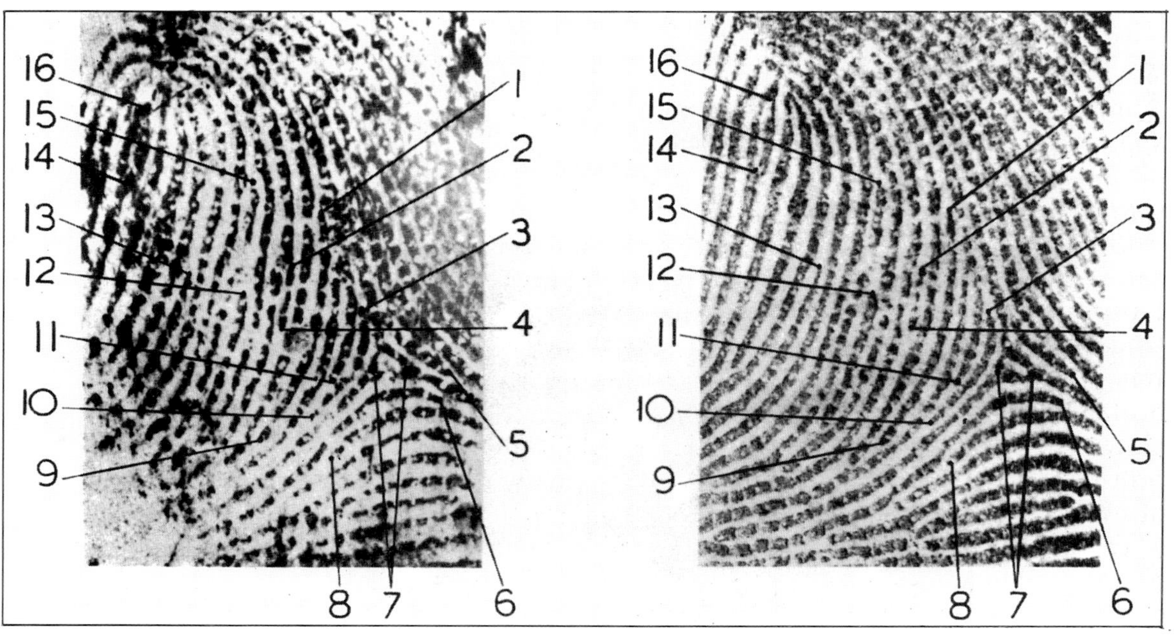

Round about the time of the trial, the chorus of a hit-song entitled *Red Sails in the Sunset* was amended in conformity with the Crown's theory as to why a *double*-murder had been committed:

> Red stains on the carpet,
> Red stains on your knife;
> Oh, Dr Buck Ruxton, you cut up your wife;
> The nursemaid, she saw you, and threatened to tell —
> So, Dr Buck Ruxton, you killed her as well.

In examination-in-chief, Ruxton, who was characteristically ornate of diction, said of the first part of the theory: 'That is an absolute and deliberate and fantastic story. You might as well say the sun was rising in the west and setting in the east.' And of the second: 'That is absolute bunkum, with a capital B, if I may say it. Why should I kill my poor Mary?' Nevertheless, he was found guilty — the jury needing only an hour to arrive at that finding — and, his appeal having been dismissed, he was hanged at Strangeways on 12 May.

Next morning, the newspaper that had won his 'exclusive story' at auction published a note he had written on the day after his arrest. Confirming part of the *Red Sails* ditty, and more of the Crown's theory, the note read:

> I killed Mrs Ruxton in a fit of temper because I thought she had been with a man. I was Mad at the time. Mary Rogerson was present at the time. I had to kill her.
>
> B. RUXTON.

In 1948, Blackburn, Lancashire, was a town of about 120,000 inhabitants, housed in some 35,000 residences. As was appropriate for the birthplace of James Hargreaves, the inventor of the spinning-jenny, Blackburn's main industry was the spinning and weaving of cotton.

On a hill overlooking the town, sensibly far from the fog of smoke emitted by the mill-chimneys, was the Queens Park Hospital (a name now prefixed by the word *Royal*). The hospital stood in seventy acres of ground surrounded by a high stone wall. The only official entrance to the area was through the porter's gate; but in May 1948 a part of the north-western wall, close to a disused quarry known as 'the Delph', had subsided, providing a way into the grounds, despite a makeshift structure of bits of old timber surmounted by barbed wire.

During the first minutes of Saturday, the 15th, a man pushed past the stop-gap and made his way to the CH3 Ward for small children, which was the ward farthest from the porter's lodge.

(Above)
CH3 Ward.

(Right)
The 'Winchester' bottle.

When he entered the ward he was alone; when he left he was holding in his arms a little girl named June Devaney, not quite four years of age, who had just recovered from pneumonia.

At about a quarter to one, Gwendoline Humphreys, the nurse on night-duty, walked into the ward from the kitchen, where she had been preparing trays for her patients' breakfasts, and at once saw that June Devaney's cot was empty. When she had last been in the ward, fifteen minutes before, all six patients had been fast asleep.

On the floor by the empty cot was a large, multi-purpose 'Winchester' bottle, normally kept on a trolley at one end of the ward; at the other end of the ward, a door to a verandah was open, as was a window in a small ante-room. The floor of the ward, recently waxed and polished, bore the imprints of adult feet that were either bare or stockinged. Nurse Humphreys noticed all those things as she searched, more and more frantically, for the missing child.

She raised the alarm, and hospital employees started searching other buildings and the grounds. They found nothing pertinent. At five minutes to two, the Blackburn police were informed, and officers were straightway dispatched to the scene; soon afterwards, an officer went to the child's home in Princess Street, awoke her parents, and then drove the father, a foundry worker, to the hospital.

At quarter-past three, the body of June Devaney was discovered in the grounds, a hundred yards or so from the ward. The child had been raped and battered to death.

Within a couple of hours, a full-scale investigation was in motion. While forensic experts respectively examined the body and scoured various parts of the grounds, officers from the Blackburn force and the Lancashire Constabulary began questioning hospital staff. Detective Inspector Colin Campbell, the Scotsman in charge of the Lancashire Constabulary Fingerprint Bureau at Preston, was already at work in CH3 Ward, which had been cleared of patients.

At 4 a.m. the Chief Constable of Blackburn, Mr C. G. Looms, arranged for a Scotland Yard 'murder specialist', Detective Chief Inspector John Capstick, to take charge of the investigation. Capstick was chosen because he had spent the past two months in the town of Farnworth, fifteen miles south of Blackburn, seeking the killer of a schoolboy, Jack Quentin Smith, who had been found stabbed and beaten to death on a railway embankment; the culprit was still at large, and it occurred to Mr Looms that the Farnworth 'moon killer' — who was suspected of being responsible for other attacks on children — might be the murderer of June Devaney.

Railway Station:—New Longton. Telephone: Preston 4811. Telegrams: 'Ecilop, Preston'.

Chief Constable's Office,
(Fingerprint Bureau)

Lancashire Constabulary,
(P.O.Box 77).

Preston, 15th June, 1948.

Communications to be addressed to the Chief Constable.

The Headquarters are situate in Saunders Lane, off Liverpool Road, Hutton.

Our Ref.: F.P. 1324/48
Your Ref.: ....

Dear Sir,

MURDER OF JUNE ANN DEVANEY AT BLACKBURN, ON THE 15th MAY, 1948

During the early hours of the 15th May, 1948, the children's ward at Queen's Park Hospital, Blackburn, was entered and June Ann Devaney, aged 3¾ years, was taken from her cot.

She was later found murdered in the hospital grounds, having been the victim of a sexual assault.

Before taking the child from her cot, the culprit carried a 'winchester' bottle from a trolley at the end of the ward and left it beside the cot from which the child was taken.

The bottle bears several digital impressions which, up to the present, have not been identified. Below are illustrated two of the impressions disclosed on the bottle and I have to ask if you will be so good as to cause them to be compared with the fingerprints in your collection with a view to establishing the identity of the offender in this case. The impression 'A', which is one of a sequence, was made by a left fore finger; the left middle finger of the same hand is an ulnar loop with at least 15 ridge counts, and the left ring finger is an ulnar loop with at least 11 ridge counts. The tip only of the left little finger appears.

The impression 'B' was made by a left thumb and it is probable, though not certain, it was made by the same hand that made the impression 'A'. The illustrations of these impressions have been enlarged two diameters.

The fingerprints of all doctors, sisters, nurses, orderlies, relatives, and visitors (642 persons in all), having legitimate access to the ward have been compared with the impressions.

If an identification is made, or thought to be made, will you please inform this office and New Scotland Yard before taking any further action?.

Yours faithfully,

J. Goodmansey.

Detective Superintendent,
for Chief Constable of Lancashire.

The Chief Constable,

Police Office,

A

A

B

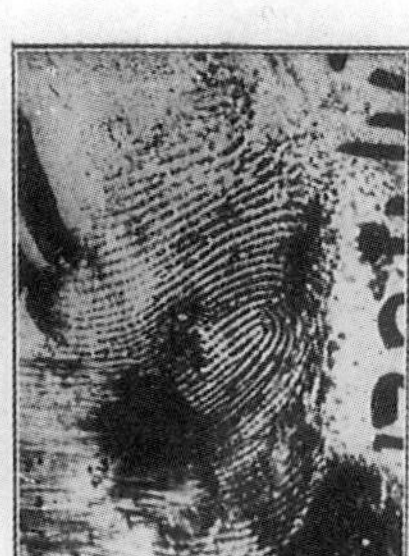

B

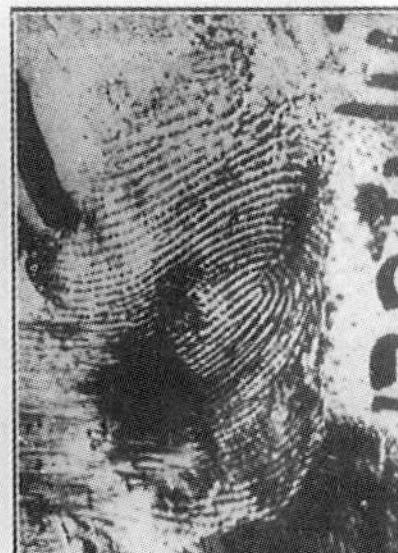

Printed by the Lancashire Constabulary, Preston.

BLACKBURN BOROUGH POLICE

DEATH OF JUNE ANN DEVANEY, AGE 3 YEARS

PARTICULARS OF PERSON INTERVIEWED

Full Name .... Nat. Regn. No ....

Address ....

Place of Employment ....

Description:—
Date of Birth .... Occupation ....

Height .... Build .... Face ....

Complexion .... Hair on Face .... Hair ....

Forehead .... Eyebrows .... Eyes .... Nose ....

Scars on Face ....

Peculiarities:—
Time of arrival home on Friday night the 14th, or a.m. Saturday, 15th May, 1948 ....

Dress ....

....

....

Movements between 11 p.m. Friday, 14th, and 2 a.m. Saturday, 15th May, 1948, and names and addresses of two persons who can verify same ....

....

....

....

....

....

....

....

If Statement Taken .... **Any bloodstains on clothing?** ....

Is any male person away from house or place of employment since Friday, 14th May, 1948? ....

....

....

....

Particulars of any person in H.M. Forces or otherwise on leave on 14th and 15th May, 1948, who has since returned home or to respective Unit ....

Any other information ....

....

....

....

Person's Signature .... Date and time of interview ....

Signature of Officer making enquiry ....

....

INFORM PERSON INTERVIEWED THAT ANY INFORMATION GIVEN TO POLICE WILL BE TREATED WITH STRICTEST CONFIDENCE.

By the afternoon, when John Capstick arrived at Queen's Park Hospital, Colin Campbell had ringed and photographed the footprints on the floor of the ward: they were ten inches long, made by a man who had walked in stockinged feet. And Campbell had isolated recently-deposited fingerprints on the Winchester bottle. He suspected — only suspected, mind — that the murderer had picked up the bottle as an impromptu weapon, and had left it by the cot before carrying the child away.

A squad of detectives, at first working almost continuously day and night, traced and recorded the fingerprints of every male member of the hospital staff; then outsiders (delivery men, patients' visitors, and the like) were included in the process of elimination — and than all men who might have been in CH3 Ward since the summer of 1946. The detectives' perseverance was based on the belief — correct, as it turned out — that the murderer was familiar with the hospital and its grounds. By 15 June, 2017 men had been traced and their fingerprints sent to Inspector Campbell.

But none of the prints tallied with those found on the Winchester bottle.

Capstick decided to do something that had never been attempted anywhere before. He told the Chief Constable: 'Mr Looms, we are going to fingerprint every male in Blackburn and district between the ages of sixteen and ninety — every male who is not actually bed-ridden.'

Though full public co-operation was expected (if for no other reason than because a refusal to assist would be viewed with suspicion), much publicity was given to the fact that the first 'volunteer' was the mayor of the town — who at the sime time gave his assurance that every 'innocent print' would be destoyed. The town was divided, like a clock-dial, into twelve triangular sections, radiating from police headquarters at the centre. Thirty officers were engaged on the task, working from eight o'clock each morning till ten each night, seven days a week. As soon as completed 'print cards' had been checked against lists of inhabitants, chiefly the local Electoral Register, they were dispatched to Preston for examination by Inspector Campbell and his helpers.

Meanwhile, men who had left Blackburn since 15 May were identified and traced. Photographs of the prints on the bottle were sent to all fingerprint bureaux in the United Kingdom and to those of foreign law-enforcement agencies; assistance was received from British and United States military policemen.

Towards the end of June, the mass fingerprinting was almost completed. And still the prints on the bottle had not been matched.

The police decided to double-check the names on the lists with the names of men who were due to receive new ration-books. This resulted in a further trickle of 'print cards' to Preston.

At about three o'clock on the afternoon of 12 August, an examiner held one of those cards aloft. 'I've got him!' he exclaimed. 'It's here!'

The card — the 46,253rd to be examined — bore the name of Peter Griffiths. He was twenty-two years of age, unmarried, and living with his parents in Birley Street, a terrace of red-brick houses in one of Blackburn's poorest districts. He had been demobilized from the Welsh Guards at the start of the year, and now worked as a packer in a flour mill. He had spent nearly two years of his childhood, between 1936 and 1938, in Queen's Park Hospital, receiving treatment for incontinence of urine.

It was the annual Wakes holiday-week in Blackburn, and John Capstick also was taking a few days off. However, as soon as he was informed of the development, he returned to the town. On the night of Friday the 13th, he and other officers arrested Griffiths and escorted him to police headquarters. As Griffiths was being taken inside, he said: 'Well, if they're my fingerprints on the bottle, I'll tell you all about it.' Shortly afterwards he made a statement to Capstick, confessing to the murder of June Devaney, which he claimed he had committed while under the influence of drink. Capstick was convinced that Griffiths had also killed the boy at Farnworth; but Griffiths refused to confess to that or any other crime.

At his trial, which occupied two days at Lancaster Assizes in October 1948, one of the five witnesses called by the defence was the estranged wife of his half-brother. Part of her examination-in-chief indicates that Griffiths's choice of a patient in CH3 Ward as his victim may have followed from a slight remark:

> Do you remember Saturday, 8 May, of this year? — Yes.
> At that time, were you separated from your husband? — Yes; we had been separated about three months.
> Do you remember going to the house [in] Birley Street? — Yes.
> Did you there see your husband? — Yes.
> Who was with him in the room? — When I walked in, Peter was laid on the settee. He was the only one who spoke to me when I walked in. There was Mr and Mrs Griffiths, and my sister came with me.
> Was there some argument between you and your husband about your children? — Yes.

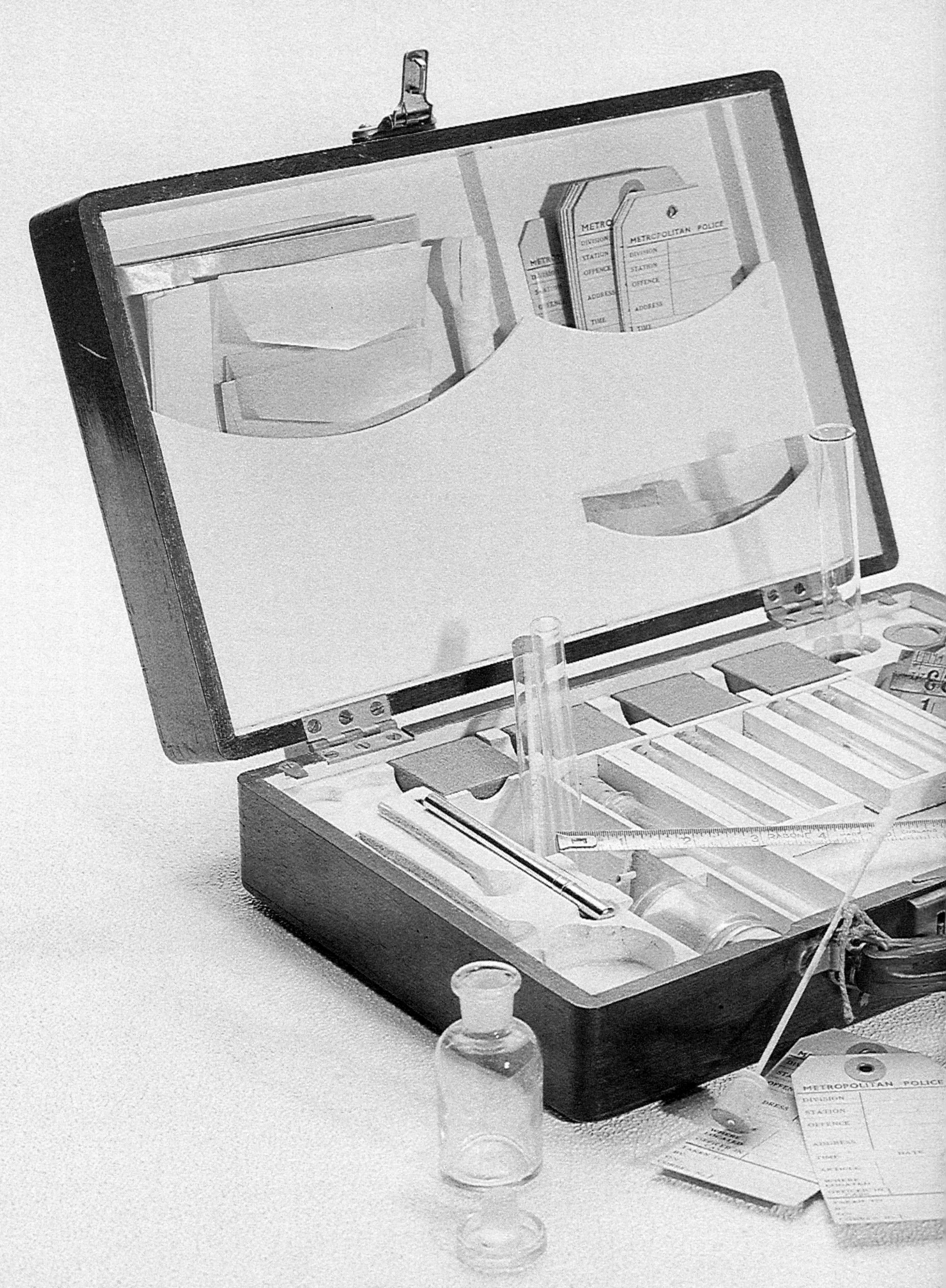
METROPOLITAN POLICE
DIVISION
STATION
OFFENCE
ADDRESS
TIME
METROPOLITAN POLICE
DIVISION
STATION
OFFENCE
ADDRESS
TIME
DATE

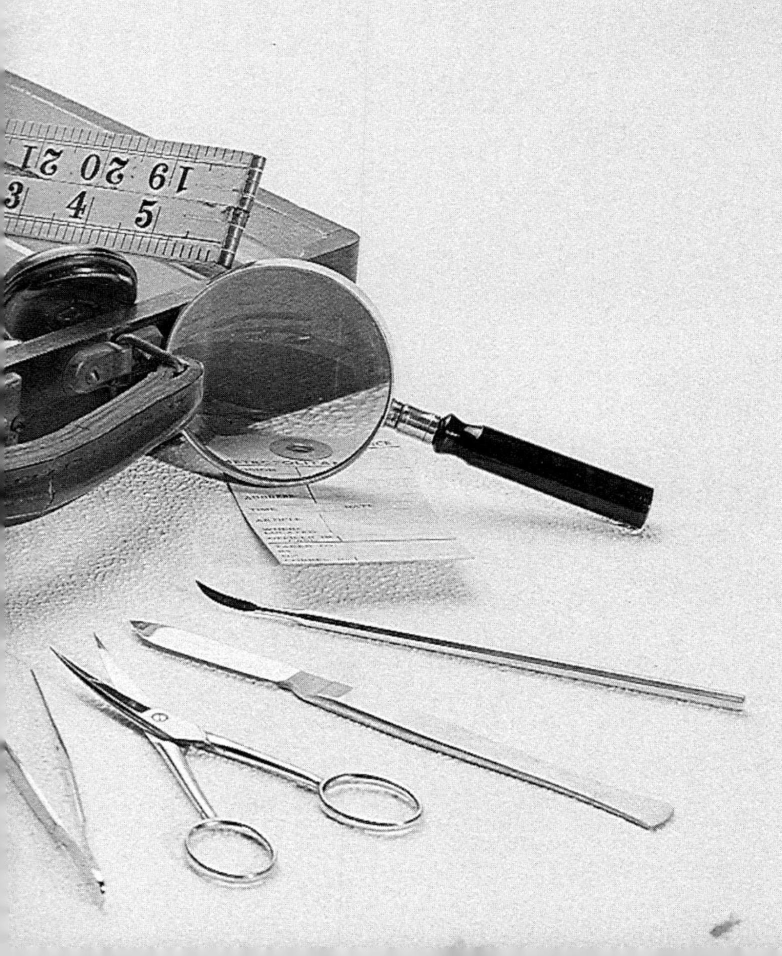

A crime case, or 'murder bag' of the sort that was carried by Scotland Yard detectives assigned to provincial inquiries, circa 1948. With each case was a leaflet containing the following information:

Contents of Crime Case

1. Scissors – 1 pair.
2. Metal probe – 1.
3. Foreceps – 1 pair.
4. Tape measure, 36 in. flexible steel – 1.
5. Magnifying glass, $2\frac{1}{2}$ in. diameter – 1.
6. Test tubes (5 in.) – 2.
7. Test tubes (3 in.) – 4.
8. Screw top glass jars – 3.
9. Glass stoppered jar – 1.
10. Cardboard boxes for specimens – 4.
11. Rubber surgical tape – 1 roll.
12. Adhesive tape, transparent – 1 roll.
13. Adhesive tape, white linen – 1 roll.
14. White cotton tape, each 9 yards in length – 2 pieces.
15. Bags, glazed and transparent, $4\frac{1}{2}$ in. $\times$ $3\frac{1}{2}$ in. – 6.
16. Bags, glazed, transparent and gussetted, 15 in. $\times$ 10 in. $\times$ 2 in. – 2.
17. Labels, adhesive, large – 24.
18. Labels, adhesive, small – 24.
19. Labels, tie-on, large – 12.
20. Labels, tie-on, small – 12.
21. White paper, plain – 24 sheets.

Replacements can be had on application to Superintendent, C.3 Branch.

In the event of loss or damage to items Nos. 1, 2, 3, 4 and 5, a report must be submitted to Superintendent, C.3 Branch, together with the article, if available.

Points to be observed in the preservation and packing of exhibits

Do not allow exhibits to become contaminated.

Label all exhibits when they are found.

Do not forget to enter on the label the name of the officer who discovered the object and its exact location.

Do not place hair, fibres and other minute articles in envelopes or containers without first placing them in the white paper provided.

Do not place objects in improper containers.

Do not use dirty containers.

Do not allow fragile fragments to become disintegrated by being placed loose in containers.

Bullets and small articles for similar tests should be first wrapped in cotton wool and then placed in the cardboard containers provided.

Indelible pencil must not be used for entering *any* particulars.

Do not use ink when labelling liquids.

Do not place fibrous or cloth articles in receptacles containing cotton wool.

Do not put corrosive fluids in metal- or cork-stoppered containers. Use the glass-stopperd container provided for this purpose and do not forget to seal the stopper with the rubber surgical tape.

Contaminated containers must be returned to C.3 Branch for cleansing.

Peter Griffiths.

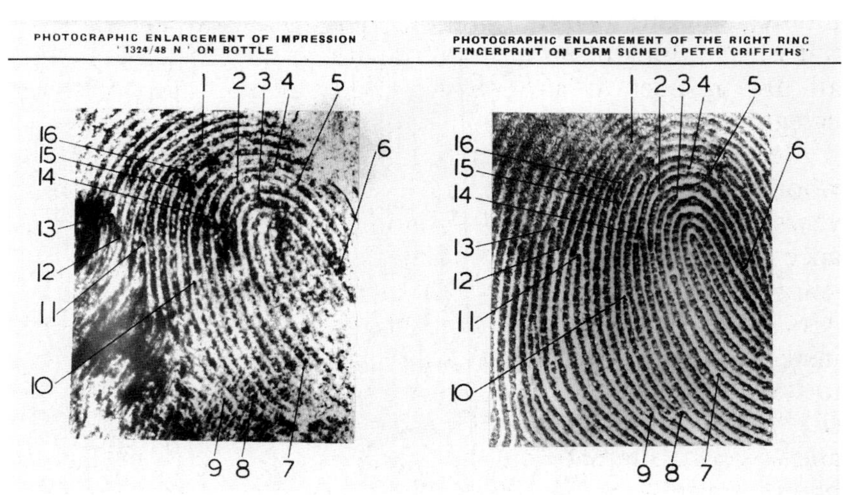
PHOTOGRAPHIC ENLARGEMENT OF IMPRESSION
'1324/48 N' ON BOTTLE
PHOTOGRAPHIC ENLARGEMENT OF THE RIGHT RING
FINGERPRINT ON FORM SIGNED 'PETER GRIFFITHS'
1 2 3 4 5 6 7 8 9 10 11 12 13 14 15 16
1 2 3 4 5 6 7 8 9 10 11 12 13 14 15 16

What was it about? — I had just been to the hospital to see the youngest one, Pauline. I was a bit vexed because he had not been to see the child, and he was arguing about that and said I could not have the children, and I said I could.
Was there any mention about where Pauline was? — Yes. He said why he had not been to see her was because he did not know where she was, *so I told him she was in CH3. . . .*

What was [Peter's] attitude towards your children? — He loved children — thought a lot about children.

Griffiths's only hope of escaping the death sentence lay with two medical witnesses who stated that they believed that he was insanely schizophrenic. As well as his confession and the fingerprint evidence, there was firm evidence that fibres on his clothes matched fibres found on the body of June Devaney; also that his feet were the exact size and shape of the footprints on the floor of the ward. The jury needed only twenty-five minutes to decide that he was sane when he committed the murder.

At the end of his statement to John Capstick, Griffiths had said: 'I hope I get what I deserve.' That hope was realized on 19 November, when he was hanged in Walton Prison, Liverpool.

Among the comparatively few gruesome exhibits in the Black Museum, the one containing parts of John Donald Merrett is probably the most eye-catching. If only because of his uniqueness in the annals of murder, it seems only right that the museum's largest remembrance of him should be unusually personal and especially conspicuous. A number of men have killed their mothers; a larger number have killed their mothers-in-law; a larger number still have killed their wives — but we can think of no murderer apart form Merrett who (with all due respect to a Scottish jury) was guilty in all three categories.

He was born in New Zealand in 1908. His parents, both of whom were English, separated in 1917 or thereabouts; seven years later, his mother brought him to Britain, and he was accepted as a boarder at Malvern College, where he earned good reports for his scholarship but poor ones for his conduct. Mrs Merrett changed her mind about sending him to Oxford; instead, she enrolled him at Edinburgh University, and, hoping to shame him away from delinquency, made it clear to him that she had chosen that college because it was non-residential — and so, once she had found a flat in the city, he would live at home, severely restricted in the opportunities for mischief.

They moved into the flat, the first floor of 31 Buckingham Terrace, on Wednesday, 10 March 1926.

Exactly a week later, soon after they had had breakfast, the daily maid, working in the kitchen, heard an explosion; then Merrett walked into the kitchen and said: 'Rita, my mother has shot herself.' Finding that hard to believe, the maid followed Merrett into the sitting-room. His mother was lying on the floor near a writing table. Blood was flowing from a wound in her right ear. There was a .25 automatic pistol on the writing-table, close to a letter that she had been in the middle of writing. It was subsequently learned that her son had bought the pistol on 13 February.

The police arrived with an ambulance and took Mrs Merrett to the Royal Infirmary. Merrett, accompanying them, attributed his mother's act to 'money matters'. She was put in the prison-like ward that was reserved for attempted suicides. During one of her brief periods of consciousness before she died on 1 April, she asked a nurse, 'What has happened? Why am I here?' Then, in answer to a question, she said, 'I was sitting writing at the time, when suddenly a bang went off in my head like a pistol.' The nurse asked, 'Was there not a pistol there?' Clearly perplexed, Mrs Merrett said, 'No; was there?' Asked whether she was sure that she was writing when the incident occurred, she said, 'Yes; quite sure. Donald can tell you — he was standing beside me, waiting to post the letter.'

Bertha Merrett was deemed to have taken her own life, and so her body was buried in unconsecrated ground. Nine months later, however, her son was charged with her murder. One of the main reasons for that charge also constituted a second charge: that, between 2 February 1926 and the following 26 March, he had forged his mother's signature on twenty-nine cheques to a total value of just over £450 (twenty-three of the cheques, totalling roughly £300, were dated prior to the day of the shooting).

He stood trial, in the High Court of Justiciary, Edinburgh, in February 1927. A large portion of the defence costs went in paying two English expert witnesses. It was money well spent. The prosecution's medical witnesses (one of whom, Professor John Glaister, of Glasgow University, would be among the scientists who helped identify the bodies in the Ruxton case) were of the opinion, based on the angle of the bullet's trajectory and the amount and pattern of the powder burns, that Mrs Merrett could not have shot herself. But Sir Bernard Spilsbury — referred to by Merrett's leading counsel as 'St Bernard', an allusion to the public's belief that he was infallible — asserted that the wound could have been self-inflicted, adding that

(Above)
The pistol found on the writing-table.

(Left)
John Donald Merrett in 1926.

women were able to shoot themselves from peculiar angles because of 'a considerable range of movement in the shoulder-joint . . . on account of the habit of pulling up their hair'. The London gunsmith Robert Churchill — who, while being far more accustomed to appearing as a defence witness than was Spilsbury, was equally unused to Sottish trial procedure — stated that 'there is nothing to exclude the possibility of suicide: I could reproduce that wound by holding the pistol with the thumb on the trigger-guard and the fingers of the hand on the butt.' The defendant did not give evidence.

After an absence of just under an hour, the jury brought in a verdict of Not Proven — which, in the view of some cynical Sassenachs, means 'we're not sure whether you did it, but don't do it again'. Though there are contradictions between reports of how the fifteen members of the jury voted, all of the reports say that the six women voted for Not Proven. Merrett was found guilty on the forgery charge, and was sent to prison for a year.

Within weeks of his release, he eloped with a seventeen-year-old ward of Chancery named Vera Bonnar, and, as soon as he was legally entitled to marry her, did so. No sooner was the honeymoon over than Vera became a grass-widow while Merrett served nine months with hard labour for having obtained £200 from shopkeepers in Newcastle-upon-Tyne by means of dud cheques. If he committed further crimes during the next ten years, he escaped punishment for them. Having inherited his mother's estate (valued, according to one account, at £50,000), he and Vera squandered most of it. He served in the Navy throughout the Second World War; when promoted to the rank of lieutenant-commander, he grew a beard that he considered apt to his nautical eminence; one admittedly biased chronicler of his service on torpedo-boats remarks that 'he was full of chase when shooting at a retreating enemy'.

After the war, he and Vera separated. She joined her mother — who, never mind her absence from *Debrett*, insisted that she was 'Lady Menzies' — in running an old people's home, 'The Sunset House', at 22 Montpelier Road, a quiet tree-lined thoroughfare in the West London suburb of Ealing.

Merrett's return to civilian life was delayed for some months, owing to the fact that a military tribunal in Germany found him guilty of the theft of a car; but as soon as he was free he took up the occupations (in some respects related) of smuggler, dealer in goods on the black market, trafficker in currency, and provider of false passports. Between 1947 and 1953 he received short prison sentences or fines, or both, for diverse offences in Belgium, France, and England. In 1949 he met and became enamoured of a German girl, Sonia Winnikes, and, in the

Merrett, the ex-Naval officer.

following year, brought her to England and introduced her to Vera; subsequently, he pleaded with Vera for a divorce, but she refused. Towards the end of 1953, the body of Heinrich Mosmann, an arms-smuggling associate of Merrett's, was fished from the river near Frankfurt, and the German police, treating his death as murder, began building a case against Merrett.

The investigation was still continuing in February 1954.

Merrett and Sonia Winnikes spent the 8th and 9th of that month in Amsterdam. They were on bad terms, for Sonia had learned not only that Merrett had lied to her, saying that he had spent the previous few days in another part of Holland, when he

The mock-pewter jug with which Merrett battered Lady Menzies.

was actually in Germany, but also that he had spent much of that time closeted with a young woman in an hotel near Dueren. On the 10th, a Wednesday, he flew to England. He had shaved off his beard and moustache. The faked passport he carried was a recent addition to his extensive collection; and the name on it, 'Leslie Chown', was not among his favourite aliases — one of which, 'Ronald John Chesney', he had used for so long and so frequently that it had become unfit for criminal purposes.

Some time between the noons of the 10th and the 11th, he crept into the Sunset House and drowned Vera in a bath. Either just before or shortly afterwards, he was seen by his mother-in-law, the self-styled Lady Menzies. For what he considered the best of reasons, he battered and strangled her to death. The first of those crimes is reminiscent, as to its mode, of George Joseph Smith,[1] and the second, as to its provocation,

1. Mentioned on page 3[illegible].

puts one in mind of Buck Ruxton's unpremeditated murder of Mary Rogerson. Merrett appears to have had two motives for killing his wife: he wanted to marry Sonia Winnikes (who, during their recent quarrel, had convincingly threatened to leave him for good), and he was keen to inherit a large share of Vera's estate.

The bodies were found soon after lunch-time on 11 February. Two hours later, Merrett arrived back in Amsterdam. Early next morning, he travelled to Germany.

If he had not been impelled to murder his mother-in-law, Vera's death might have been ascribed to accident or suicide: in which case, the bathroom would not have been searched for fingerprints. But, of course, such an examination *was* carried out — fruitlessly, because Merrett had scoured the edges of the bath with Vim, and swabbed all other surfaces.

Suspicion fell upon him almost at once. But because neither his real name nor any of his known aliases appeared on Customs records of persons who had entered the country since the first week of the month or departed since the murders, the police kept their suspicion to themselves, saying that they wished to interview a man of 'buccaneer-like' appearance *and* (ostensibly as an afterthought) Vera Merrett's husband. The popular press, undeceived by that ruse, found ways of indicating that Merrett was guilty without actually saying so. A Sunday paper published a story purchased from a man who, years before, had shared a cell with him in Wandsworth Prison; Merrett, so the man said, had offered him £1000 to kill Vera.

Next day — Monday, 15 February — Merrett bought a copy of that paper at the main railway station in Cologne. After writing two letters, one to Sonia, the other to his solicitor in England, he went to a wood outside the city and shot himself through the head with a Colt .45 revolver. His body was found the following morning,

The Cologne police informed Scotland Yard. The officer working on the Sunset House case, worried by the information that the dead man was clean-shaven, and so not at all buccaneer-like, asked for the fingerprints to be forwarded. Either something was lost (or rather, added) in the translation of that request or the response exemplified Teutonic thoroughness. The large parcel sent from Germany contained, not fingerprints, but a complete set of the fingers — still attached to hands which were still attached to arms that extended as far as the funny-bones. A fingerprint man, holding his breath as he worked, took the impressions he needed, and found that they established the truth of what the Germans had said in the first place.

Because the letter that Merrett had written to his solicitor was inadequately stamped, it did not arrive at its destination till after his arms had arrived at theirs. The letter read, in part:

> . . . I realise that although I am innocent I have not the chance of the proverbial snowball in Hades of getting out of the mess. I have seen so much of prison that I have no wish to return there even for a day, and the prospects of hanging appeal to me still less.
>
> I assure you that although the way I shall have taken to get out of it may seen cowardly, it does, all the same, need some courage.
>
> Nevertheless, it may be taken to indicate my guilt, but this is not the case.
>
> I hope that eventually the police do find the doer of the deeds.
>
> I wish only to make sure that Miss Sonia Winnikes gets *everything* which devolves upon me. . . .

Merrett's assertion of his innocence was contradicted by evidence (for instance, fibres identical with those of Lady Menzies' pink cardigan had been found on his clothes; Customs investigators had discovered how and when he had entered and left England; he had been seen in the vicinity of Sunset House), and a coroner's jury needed only a few minutes to decide that he had murdered his wife and his mother-in-law.

In Scotland, the suggestion was made that a high-court jury's verdict, delivered twenty-seven years before, should be set aside; but the justiciary took no notice, of course.

Between September 1967 and November 1974, one man carried out more than twenty armed robberies, almost invariably of small post offices in the Midlands and the North of England, and, in the course of those crimes, shot to death three sub-postmasters and severely wounded a number of other persons. Most of the eye-witness descriptions of the criminal referred only to his apparel, which usually consisted of black plimsolls, a camouflaged combat-suit, white gloves, and a black hood with a slit for the eyes. Inspired by that last-mentioned item, a reporter called the criminal the Black Panther — a sobriquet that so appealed to the reporter's rivals that they, *en masse*, followed suit. (If only as an example of how legends are made, it it worth mentioning that one of the reporters subsequently concocted a 'police mnemonic *aide-memoire*' which used the letters of the word PANTHER in this way: *P*ost offices, *A*rmed with shotgun, *N*o apparent accomplices, *T*iming: early morning, *H*ooded intruder, *E*ntry: drills window-frames, *R*ouses occupants for keys. The reporter neglected to explain what use the mnemonic was to the investigators who were said to be using it.)

Leonard 'Nipper' Read, who was the National Co-ordinator of Regional Crime Squads for England and Wales when the Black Panther was busiest, has stated that the case 'highlighted a glaring inadequacy in the operational efficiency of the police service in Britain — namely the failure, once the common denominator had been established, to appoint one selected officer to co-ordinate and overlord the various operations, irrespective of police force boundaries. The system allowed five different sites of investigation to be maintained and it is hardly surprising that sometimes investigating officers were pulling in different directions.' It is impossible to say whether greater co-operation between the different forces would have resulted

A policeman wearing Black Panther gear and holding one of his firearms.

in the Black Panther's activities being less prolonged — but, anyway, he was still at large on Tuesday, 14 January 1975.

In the early hours of that day, he kidnapped a seventeen-year-old girl named Lesley Whittle from her home, a large, detached house, 'Beech Croft', in the Shropshire village of Highley, to the west of Wolverhampton. He appears to have been prompted to turn from robbery to kidnapping, and to choose Lesley as his victim, by press reports of a squabble over money between members of the Whittle family, which suggested that the Whittles were far richer than was so. He left in the house a number of messages punched on strips of red plastic Dymo-tape. The ransom he demanded was £50,000. Despite the instruction, 'NO POLICE', and the threat, 'YOU ARE ON A TIME LIMIT IF POLICE OR TRICKS. DEATH', Lesley's elder brother telephoned the West Mercia Constabulary.

Plans made by the police to keep both the kidnapping and their knowledge of it secret were rendered useless by a local freelance reporter, who having obtained information concerning the crime from an 'anonymous source', sold the story to a Birmingham newspaper and to the BBC. The latter, without bothering to ascertain whether the story was true (let alone whether the broadcasting of it might imperil a life), interrupted television programmes with a newsflash. Almost at once the Whittles received the first of hundreds of telephone calls, mostly from idiots but also from petty criminals pretending to be the kidnapper and explaining how the ransom was to be paid to them. (One of the latter, a woman, was caught, tried, and sentenced to four years' imprisonment.) Efforts by the police to trap the real kidnapper at the 'ransom rendezvous' given in the Dymo-tape message turned into fiascoes — chiefly because of the presence of almost as many reporters and spectators as plain-clothes policemen.

An 'incident room' was set up at Bridgnorth Police Station. Members of Scotland Yard's Criminal Intelligence Bureau, experts in undercover surveillance methods, arrived there on the day after the kidnapping.

That night, a serious crime was committed at a place fifteen miles east of Highley. It led to two discoveries, one of great importance, regarding the kidnapping. Gerald Smith, an overseer at the depot for Freightliner railroad containers at Dudley, Worcestershire, approached a man loitering near the perimeter fence. Made more suspicious by the man's incomprehensible replies to his questions, Smith turned away, intending to telephone the police. As he did so, the man produced a small pistol. Smith started to run. A shot hit him in the buttocks. He squared up to the man — who thereupon fired five more shots into his body, and then, the pistol empty, ran away. Smith managed to hobble to within earshot of workmen, one of whom made a 999 call. Even before Smith was taken to hospital, policemen were combing the area for his attacker. There was no sign of him.

Next day, bullets found at the scene of the crime were sent to a forensic science laboratory. The ejection marks on them, as unique as fingerprints, matched those on bullets recovered from the scenes of two earlier crimes — both committed by the Black Panther.

The registration number of a green Morris 1300 saloon parked near the Freightliner depot was found to be false. Using duplicate keys to unlock the small car, the police discovered a motley collection of items — among them, a length of rope, a pair of new but inexpertly shortened corduroy trousers, a foam-rubber mattress, a tape-recorder and cassette. And four buff-coloured envelopes, each with handwritten notes on the front, and each containing a strip of punched Dymo-tape. The strips read like clues in a treasure-hunt. One of the messages referred to 'SECOND TRAFFIC LIGHTS TO FREIGHT-LINER LIMITED DUDLEY'. Clearly, the messages were, in the words of one of the detectives, 'part of a ransom trail'.

All of the contents of the car, as well as the vehicle itself, were tested for fingerprints; none of those found was complete enough or sufficiently clear to be identified. The cassette was not played till it had been examined. Lesley Whittle's voice was heard. After giving instructions that were similar to those on one of the strips of Dymo-tape, she said: 'Please, Mum. . . . There's no need to worry, Mum. I'm OK. I got a bit wet but I'm quite dry now. I'm being treated very well. OK?'

There was no longer any doubt that Lesley Whittle had been kidnapped by the Black Panther.

During the next seven weeks, every millimetre of the Morris saloon was examined for fibres and other 'transfer evidence'; an appeal for information regarding the car's whereabouts from the time it was stolen produced dozens of reported sightings; efforts were made to trace the maker of the false number plates; a sketch of the Black Panther, based on Gerald Smith's description of him, was shown on television and published in newspapers, resulting in more than seven hundred 'recognitions'; house-to-house inquiries were made in Dudley and Highley; etc. Meanwhile, Lesley Whittle's brother followed several 'ransom trails', all but one of which proved to have been laid by hoaxers. The exception — instigated by a telephone call that was made just before midnight on 16 January — led to the

town of Kidsgrove, Staffordshire, more than forty miles north-east of Highley; the trail, marked by Dymo-tape messages, petered out in Bathpool Park, an area of common land that was once a coal-mine.

For reasons that he thought sensible, the head of the West Mercia CID delayed a full-scale search of the park until 4 March. The publicity given to the search caused a number of local schoolboys to come forward: one handed over a strip of Dymo-tape, stamped with the message 'DROP SUITCASE INTO HOLE', which he had picked up in the park two days after the kidnapping; another surrendered a lantern-type torch which he had prised from between the bars of a grille that guarded a drainage shaft in the park.

The shaft, known locally as the Glory Hole, was one of three, connected by culverts. The naked body of Lesley Whittle was found near the foot of the largest shaft. It was suspended by wire noosed around the neck and tied to a rung of the ladder.

Of several articles found close to the body and in the culverts, one was a Woolworth's notebook, from which sheets had been torn. The existing pages were blank, but the first of them bore the imprint of writing on a missing page — a message, word for word the same as one of those on the strips of Dymo-tape.

There was a fingerprint on the inside of the front cover of the notebook. Almost certainly it was the Black Panther's. For the first time in his long career, he had left an unequivocal clue to his identity. Photographs of the print were sent to Scotland Yard and provincial criminal records offices. The importance attached to the task of trying to match the print is indicated by the fact that virtually all routine operations in the fingerprint department at the Yard were suspended for four months. Commander John Morrison — who, immediately after the discovery of the body, was appointed head of the entire Black Panther investigation — would say: 'I don't think there has ever been anything like the contribution made by the fingerprint officers of this country, both at the Yard and at fingerprint branches throughout Britain. It is probably the biggest involvement ever.' But when, in the middle of July, the last of nearly two million comparisons were made, the print in the notebook had not been matched. The investigators could only hope that the Black Panther would make another mistake: then, perhaps, the print could be used towards snaring him. They waited for him to strike again.

They waited throughout the summer and autumn; the first weeks of winter.

On the night of Thursday, 11 December, Police Constables Tony White and Stuart Mackenzie, patrolling the Nottinghamshire mining village of Mansfield Woodhouse in a Panda car, saw a little man hurrying along a footpath. He was carrying a holdall. White called out to him to stop. The man obeyed — but after saying that his name was John Moxon, he suddenly

(Opposite)
Three photofit impressions of the Black Panther and a sketch of him that was issued after the shooting at the Dudley Freightliner depot.

produced a sawn-off shotgun. He ordered White into the back of the car, took his place, and, prodding Mackenzie in the ribs with the gun, uttered one word: 'Drive.' Mackenzie did as he was told. As the car travelled towards Sherwood Forest, the policemen used the driving mirror for an exchange of signals. At the approach to a T-junction, Mackenzie asked, 'Which way?' and turned the steering-wheel left, then back again. White shouted, 'Don't do anything daft, Mac.' Losing his concentration, the gunman looked round. Mackenzie plunged his foot down on the brake-pedal, and the man was jolted forward. White lunged towards him — managed to grab the muzzle of the shotgun. An instant later, there was an explosion; ragged holes appeared in the roof of the car, in the windscreen. Though some of the pellets had pierced White's right hand, he held on to the gun; he hooked his left arm round the man's neck, pulled him into the back, and fought with him. Mackenzie had rolled out into the road; the blast from the explosion had perforated one of his eardrums and bruised the other. He ran to help White. The car had come to a halt near a fish and chip shop. One of the customers, a miner, dashed out. With his assistance, the ferocity of the gunman was subdued.

When searched, he was found to be carrying other weapons: a large sheath-knife was tucked in his belt, a small one was concealed in one of his boots; he was wearing a cowboy-style waistband to which was clipped ten 12-bore shells. His holdall contained, among other things, hoods, torches, a collection of tools, and a plastic bottle of ammonia. He was taken to Mansfield Police Station.

The detective who interviewed him suspected at once that 'John Moxon' was the Black Panther. That suspicion was confirmed by the print of the man's left middle finger, which — a complete set of his prints having been rushed to Scotland Yard — was matched with the print in the notebook.

During the first hours of interrogation, the man said little — and what he did say was spoken with a sort of mid-European accent: 'I no shoot anybody. . . . I would shoot dog but no policeman. I no Black Panther. When Black Panther work, he shoot to kill.' But, late on Friday night, speaking with a North-Country accent, he admitted that his name was Donald Neilson, and said that he lived at an address in Bradford, Yorkshire. Subsequently the police learned that, though he had called himself Neilson for about ten years, his real name was Nappey. Born in 1936, near Bradford, the first child of working-class parents (the father a machine operator in a woollen mill), he left school when he was fourteen and became an apprentice-carpenter; he was serving his third appren-

Donald Neilson.

ticeship when, in 1955, he was conscripted into the army for two years — some months of which he spent in Cyprus, fighting the EOKA terrorists. When demobilized, he returned to the Bradford area and within a few months married a girl whom he had known since before his call-up: after trying to earn a living as a window-cleaner, and then as a minicab-driver, he set up as a jobbing carpenter. His wife, who helped to make both ends meet by taking in lodgers, gave birth to a daughter in 1960.

The police search of Neilson's house revealed so many items of positive or possible evidential value that a furniture van was needed to take them away. They included an exercise book containing notes of premises that had been 'cased' ('Lights go out at 11 p.m.', 'If boxed in here, no way out'; among the premises referred to was a public-house in Mansfield Woodhouse), Dymo-tape punches, firearms, hundreds of rounds of ammunition, a kit for making vehicle-registration plates — and a pottery model of a black panther.

Two days after his capture, Neilson made statements in which he confessed to several of his crimes. He was, he claimed, accident-prone: the people who had been killed or wounded during the robberies were victims of that unfortunate condition, which was manifested by the fact that each of his various guns had fired of their own accord; he had only meant to tether Lesley Whittle with the wire around her neck, but she had slipped.

In July 1976, Neilson was tried twice — first, for the kidnapping and murder of Lesley Whittle, and second, for a selection of earlier crimes. At the end of the second trial, he was sentenced to five terms of life imprisonment; other sentences totalled sixty-one years. In the following month, his wife pleaded guilty to six charges of dishonestly cashing stolen postal-orders, asking for seventy-six similar crimes to be taken into consideration, and admitted that she had also dishonestly disposed of a quantity of stolen postal-orders. She was sentenced to a year in prison, and was released after serving eight months.

A charge against Neilson that he had attempted to murder Gerald Smith — who had died in March 1976[1] — was not proceeded with. The judge ordered that the charge should lie on the file. If Neilson is ever released, on the say-so of psychiatrists or a politician, the charge can be brought against him.

1. More than a year and a day after the injuries were inflicted — which is the statutory period in which death must occur for it to be classed as murder.

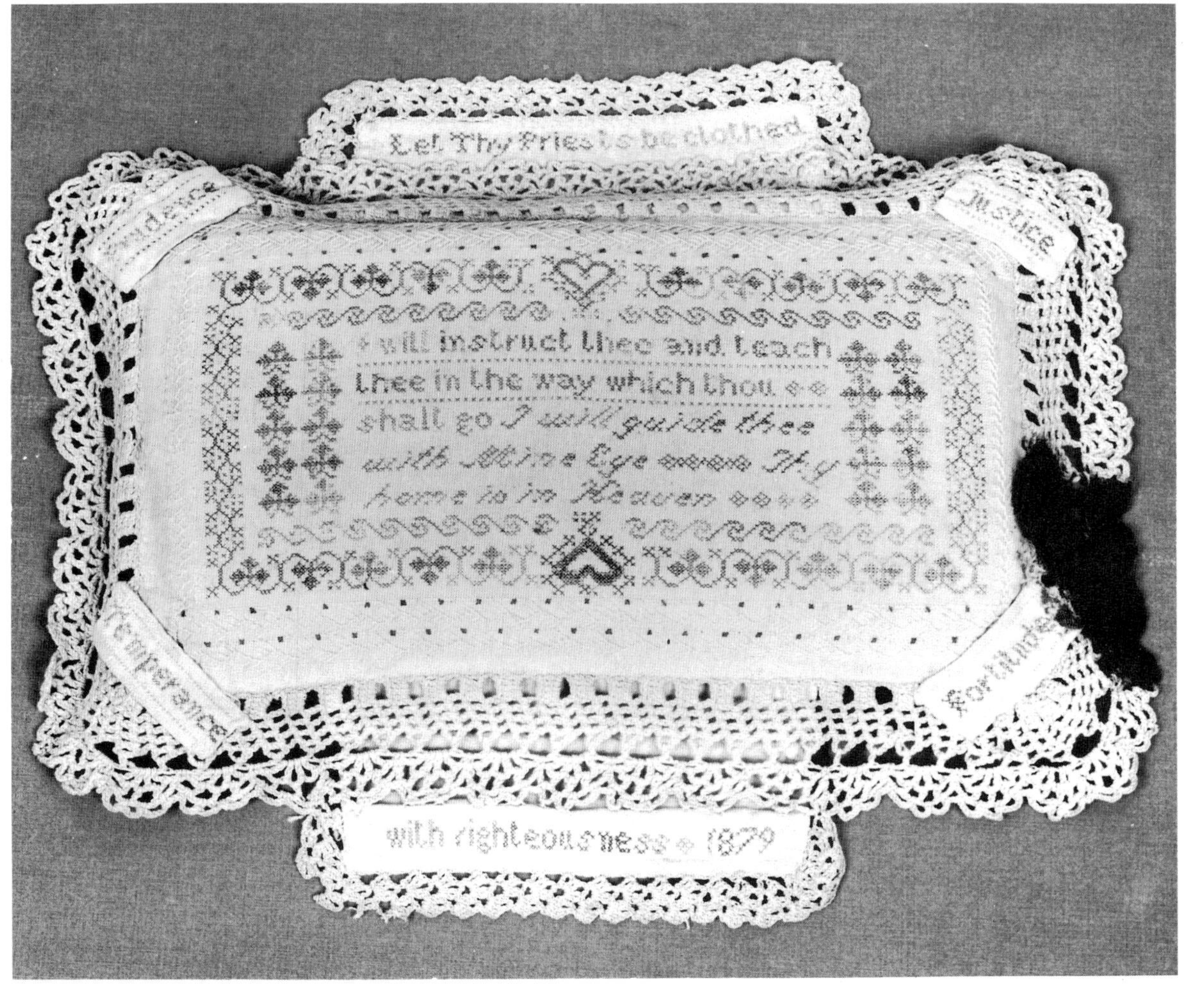
Let Thy Priests be clothed
Justice
I will instruct thee and teach
thee in the way which thou
shall go I will guide thee
with Mine Eye Thy
home is in Heaven
Temperance
Fortitude
with righteousness 1879

LAST WORD

To end on an uplifting note, let us speak of one of the Black Museum's few intendedly pretty exhibits — a pin-cushion, religiously embroidered in 1879 by Annie Parker, who, lacking cotton, made do with hair from her head.

Almost certainly, she made the pin-cushion while in prison — for, sad to say, she was rarely elsewhere. No sooner had she served one sentence for drunkenness than, drunk again, and meanwhile arrested again, she was put inside again: that, at any rate, was her destination after three hundred of her four hundred appearances before the Greenwich magistrates. She died, aged thirty-five, in 1885; the cause of her death was said to be consumption.

SELECTED BIBLIOGRAPHY

1. Adam, Hargrave Lee (ed.): *Trial of George Chapman*, Edinburgh, 1930
2. Adam. Hargrave Lee (ed.): *Trial of George Henry Lamson*, Edinburgh, 1912
3. Altick, Richard D.: *Victorian Studies in Scarlet*, London 1971
4. Anon.: *The Bermondsey Tragedy*, London, nd (1849)
5. Anon.: *The Man They Could Not Hang: The Life Story of John Lee*, London, 1908
6. Barker, Felix, and Jackson, Peter: *London: 2000 Years of a City and Its People*, London, 1974
7. Berry, James: *My Experiences as an Executioner*, London, nd,: Newton Abbot, 1972
8. Birmingham, George A.: *Murder Most Foul!*, London, 1929
9. Blundell, R. H., and Wilson, G. Haswell (eds.): *Trial of Buck Ruxton*, Edinburgh, 1937
10. Borowitz, Albert: *The Woman Who Murdered Black Satin*, Columbus, Ohio, 1981
11. Bresler, Fenton: *Reprieve: A Study of a System*, London, 1965
12. Browne, Douglas G., and Brock, Alan: *Fingerprints: Fifty Years of Scientific Crime Detection*, London, 1953
13. Browne, Douglas G., and Tullett, E. V.: *Bernard Spilsbury: His Life and Cases*, London, 1951
14. Calvert, E. Roy: *Capital Punishment in the Twentieth Century*, London, 1927
15. Camps, Francis E.: *Medical and Scientific Investigations in the Christie Case*, London, 1953
16. Curtis, J.: *An Authentic and Faithful History of the Mysterious Murder of Maria Marten. . . .*, London, 1828 and 1928
17. Dew, Ex-Chief Inspector Walter: *I Caught Crippen*, London, 1938
18. Gattey, Charles Neilson: *The Incredible Mrs Van der Elst*, London, 1972
19. Gillen, Mollie: *Assassination of the Prime Minister: The Shocking Death of Spencer Perceval*, London, 1972
20. Glaister, John, and Brash, James Couper: *Medico-Legal Aspects of the Ruxton Case*, Edinburh, 1937
21. Godwin, George (ed.): *Trial of Peter Griffiths*, Edinburgh, 1950
22. Goodman, Jonathan: *Acts of Murder*, London, 1986
23. Goodman, Jonathan (ed.): *The Christmas Murders*, London, 1986
24. Goodman, Jonathan: *Posts-Mortem: The Correspondence of Murder*, Newton Abbot, 1971
25. Goodman, Jonathan: *The Crippen File*, London, 1985
26. Goodman, Jonathan (ed.): *The Pleasures of Murder*, London, 1983
27. Goodman, Jonathan (ed.): *The Railway Murders*, London, 1984
28. Goodman, Jonathan (ed.): *The Seaside Murders*, London, 1985

29. Goodman, Jonathan, and Pringle, Patrick (eds.): *The Trial of Ruth Ellis*, Newton Abbot, 1974
30. Gowers, Sir Ernest: *A Life for a Life: The Problem of Capital Punishment*, London, 1956
31. Hastings, Macdonald: *The Other Mr Churchill*, London, 1963
32. Hawkes, Harry: *The Capture of the Black Panther*, London, 1978
33. Hyde, H. Montgomery (ed.): *Trial of Christopher Craig and Derek William Bentley*, Edinburgh, 1954
34. Hyde, H. Montgomery (ed.): *Trial of Sir Roger Casement*, Edinburgh, 1960
35. Irving, H. B. (ed.): *Trial of Franz Müller*, Edinburgh, 1911
36. Jackson, Robert: *Coroner*, London, 1963
37. Jesse, F. Tennyson (ed.): *Trial of Samuel Herbert Dougal*, Edinburgh, 1928
38. Jesse, F. Tennyson (ed.): *Trials of Timothy John Evans and John Reginald Halliday Christie*, Edinburgh, 1957
39. Jones, Elwyn: *The Last Two to Hang*, London, 1966
40. Kennedy, Ludovic: *Ten Rillington Place*, London, 1961
41. Knott, George, H. (ed.): *Trial of Sir Roger Casement*, Edinburgh, 1917
42. Knott, George, H. (ed.): *Trial of William Palmer*, Edinburgh, 1912
43. Lambton, Arthur: *Echoes of Causes Célèbres*, London, nd
44. Laurence, John: *A History of Capital Punishment*, London, nd
45. MacNaghten, Sir Melville: *Days of My Years*, London, 1914
46. Marks, Alfred: *Tyburn Tree: Its History and Annals*, London, 1905
47. O'Donnell, Elliot (ed.): *Trial of Kate Webster*, Edinburgh, 1925
48. Pierrepoint, Albert: *Executioner: Pierrepoint*, London, 1974
49. Poland, Sir Harry, KC (introduction by): *Trial of Courvoisier for the Murder of Lord William Russell*, London, 1918
50. Rhodes, Henry, T. F.: *Alphonse Bertillon, Father of Scientific Detection*, London, 1956
51. Roughead, William (ed.): *Trial of John Donald Merrett*, Edinburgh, 1929
52. St Aubyn, Giles: *Infamous Victorians*, London, 1971
53. Shore, W. Teignmouth (ed.): *Trial of James Blomfield Rush*, Edinburgh, 1928
54. Shore, W. Teignmouth (ed.): *Trial of Thomas Neill Cream*, Edinburgh, 1923
55. Shore, W. Teignmouth (ed.): *Trials of Charles Peace*, Edinburgh, 1926
56. Tod, T. M.: *The Scots Black Kalendar*, Perth, Scotland, 1938
57. Van der Elst, Violet: *On the Gallows*, London, 1937
58. Watson, Eric R. (ed.): *Trial of George Joseph Smith*, Edinburgh, 1922
59. Whipple, Sidney B. (ed.): *The Trial of Richard Bruno Hauptmann*, London, nd
60. Whittington-Egan, Richard: *A Casebook on Jack the Ripper*, London, 1975

61. Wilton, George W.: *Fingerprints: History, Law and Romance*, Edinburgh, 1938
62. Young, Filson (ed.): *Trial of Frederick Bywaters and Edith Thompson*, Edinburgh, 1923
63. Young, Filson (ed.): *Trial of Hawley Harvey Crippen*, Edinburgh, 1919

INDEX

Note: B (followed by number) after a name denotes a relevant book listed in Selected Bibliography (pp. 216-18); page numbers in italics refer to illustrations.